SUNDAY-SCHOOL BOOK.

FOR THE USE OF

EVANGELICAL LUTHERAN CONGREGATIONS.

BY AUTHORITY OF THE

GENERAL COUNCIL OF THE EVANGELICAL LUTHERAN CHURCH IN NORTH AMERICA.

REVISED AND ENLARGED.

PHILADELPHIA:

GENERAL COUNCIL PUBLICATION BOARD.

IN the compilation of the Sunday School Book, the greatest care has been taken not to infringe upon any copyrights, and nothing thus protected has been included without permission. If, however, notwithstanding the caution exercised, any infringements of such rights are discovered, it is hoped that the assurance that they are unintentional will be received with the sincerity with which it is made. It is desired that every such trespass should be brought to the notice of the proper persons, in order that just and proper acknowledgments may be made.

TABLE OF CONTENTS.

————※————

Directions and Explanations Concerning the Chants.

---※---

The Sunday School Book contains a very ample provision of chants, both Anglican, single and double, and Gregorian.

The double Anglican chants may be sung to the Psalms and Canticles, all the voices uniting in all the verses, in the manner customary among us. The single Anglican chants are usually sung antiphonally, one choir or set of singers singing one verse, and another singing the next verse, and so on through the Psalm or Canticle; and at the close both unite in the Gloria Patri. The double and single chants are sung in four-part harmony.

Gregorian Tones consist of four parts: the *Intonation*, the opening notes separated from the rest of the chant by a colon :, which is used on Sundays and Festivals to every verse of the Benedictus, Magnificat, and Nunc Dimittis; to both verses of the Gloria Patri; to the first verse of every other Canticle, and of each Psalm or portion of Psalm. The Psalms and Canticles in this book are marked with the colon so that the proper place for the *Intonation* is readily and plainly seen.

The *Dominant*, or reciting note, follows the *Intonation*. In some of the Tones—the 2nd, 5th, and 8th—it runs through two bars. When this occurs, the bar between these notes is considered left out in the words, and the recitation is kept up to the second bar. Then comes the *Mediation*, a short cadence in the middle; and the chant closes with the *Finalis, i. e.*, Ending, or Final Cadence.

The Gregorian Tones are usually sung in unison, though they may be sung in four-part harmony. One set of singers, sings the first part of a verse to the colon, or line division ||, and another takes up the second part and carries it to the end of the verse. At the end of the Psalm or Canticle both sets of singers unite in the Gloria Patri.

v

SUNDAY SCHOOL SERVICE.

OPENING SERVICE.

¶ *A Hymn of Invocation to the Holy Spirit, or another suitable Hymn, may be sung. Or*

¶ *The Service shall begin with the* VERSICLE *and* GLORIA PATRI, *sung or said responsively as here followeth, all standing to the end of the* PSALMS. *The Superintendent of the Sunday School shall lead the Service.*

The Versicle.

SUPERINTENDENT.—O Lord, open Thou my lips.

TALLIS.

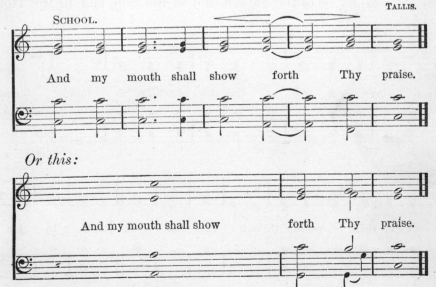

1

Sup'T.—Make haste, O God, to deliver me.

Sup'T.—Glory be to the Father, and to the Son, and to the Holy Ghost.

Or this:

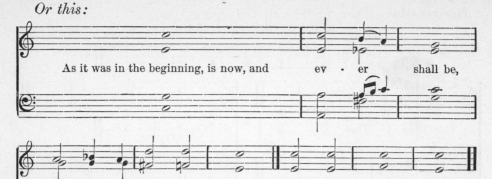

As it was in the beginning, is now, and ev • er shall be,

world with • out end. A • men. Hal • le • lu • jah.

¶ *During the Passion Season the* HALLELUJAH *is omitted.*

¶ *Then shall be sung or said one or more of the* PSALMS *as selected for the different seasons of the Church Year. At the close of each* PSALM *shall be sung or said the* GLORIA PATRI.

The Psalm and the Gloria Patri.

¶ *When the* PSALM *is said, the* GLORIA PATRI *may be sung as here given, or a suitable chant may be used.*

ENDLICH'S CHORAL BUCH.

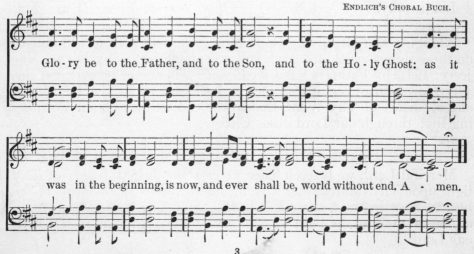

Glo • ry be to the Father, and to the Son, and to the Ho • ly Ghost: as it

was in the beginning, is now, and ever shall be, world without end. A • men.

3

¶ *Then shall follow*

The Scripture Lesson,

which may be read responsively. At its close shall be sung or said:

Or this:

Thanks be to Thee, O God.   Thanks be to Thee, O God.

¶ *Then shall be said*

The Catechism,

each part being used successively, the first part on the first Sunday of the month, the second part on the second, and so on to the end of the month.

¶ *Then shall follow*

The Prayer,

which may be one of the COLLECTS *here given, or any suitable prayer.*

¶ *The Superintendent shall say:*

Let us pray.

1.

Almighty and Everliving God, Who makest us both to will and to do those things which are good, and acceptable unto Thy Divine Majesty: Let Thy Fatherly hand, we beseech Thee, ever be over us; let Thy Holy Spirit ever be with us; and so lead us in the knowledge and obedience of Thy Word, that in the end we may obtain everlasting life; through our Lord Jesus Christ.

2.

Merciful Lord, we beseech Thee to cast the bright beams of Thy light upon Thy Church, that it being instructed by the doctrine of the blessed Apostles, may so walk in the light of Thy truth, that it may at length attain to the light of everlasting life; through Jesus Christ our Lord.

3.

Almighty and Everlasting God, Who dost will that not one of these little ones should perish, and hast sent Thine Only Son to seek and to save that which was lost, and through Him hast said, Suffer the little children to come unto Me, and forbid them not; for of such is the kingdom of God: Most heartily we beseech Thee so to bless and govern the children of Thy Church, by Thy Holy Spirit, that they may grow in grace and in the knowledge of Thy Word; protect and defend them against all danger and harm, giving Thy holy Angels charge over them; through Jesus Christ our Lord.

4.

Almighty God, without Whose help we can do nothing good: Grant us grace, we beseech Thee, faithfully to perform the duties that now devolve upon us. Engraft Thy saving truth upon our hearts, that it may bring forth fruit in those who teach and in those who hear; and graciously build us up in faith and good works, to the praise of Thy Holy Name; through Jesus Christ, Thy Son, our Lord.

¶ *The school shall sing*

A - men.

¶ *Then shall be sung*

A Hymn.

¶ *Then shall follow*

The Instruction for the Day,

either on the Epistle *or* Gospel *for the day, or any suitable* Scripture Lesson *that may have been appointed, or the* Catechism.

5

Additional Prayers and Collects,

From which selections may be made for opening or closing.

1.

Almighty and everlasting God, from Whom cometh every good and perfect gift, grant us, we beseech Thee, the healthful Spirit of Thy grace, that we may renounce the devil, and all his works, and all his ways, and keep Thy holy will and commandments all the days of our lives. Graft in our hearts the love of Thy Name; increase in us true religion; nourish us in all goodness; and, of Thy great mercy, keep us, that, in the end, we may obtain everlasting life; through Jesus Christ, Thy Son our Lord.

2.

O Lord, most loving and merciful Redeemer, Who didst receive little children, and didst lay Thine hands upon them, look upon us, Thy children, who have been baptized in Thy Name. Enable us to remember our Creator in the days of our youth, and make us dutiful, as Thou, O Lord Jesus, wast dutiful. Preserve us from all errors and dangers, that, the longer we live, the better we may be, to the honor and glory of Thee, and to our own happiness here and forever, O Thou, Who, with the Father and the Holy Ghost, livest and reignest, ever one God, world without end.

3.

O Lord Jesus Christ, Who, when a child, wast seated in the midst of the doctors, both hearing them and asking them questions; so rule us, we beseech Thee, by Thy Holy Spirit, that following Thy example, we may love the habitation of Thy house and the place where Thine honor dwelleth, hear Thy word with gladness, and faithfully keep it to the saving of our souls.

4.

O Lord Jesus Christ, Who wast given both to be a sacrifice for sin, and an example of godly life, and Who dost bid us take up our cross daily and follow Thee; conform us to Thy likeness; and give us grace that we may keep Thy way, and carry Thine image in our hearts.

6

5.

Almighty Father, Who hast promised that they who seek Thy heavenly wisdom shall find it; send down upon us Thy heavenly grace, that we, being trained up in the nurture and admonition of the Lord, may choose and love Thy way, and never depart therefrom; that when Thou makest up Thy jewels in Thy glorious kingdom, we may be Thine, for the sake of Thy Holy Child Jesus, our Saviour.

6.

Almighty and most merciful God, our Heavenly Father, we give Thee thanks that in the sacrament of Holy Baptism, Thou hast received us as Thy children, and granted us, for Christ's sake, forgiveness of sins; and we implore Thy help, that we may never be unmindful of our Baptism, but daily renouncing every evil way, may serve Thee in true holiness, until we come into Thy Heavenly kingdom; through Jesus Christ our Lord.

7.

O Lord Jesus, Who art the Good Shepherd, and didst lay down Thy life for the sheep; look mercifully upon this, Thy flock, and make it Thine forever, that we may love and serve Thee in constant obedience to Thy word, and, finally, be with those that come into Thy kingdom of glory.

8.

O Lord, we beseech Thee to keep our feet when we go into Thy house, that we may be ready to hear, and to offer the sacrifice of praise. Guard us from all wandering thoughts and unseemly actions, and make our service acceptable unto Thee; through Jesus Christ, Thine only Son our Lord.

9.

O Lord, Who didst come to seek and to save that which was lost, and to Whom all power is given in Heaven and on earth; hear, we beseech Thee, the prayers of Thy Church for those who, at Thy command, go forth to preach the Gospel in all the world. Preserve them from all dangers, to which they may be exposed; and, while they plant and water, send Thou the increase, gathering in the multitude of the heathen; so that Thy Name may be glorified, and Thy kingdom come.

10.

Almighty God our Heavenly Father, we thank Thee that Thou hast given us godly parents and faithful teachers, so that in our childhood we know the holy Scriptures whereby we are made wise unto salvation; and, we beseech Thee, help us by Thy Holy Spirit to understand Thy Word, and to treasure its truths in our hearts, so that, as we increase in stature, we may also grow in grace, and in favor with God and man, until we come to eternal life, through Jesus Christ our Lord.

For Catechumens.

11.

Almighty and everlasting God, Who dost always multiply Thy Church, and with Thy light and grace dost strengthen the hearts of those whom Thou hast regenerated, confirming unto them Thy covenant and faithfulness: Grant unto our Catechumens increase both of faith and knowledge, that they may rejoice in their Baptism and really and heartily renew their covenant with Thee, through Jesus Christ our Lord.

For the Sick.

12.

Almighty and gracious God, whose mercies are over all Thy creatures, look in tender compassion, we beseech Thee, upon Thy servant, *N. N.*, who is sick. Sustain *him* in the trial through which *he* is passing, and sanctify it to *his* good. Deliver *him* from suffering, and, if in accordance with Thy holy will, restore *him* to health and strength that *he* may joyfully serve Thee in Thy Church, to the honor of Thy Name, through Jesus Christ Thy Son, our Lord.

8

For Teachers' Meetings.

13.

Almighty God, the source of all wisdom, grace and strength, without Whom nothing can prosper, and on Whom we are dependent in all our efforts to serve and glorify Thee; Accept, we pray Thee, the thanks of Thine unworthy servants, for the gift of Thy Son Jesus Christ our Saviour, for the establishment of Thy Church on the earth, and that Thou hast made it our privilege to labor therein for the dissemination of Thy truth and the leading of souls in the way of salvation. Have mercy upon us in our weakness, ignorance and sins, and graciously strengthen and prosper us in our endeavors to fulfill the duties to which Thou in Thy providence hast called us.

Bless Thy Church, we pray Thee, its Pastors, and all who labor and give for its prosperity and extension. Raise up for it many friends who may joyfully serve it in its various necessities. Increase the number of those who preach and uphold Thy Word, that it may have free course, and win many to righteousness.

Let Thy special benediction be upon this congregation,—upon its officers, its schools, its teachers, and upon all its interests and efforts, that streams of blessing may issue from it, to the honor and glory of Thy Name; Through Jesus Christ our Lord.

14.

Almighty God, Who hast promised to hear the petitions of those who ask in Thy Son's Name; we beseech Thee mercifully to incline Thine ear to us who have now made our prayers and supplications unto Thee; and grant that those things which we have faithfully asked according to Thy will, may be effectually obtained, to the relief of our necessity, and to the setting forth of Thy glory; through Jesus Christ our Lord, Who liveth and reigneth with Thee and The Holy Ghost, ever one God, world without end. Amen.

Closing Service.

¶ *The Instruction being ended, and the Offerings gathered, there shall be sung*

A Hymn.

¶ *Then, all standing to the end of the Prayers, shall be sung or said*

The Canticle.

¶ *If the Service be held in the morning the* Benedictus *shall be used; but if the Service be held in the afternoon the* Magnificat *with its* Versicle *shall be used. Other* Canticles *may occasionally be sung at this place. The* Versicle *may be used with the* Nunc Dimittis.

I. Benedictus.

Blessed : be the Lord | God of | Israel; ||
For He hath visited | and re- | deemed . His | people,
    And hath : raised up a horn of sal- | vation | for us ||
In the house of His | servant | Da- | vid;

10

As HE **:** spake by the mouth of His | holy | prophets, ||
Which have been | since the | world be- | gan:

THAT **:** we should be saved | from our | ene - mies, ||
And from the | hand of | all that | hate us;

To PER-**:** form the mercy promised | to our | fathers, ||
And to remember His | holy | cove- | nant;

THE **:** oath which He sware to our father | Abra- | ham, ||
That He would | grant | unto | us,

THAT **:** we, being delivered out of the | hand of . our | ene - mies, ||
Might | serve Him | without | fear,

IN **:** holiness and righteousness be- | fore | Him, ||
All the | days of | our | life.

AND THOU, **:** child, shalt be called the prophet | of the | Highest: ||
For thou shalt go before the face of the | Lord . to pre- | pare His | ways:

To GIVE **:** knowledge of salvation | unto His | people ||
By the re- | mission | of their | sins,

THROUGH THE **:** tender mercy | of our | God; ||
Whereby the dayspring from on | high hath | visit - ed | us,

To GIVE **:** light to them that sit in darkness and in the | shadow . of |
death, ||
To guide our feet | into the | way of | peace.

GLORY **:** be to the Father, and | to the | Son, ||
And | to the | Holy | Ghost,

As IT **:** was in the beginning, is now, and | ever | shall be, ||
World | without | end.   A- | men.

The Versicle.

SUP'T.—Let my prayer be set forth before Thee as incense.

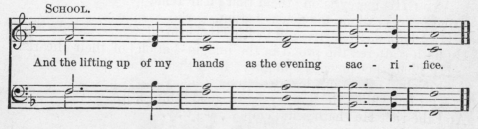

And the lifting up of my hands as the evening sac - ri - fice.

II. Magnificat.

TONUS REGIUS.

1.

ROBERT COOKE.

2.

B. COOKE.   4.   TURLE.

3.

My : soul doth magni- | fy the | Lord; ||
And my spirit hath re- | joiced in | God my | Saviour.

For : He | hath re- | garded ||
The low es- | tate of | His hand- | maiden.

For : behold, | from hence- | forth ||
All gener- | ations . shall | call me | blessed.

For : He that is mighty hath done to | me great | things: ||
And | holy | is His | Name.

And : His mercy is on | them that | fear Him, ||
From gener- | ation . to | gener- | ation.

He : hath showed strength | with His | arm: ||
He hath scattered the proud in the imagin- | ation | of their | hearts.

He : hath put down the mighty | from their | seats, ||
And exalted | them of | low de- | gree.

He : hath filled the hungry | with good | things, ||
And the rich He | hath sent | empty . a- | way.

12

HE **:** hath holpen His | servant | Israel, ||
In re- | membrance | of His | mercy:
　　As **:** He spake | to our | fathers, ||
To Abraham, and | to his | seed, for | ever.
　　GLORY **:** be to the Father, and | to the | Son, ||
And | to the | Holy | Ghost,
　　As IT **:** was in the beginning, is now, and | ever | shall be ||
World | without | end.　A- | men.

¶ *Then shall be said the Prayers here following, or other suitable prayers, but the* LORD'S PRAYER *shall always be used.*

The Prayers.

MERBECKE.

SUP'T.—Lord, have mercy upon us.

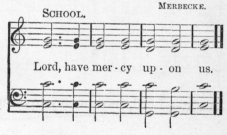

SUP'T.—Christ, have mercy upon us.

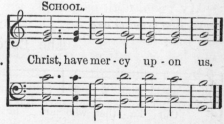

SUP'T.—Lord, have mercy upon us.

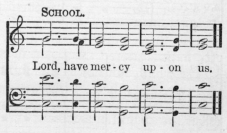

Or this:

EDWIN POTTER.

SUP'T.—Lord, have mercy upon us.

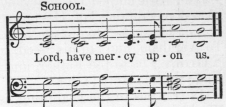

SCHOOL.

Lord, have mer - cy up - on us.

SUP'T.—Christ, have mercy upon us.

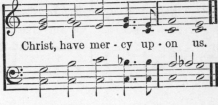

SCHOOL.

Christ, have mer - cy up - on us.

SUP'T.—Lord, have mercy upon us.

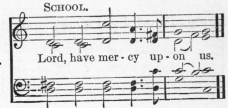

SCHOOL.

Lord, have mer - cy up - on us.

¶ *Then shall be said or sung*

The Lord's Prayer.

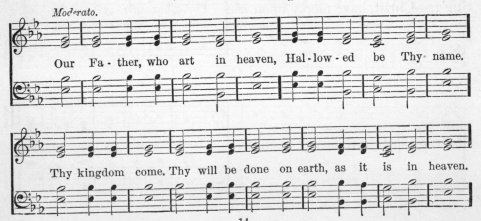

Moderato.

Our Fa - ther, who art in heaven, Hal - low - ed be Thy name.

Thy kingdom come. Thy will be done on earth, as it is in heaven.

14

Give us this day our dai - ly bread. And for - give us our tres - passes, as we for - give those who tres - pass a - gainst us. And lead us not in - to temp - ta - tion, but de - liv - er us from e - vil. For Thine is the king - dom, and the pow - er, and the glo - ry, for - ev - er and ev - er. A - men.

Or this:

The Lord's Prayer.

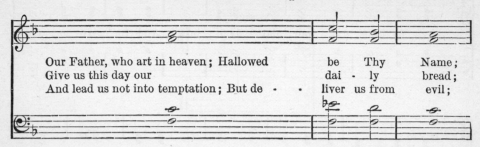

Our Father, who art in heaven; Hallowed be Thy Name;
Give us this day our dai - ly bread;
And lead us not into temptation; But de - - liver us from evil;

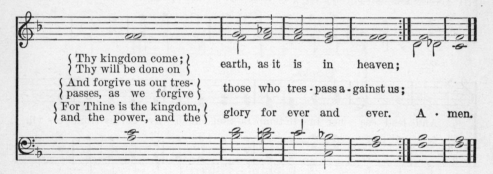

{ Thy kingdom come; }
{ Thy will be done on } earth, as it is in heaven;

{ And forgive us our tres- }
{ passes, as we forgive } those who tres - pass a - gainst us;

{ For Thine is the kingdom, }
{ and the power, and the } glory for ever and ever. A - men.

¶ *Then may be said:*

Sup't.—The Lord be with you.

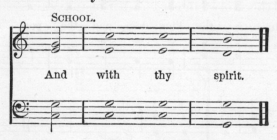

SCHOOL.

And with thy spirit.

Sup't.—Let us pray.

¶ *Then shall be said*

The Collect for the Day.

¶ *Then may two more Collects be said. At the end of each Collect, or at the end of all of the Collects shall be sung or said*

¶ *Then may be said:*

SUP'T.—Bless we the Lord.

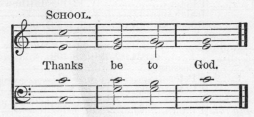

¶ *This may end the Service; or there may be*

A Closing Hymn,

after which may be said:

The Grace of the Lord Jesus Christ, the Love of God, and the Communion of the Holy Ghost, be with us all.

¶ *The School shall sing or say:*

and shall offer silent prayer.

17

TABLE OF THE EPISTLES AND GOSPELS

FOR THE SUNDAYS AND FESTIVALS OF THE CHURCH YEAR.

SUNDAYS AND CHIEF FESTIVALS.	EPISTLES.	GOSPELS.
1 *Sunday in Advent,*	Romans ....xiii. 11–14.	Matthew.................xxi. 1–9
2	................................xv. 4–13.	Luke....................xxi. 25–36.
3	1 Corinthians.............iv. 1–5.	Matthew...................xi. 2–10.
4	Philippians................iv. 4–7.	John.......................i. 19–28
Christmas Day................	Titus ii. 11–14; Isaiah ix. 2–7.	Luke........................ii. 1–14
2	Titus ....iii. 4–7.	..........................ii. 15–20.
Sunday after Christmas,.....	Galatians................iv. 1–7.	..........................ii. 33–40.
Circumcision, New Year,......	........................iii. 23–29.	..............................ii. 21.
Sunday after New Year,......	1 Peter...............iv. 12–19.	Matthew...............ii. 13–23.
Epiphany,....................	Isaiah....................lx. 1–6.	.............................ii. 1–12.
1 *Sun. after Epiphany,*....	Romans ....xii. 1–5.	Luke.....................ii. 41–52.
2	..........................xii. 6–16.ᵃ	John........................ii. 1–11.
3	........................xii. 16–21.ᵇ	Matthew..................viii. 1–13.
4	......................xiii. 8–10.	.........................viii. 23–27.
5	Colossians............iii. 12–17.	.........................xiii. 24–30.
6	2 Peter...................i. 16–21.	.........................xvii. 1–9.
Septuagesima Sunday,.........	1 Corinthians........ix. 24–x. 5.	............................xx. 1–16.
Sexagesima Sunday,.........	2 ....xi. 19–xii. 9.	Luke.....................viii. 4–15.
Quinquagesima Sunday.......	1 ....xiii. 1–13.	.......................xviii. 31–43.
Ash Wednesday,..............	Joel....................ii. 12–19.	Matthew...............vi. 16 21
Sundays in Lent.		
1 *Invocavit,*..............	2 Corinthians..........vi. 1–10.	...........................iv. 1–11.
2 *Reminiscere,*..............	1 Thessalonians.........iv. 1–7.	..........................xv. 21–28.
3 *Oculi,*................	Ephesians..................v. 1–9.	Luke.....................xi. 14–28.
4 *Laetare,*................	Galatians...............iv. 21–31.	John........................vi. 1–15.
5 *Judica,*................	Hebrews................ix. 11–15.	.........................viii. 46–59.
6 *Palmarum,*................	Philippians...............ii. 5–11.	Matthew................xxi. 1–9.
Monday in Holy Week,.......	Isaiah......................l. 5–10.	John......................xii. 1–23.
Tuesday,..................	Jeremiah..............xi. 18–20.	..........................xii. 24–43.
Wednesday,..............	Isaiah..........lxii. 11; lxiii. 1–7.	Luke.........xxii. 1–xxiii. 42.
Holy Thursday,.............	1 Corinthians........xi. 23–32.	John......................xiii. 1–15.
Good Friday,................	Isaiah............liii. 13–liii. 12.	John.........xviii. 1–xix. 42.
Easter Sunday,.............	1 Corinthians............v. 6–8.	Mark.....................xvi. 1–8.
Easter Monday,..............	Acts.....................x. 34–41.	Luke.....................xxiv. 13–35.
Sundays after Easter.		
1 *Quasimodogeniti,*..........	1 John ....v. 4–12.	John.......................xx. 19–31.
2 *Misericordias,*..............	1 Peter...............ii. 21–25.	...........................x. 11–16.
3 *Jubilate,*	........................ii. 11–20.	.......................xvi. 16–23.ᶜ
4 *Cantate,*................	James..................i. 16–21.	..........................xvi. 5–15.
5 *Rogate,*................	........................i. 22–27.	.......................xvi. 23–30.ᵈ
Ascension Day,..............	Acts.......................i. 1–11.	Mark.....................xvi. 14–20.
Sunday after Ascension......	1 Peter...............iv. 7–11.ᵉ	John.............xv. 26–xvi. 4.
Whitsunday,................	Acts....................ii. 1–13.	.......................xiv. 23–31.
Whitmonday,................	...................x. 42–48.ᶠ	..........................iii. 16–21.

ᵃ End: "men of low estate."
ᵇ Begin: "Be not wise in your own conceits."
ᶜ End: "ye shall ask Me nothing."

ᵈ Begin: "Verily, verily, I say."
ᵉ   "   "Be ye therefore sober."
ᶠ End: "In the name of the Lord."

TABLE OF THE EPISTLES AND GOSPELS.—Concluded.

SUNDAYS AND CHIEF FESTIVALS.	EPISTLES.	GOSPELS.
Trinity Sunday, ...	Romans .... xi. 33–36.	John .... iii. 1–15.
1 *Sunday after Trinity,* ...	1 John .... iv. 16–21.*g*	Luke .... xvi. 19–31.
2	1 John .... iii. 13–18.	.... xiv. 16–24.
3	1 Peter .... v. 6–11.	.... xv. 1–10.
4	Romans .... viii. 18–23.	.... vi. 36–42.
5	1 Peter .... iii. 8–15.*h*	.... v. 1–11.
6	Romans .... vi. 3–11.	Matthew .... v. 20–26.
7	.... vi. 19–23.	Mark .... viii. 1–9.
8	.... viii. 12–17.	Matthew .... vii. 15–23.
9	1 Corinthians .... x. 6–13.	Luke .... xvi. 1–9.
10	.... xii. 1–11.	.... xix. 41–48.
11	.... xv. 1–10.	.... xviii. 9–14.
12	2 Corinthians .... iii. 4–11.	Mark .... vii. 31–37.
13	Galatians .... iii. 15–22.	Luke .... x. 23–37.
14	.... v. 16–24.	.... xvii. 11–19.
15	.... v. 25–vi. 10.	Matthew .... vi. 24–34.
16	Ephesians .... iii. 13–21.	Luke .... vii. 11–17.
17	.... iv. 1–6.	.... xiv. 1–11.
18	1 Corinthians .... i. 4–9.	Matthew .... xxii. 34–46.
19	Ephesians .... iv. 22–28.	.... ix. 1–8.
20	.... v. 15–21.	.... xxii. 1–14.
21	.... vi. 10–17.	John .... iv. 46–54.*i*
22	Philippians .... i. 3–11.	Matthew .... xviii. 23–35.
23	.... iii. 17–21.	.... xxii. 15–22.
24	Colossians .... i. 9–14.	.... ix. 18–26.
25	1 Thessalonians .... iv. 13–18.	.... xxiv. 15–28.
26	2 Peter .... iii. 3.–14, or 2 Thessalonians .... i. 3–10.	.... xxv. 31–46.
27	1 Thessalonians .... v. 1–11.	Matthew .... xxv. 1–13.
Reformation, ...	Galatians .... ii. 16–21, Revelation .... xiv. 6–7.	John .... ii. 13–17.

g Begin: "God is love."   *h* End: "sanctify the Lord God in your hearts."
i Begin: "And there was a certain nobleman."

LUTHER'S SMALL CATECHISM.

PART I.

THE TEN COMMANDMENTS.

In the plain form in which they are to be taught by the head of a family.

THE FIRST COMMANDMENT.

I am the Lord thy God. Thou shalt have no other gods before Me.

[Thou shalt not make unto thee any graven image, or any likeness of anything that is in heaven above, or that is in the earth beneath, or that is in the water under the earth; thou shalt not bow down thyself to them, nor serve them: for I the Lord thy God am a jealous God, visiting the iniquity of the fathers upon the children unto the third and fourth generation of them that hate Me; and shewing mercy unto thousands of them that love Me, and keep My commandments.]

What is meant by this Commandment?

Answer. We should fear, love, and trust in God above all things.

THE SECOND COMMANDMENT.

Thou shalt not take the Name of the Lord thy God in vain; for the Lord will not hold him guiltless that taketh His Name in vain.

What is meant by this Commandment?

Answer. We should so fear and love God as not to curse, swear, conjure, lie, or deceive, by His Name, but call upon Him in every time of need, and worship Him with prayer, praise, and thanksgiving.

THE THIRD COMMANDMENT.

Remember the Sabbath day, to keep it holy.

[Six days shalt thou labor, and do all thy work: but the seventh day is the sabbath of the Lord thy God: in it thou shalt not do any work, thou, nor thy son, nor thy daughter, thy manservant, nor thy maidservant, nor thy cattle, nor thy stranger that is within thy gates: for in six days the Lord made heaven and earth, the sea, and all that in them is, and rested the seventh day; wherefore the Lord blessed the sabbath day, and hallowed it.]

What is meant by this Commandment?

Answer. We should so fear and love God as not to despise His Word and the preaching of the Gospel, but deem it holy, and willingly hear and learn it.

THE FOURTH COMMANDMENT.

Honor thy father and thy mother, that thy days may be long upon the land which the Lord thy God giveth thee.

What is meant by this Commandment?

Answer. We should so fear and love God as not to despise nor displease our parents and superiors, but honor, serve, obey, love, and esteem them.

THE FIFTH COMMANDMENT.

Thou shalt not kill.

What is meant by this Commandment?

Answer. We should so fear and love God as not to do our neighbor any bodily harm or injury, but rather assist and comfort him in danger and want.

THE SIXTH COMMANDMENT.

Thou shalt not commit adultery.

What is meant by this Commandment?

Answer. We should so fear and love God as to be chaste and pure in our words and deeds, each one also loving and honoring his wife or her husband.

THE SEVENTH COMMANDMENT.

Thou shalt not steal.

What is meant by this Commandment?

Answer. We should so fear and love God, as not to rob our neighbor of his money or property, nor bring it into our possession by unfair dealing or fraudulent means, but rather assist him to improve and protect it.

THE EIGHTH COMMANDMENT.

Thou shalt not bear false witness against thy neighbor.

What is meant by this Commandment?

Answer. We should so fear and love God as not deceitfully to belie, betray, slander, nor raise injurious reports against our neighbor, but apologize for him, speak well of him, and put the most charitable construction on all his actions.

THE NINTH COMMANDMENT.

Thou shalt not covet thy neighbor's house.

What is meant by this Commandment?

Answer. We should so fear and love God as not to desire by craftiness to gain possession of our neighbor's inheritance or home, or to obtain it under the pretext of a legal right, but be ready to assist and serve him in the preservation of his own.

THE TENTH COMMANDMENT.

Thou shalt not covet thy neighbor's wife, nor his manservant, nor his maidservant, nor his ox, nor his ass, nor any thing that is thy neighbor's.

What is meant by this Commandment?

Answer. We should so fear and love God as not to alienate our neighbor's wife from him, entice away his servants, nor let loose his cattle, but use our endeavors that they may remain and discharge their duty to him.

What does God declare concerning all these Commandments?

Answer. He says: I the Lord thy God am a jealous God, visiting the iniquity of the fathers upon the children unto the third and fourth generation of them that hate Me: and shewing mercy unto thousands of them that love Me and keep My commandments.

What is meant by this declaration?

Answer. God threatens to punish all those who transgress these commandments. We should, therefore, dread His displeasure, and not act contrarily to these commandments. But He promises grace and every blessing to all who keep them. We should, therefore, love and trust in Him, and cheerfully do what He has commanded us.

PART II.

THE CREED.

In the plain form in which it is to be taught by the head of a family.

The First Article.
Of Creation.

I believe in God the Father Almighty, Maker of heaven and earth.

What is meant by this Article?

Answer. I believe that God has created me and all that exists; that He has given and still preserves to me my body and soul, with all my limbs and senses, my reason and all the faculties of my mind, together with my raiment, food, home, and family, and all my property; that He daily provides me abundantly with all the necessaries of life, protects me from all danger, and preserves me and guards me against all evil; all which He does out of pure, paternal, and divine goodness and mercy, without any merit or worthiness in me; for all which I am in duty bound to thank, praise, serve, and obey Him. This is most certainly true.

The Second Article.
Of Redemption.

And in Jesus Christ His only Son, our Lord; Who was conceived by the Holy Ghost, born of the Virgin Mary; suffered under Pontius Pilate, was crucified, dead, and buried; He descended into hell; the third day He rose again from the dead; He ascended into heaven, and sitteth on the right hand of God the Father Almighty; from thence He shall come to judge the quick and the dead.

What is meant by this Article?

Answer. I believe that Jesus Christ, true God, begotten of the Father from eternity, and also true man, born of the Virgin Mary, is my Lord; who has redeemed me, a lost and condemned creature, secured and delivered me from all sins, from death, and from the power of the devil, not with silver and gold, but with His holy and precious blood, and with His innocent sufferings and death; in order that I might be His, live under Him in His kingdom, and serve Him in everlasting righteousness, innocence and blessedness; even as He is risen from the dead, and lives and reigns to all eternity. This is most certainly true.

The Third Article.
Of Sanctification.

I believe in the Holy Ghost; the holy Christian Church, the Communion of Saints; the Forgiveness of sins; the Resurrection of the body; and the Life everlasting. Amen.

What is meant by this Article?

Answer. I believe that I cannot by my own reason or strength believe in Jesus Christ my Lord, or come to Him; but the Holy Ghost has called me through the gospel, enlightened me by His gifts, and sanctified and preserved me in the true faith; in like manner as He calls, gathers, enlightens, and sanctifies the whole Christian Church on earth, and preserves it in union with Jesus Christ in the true faith; in which Christian Church He daily forgives abundantly all my sins, and the sins of all believers, and will raise up me and all the dead at the last day, and will grant everlasting life to me and to all who believe in Christ. This is most certainly true.

PART III.

THE LORD'S PRAYER.

In the plain form in which it is to be taught by the head of a family.

INTRODUCTION.

Our Father who art in heaven.

What is meant by this Introduction?

Answer. God would thereby affectionately encourage us to believe that He is truly our Father, and that we are His children indeed, so that we may call upon Him with all cheerfulness and confidence, even as beloved children entreat their affectionate parent.

FIRST PETITION.

Hallowed be Thy name.

What is meant by this Petition?

Answer. The name of God is indeed holy in itself; but we pray in this petition that it may be hallowed also by us.

How is this effected?

Answer. When the Word of God is taught in its truth and purity, and we, as the children of God, lead holy lives in accordance with it; to this may our blessed Father in heaven help us! But whoever teaches and lives otherwise than as God's Word prescribes, profanes the name of God among us; from this preserve us, Heavenly Father!

SECOND PETITION.

Thy kingdom come.

What is meant by this Petition?

Answer. The kingdom of God comes indeed of itself, without our prayer; but we pray in this petition that it may come unto us also.

When is this effected?

Answer. When our heavenly Father gives us His Holy Spirit, so that by His grace we believe His holy Word, and live a godly life here on earth, and in heaven for ever.

THIRD PETITION.

Thy will be done on earth, as it is in heaven.

What is meant by this Petition?

Answer. The good and gracious will of God is done indeed without our prayer; but we pray in this petition that it may be done by us also.

When is this effected?

Answer. When God frustrates and brings to naught every evil counsel and purpose, which would hinder us from hallowing the name of God, and preventing His kingdom from coming to us, such as the will of the devil, of the world, and of our own flesh; and when He strengthens us, and keeps us steadfast in His Word and in the faith, even unto our end. This is His gracious and good will.

FOURTH PETITION.

Give us this day our daily bread.

What is meant by this Petition?

Answer. God gives indeed without our prayer, even to the wicked also their daily bread; but we pray in this petition that He would make us sensible of His benefits, and enable us to receive our daily bread with thanksgiving.

What is implied in the words: "Our daily bread?"

Answer. All things that pertain to the wants and the support of this present life; such as food, raiment, money, goods, house and land, and other property; a believing spouse and good children; trustworthy servants and faithful magistrates; favorable seasons, peace and health; education and honor; true friends, good neighbors, and the like.

FIFTH PETITION.

And forgive us our trespasses, as we forgive those who trespass against us.

What is meant by this Petition?

Answer. We pray in this petition, that our heavenly Father would not regard our sins, nor deny us our requests on account of them; for we are not worthy of any thing for which we pray, and have not merited it; but that He would grant us all things through grace, although we daily commit much sin, and deserve chastisement alone. We will therefore, on our part, both heartily forgive, and also readily do good to, those who may injure or offend us.

SIXTH PETITION.

And lead us not into temptation.

What is meant by this Petition?

Answer. God indeed tempts no one to sin; but we pray in this petition that God would so guard and preserve us, that the devil, the world, and our own flesh, may not deceive us, nor lead us into error and unbelief, despair, and other great and shameful sins; and that, though we may be thus tempted, we may nevertheless finally prevail and gain the victory.

SEVENTH PETITION.

But deliver us from evil.

What is meant by this Petition?

Answer. We pray in this petition, as in a summary, that our heavenly Father would deliver us from all manner of evil, whether it affect the body or soul, property or character, and, at last, when the hour of death shall arrive, grant us a happy end, and graciously take us from this world of sorrow to Himself in heaven.

CONCLUSION.

For Thine is the kingdom, and the power, and the glory, for ever and ever. Amen.

What is meant by the word "Amen?"

Answer. That I should be assured that such petitions are acceptable to our heavenly Father, and are heard by Him; for He Himself has commanded us to pray in this manner, and has promised that He will hear us. Amen, Amen, that is, Yea, yea, it shall be so.

PART IV.

THE SACRAMENT OF HOLY BAPTISM.

In the plain form in which it is to be taught by the head of a family.

I. *What is Baptism?*

Answer. Baptism is not simply water, but it is the water comprehended in God's command, and connected with God's Word.

What is that Word of God?

Answer. It is that which our Lord Jesus Christ spake, as it is recorded in the last chapter of Matthew, verse 19: "Go ye, and teach all nations, baptizing them in the Name of the Father, and of the Son, and of the Holy Ghost."

II. *What gifts or benefits does Baptism confer?*

Answer. It worketh forgiveness of sins, delivers from death and the devil, and confers everlasting salvation on all who believe as the Word and promise of God declare.

What are such words and promises of God?

Answer. Those which our Lord Jesus Christ spake, as they are recorded in the last chapter of Mark, verse 16 : "He that believeth and is baptized, shall be saved; but he that believeth not shall be damned."

III. *How can water produce such great effects?*

Answer. It is not the water indeed that produces these effects, but the Word of God, which accompanies and is connected with the water, and our faith, which relies on the Word of God, connected with the water. For the water without the Word of God, is simply water and no baptism. But when connected with the Word of God, it is a baptism, that is, a gracious water of life, and a "washing of regeneration" in the Holy Ghost; as St. Paul says to Titus, in the third chapter, verses 5–8 : "According to His mercy He saved us, by the washing of regeneration, and renewing of the Holy Ghost; which He shed on us abundantly through Jesus Christ our Saviour; that being justified by His grace, we should be made heirs according to the hope of eternal life. This is a faithful saying."

IV. *What does such baptizing with water signify?*

Answer. It signifies that the old Adam in us is to be drowned and destroyed by daily sorrow and repentance, together with all sins and evil lusts; and that again the new man should daily come forth and rise, that shall live in the presence of God in righteousness and purity for ever.

Where is it so written?

Answer. St. Paul, in the Epistle to the Romans, chapter 6, verse 4, says: "We are buried with Christ by baptism into death; that like as He was raised up from the dead by the glory of the Father, even so we also should walk in newness of life."

OF CONFESSION.

What is confession?

Answer. Confession consists of two parts: the one is, that we confess our sins; the other, that we receive absolution or forgiveness through the pastor as of God himself, in no wise doubting, but firmly believing, that our sins are thus forgiven before God in heaven.

What sins ought we to confess?

Answer. In the presence of God we should acknowledge ourselves guilty of all manner of sins, even of those which we do not ourselves perceive; as we do in the Lord's Prayer. But in the presence of the pastor we should confess those sins alone of which we have knowledge, and which we feel in our hearts.

Which are these?

Answer. Here reflect on your condition, according to the Ten Commandments, namely: Whether you are a father or mother, a son or daughter, a master or mistress, a manservant or maidservant— whether you have been disobedient, unfaithful, slothful—whether you have injured any one by words or actions—whether you have stolen, neglected, or wasted aught, or done other evil.

PART V.

THE SACRAMENT OF THE ALTAR,

OR

THE LORD'S SUPPER.

In the plain form in which it is to be taught by the head of a family.

What is the Sacrament of the Altar?

Answer. It is the true body and blood of our Lord Jesus Christ, under the bread and wine, given unto us Christians to eat and drink, as it was instituted by Christ himself.

Where is it so written?

Answer. The holy Evangelists, Matthew, Mark, and Luke, together with St. Paul, write thus:

"Our Lord Jesus Christ, the same night in which He was betrayed, took bread: and when He had given thanks, He brake it, and gave it to the disciples, and said, Take, eat; this is My body, which is given for you: this do, in remembrance of Me."

"After the same manner also He took the cup, when He had supped, gave thanks, and gave it to them, saying, Drink ye all of it; this cup is the new testament in My blood, which is shed for you, for the remission of sins: this do ye, as oft as ye drink it, in remembrance of Me."

What benefits are derived from such eating and drinking?

Answer. They are pointed out in these words: "Given and shed for you, for the remission of sins." Namely, through these words, the remission of sins, life and salvation are granted unto us in the Sacrament. For where there is remission of sins, there are also life and salvation.

How can the bodily eating and drinking produce such great effects?

Answer. The eating and the drinking, indeed, do not produce them, but the words which stand here, namely: "Given, and shed for you, for the remission of sins." These words are, besides the bodily eating and drinking, the chief things in the Sacrament; and he who believes these words, has that which they declare and set forth, namely, the remission of sins.

Who is it, then, that receives this Sacrament worthily?

Answer. Fasting and bodily preparation are indeed a good external discipline; but he is truly worthy and well prepared, who believes these words: "Given, and shed for you, for the remission of sins." But he who does not believe these words, or who doubts, is unworthy and unfit; for the words: "FOR YOU," require truly believing hearts.

MORNING AND EVENING PRAYER.

In the plain form in which it is to be taught by the head of a family.

MORNING.

¶ *In the Morning, when thou risest, thou shalt say:*

IN the Name of the Father, and of the Son, and of the Holy Ghost. Amen.

¶ *Then, kneeling or standing, thou shalt say the* Apostles' Creed *and the* Lord's Prayer.

¶ *Then mayest thou say this Prayer:*

I give thanks unto Thee, heavenly Father, through Jesus Christ Thy dear Son, that Thou hast protected me through the night from all danger and harm; and I beseech Thee to preserve and keep me, this day also, from all sin and evil; that in all my thoughts, words, and deeds, I may serve and please Thee. Into Thy hands I commend my body and soul, and all that is mine. Let Thy holy angel have charge concerning me, that the wicked one have no power over me. *Amen.*

¶ *And then shouldst thou go with joy to thy work, after a Hymn, or the* Ten Commandments, *or whatever thy devotion may suggest.*

EVENING.

¶ *In the Evening, when thou goest to bed, thou shalt say:*

In the Name of the Father, and of the Son, and of the Holy Ghost. Amen.

¶ *Then, kneeling or standing, thou shalt say the* Apostles' Creed *and the* Lord's Prayer.

¶ *Then mayest thou say this Prayer:*

I give thanks unto Thee, heavenly Father, through Jesus Christ Thy dear Son, that Thou hast this day so graciously protected me, and I beseech Thee to forgive me all my sins, and the wrong which I have done, and by Thy great mercy defend me from all the perils and dangers of this night. Into Thy hands I commend my body and soul, and all that is mine. Let Thy holy angel have charge concerning me, that the wicked one have no power over me. *Amen.*

¶ *And then lie down in peace, and sleep.*

BLESSING AND THANKSGIVING AT TABLE.

In the plain form in which they are to be taught by the head of a family.

BEFORE MEAT.

¶ *Before meat, the members of the family standing at the table reverently and with folded hands, there shall be said:*

The eyes of all wait upon Thee, O Lord: and Thou givest them their meat in due season. Thou openest Thine hand, and satisfiest the desire of every living thing.

¶ *Then shall be said the* Lord's Prayer, *and after that this Prayer:*

O Lord God, heavenly Father, bless unto us these Thy gifts, which of Thy tender kindness Thou hast bestowed upon us, **through Jesus Christ our Lord. Amen.**

AFTER MEAT.

¶ *After meat, all standing reverently, and with folded hands, there shall be said:*

O give thanks unto the Lord, for He is good; for His mercy endureth for ever. He giveth food to all flesh; He giveth to the beast his food, and to the young ravens which cry. He delighteth not in the strength of the horse; He taketh not pleasure in the legs of a man. The Lord taketh pleasure in them that fear Him: in those that hope in His mercy.

¶ *Then shall be said the* Lord's Prayer, *and after that this Prayer:*

We give thanks to Thee, O God our Father, for all Thy benefits, through Jesus Christ our Lord, Who with Thee liveth and reigneth, for ever and ever. Amen.

TABLE OF DUTIES.

Or, certain passages of the Scriptures, selected for various orders and conditions of men, wherein their respective duties are set forth.

BISHOPS, PASTORS, AND PREACHERS.

A bishop must be blameless, the husband of one wife, vigilant, sober, of good behavior, given to hospitality, apt to teach; not given to wine, no striker, not greedy of filthy lucre; but patient, not a brawler, not covetous; one that ruleth well his own house, having his children in subjection with all gravity; not a novice, but holding fast the faithful Word as he hath been taught, that he may be able by sound doctrine both to exhort and to convince the gainsayers. 1 *Tim.* iii. 2–6; *Tit.* i. 9.

WHAT DUTIES HEARERS OWE THEIR BISHOPS.

Even so hath the Lord ordained that they which preach the Gospel should live of the Gospel, 1 *Cor.* ix. 14. Let him that is taught in the Word communicate unto him that teacheth in all good things, *Gal.* vi. 6. Let the elders that rule well be counted worthy of double honor, especially they who labor in word and doctrine. For the Scripture saith, Thou shalt not muzzle the ox that treadeth out the corn. And, The laborer is worthy of his reward, 1 *Tim.* v. 17, 18. Obey them that have the rule over you, and submit yourselves; for they watch for your souls, as they that must give account, that they may do it with joy and not with grief; for that is unprofitable for you. *Heb.* xiii. 17.

MAGISTRATES.

Let every soul be subject unto the higher powers. For there is no power but of God; the powers that be are ordained of God; for rulers are not a terror to good works, but to the evil. Wilt thou then not be afraid of the power? Do that which is good, and thou shalt have praise of the same; for he is the minister of God to thee for good. But if thou do that which is evil, be afraid; for he beareth not the sword in vain; for he is the minister of God, a revenger to execute wrath upon him that doeth evil. *Rom.* xiii. 1–4.

WHAT DUTIES SUBJECTS OWE MAGISTRATES.

Render therefore unto Cæsar the things that are Cæsar's, *Matt.* xxii. 21. Let every soul be subject unto the higher powers, etc. Wherefore we must needs be subject, not only for wrath, but also for conscience' sake. For this cause pay ye tribute also; for they are God's ministers, attending continually upon this very thing. Render therefore to all their dues; tribute to whom tribute is due; custom to whom custom; fear to whom fear; honor to whom honor, *Rom.* xiii. 1, 5. I exhort, therefore, that, first of all, supplications, prayers, intercessions, and giving of thanks be made for all men; for kings and for all that are in authority, that we may lead a quiet and peaceable life in all godliness and honesty, 1 *Tim.* ii. Put them in mind to be subject to principalities and powers, etc., *Tit.* iii. 1. Submit yourselves to every ordinance of man for the Lord's sake: whether it be to the king as supreme; or unto governors as unto them that are sent, etc., 1 *Pet.* ii. 13.

HUSBANDS.

Ye husbands, dwell with your wives according to knowledge, giving honor unto the wife as unto the weaker vessel, and as being heirs together of the grace of life; that your prayers be not hindered, 1 *Peter* iii. 7. And be not bitter against them. *Col.* iii. 19.

WIVES.

Wives, submit yourselves unto your husbands, as unto the Lord. Even as Sarah obeyed Abraham, calling him lord: whose daughters ye are, as long as ye do well, and are not afraid with any amazement. *Eph.* v. 22; 1 *Pet.* iii. 6.

PARENTS.

Ye fathers, provoke not your children to wrath: but bring them up in the nurture and admonition of the Lord. *Eph.* vi. 4.

28

CHILDREN.

Children, obey your parents in the Lord: for this is right. Honor thy father and mother; which is the first commandment with promise; that it may be well with thee, and thou mayest live long on the earth. *Eph.* vi. 1-3.

MALE AND FEMALE SERVANTS, AND LABORERS.

Servants, be obedient to them that are your masters according to the flesh, with fear and trembling, in singleness of your heart, as unto Christ; not with eye-service, as men-pleasers; but as the servants of Christ, doing the will of God from the heart; with good will doing service, as to the Lord, and not to men; knowing that whatsoever good thing any man doeth, the same shall he receive of the Lord, whether he be bond or free. *Eph.* vi. 5-8.

MASTERS AND MISTRESSES.

Ye masters, do the same things unto them, forbearing threatening; knowing that your Master also is in heaven; neither is there respect of persons with Him. *Eph.* vi. 9.

YOUNG PERSONS, IN GENERAL.

Likewise, ye younger, submit yourselves unto the elder. Yea, all of you be subject one to another, and be clothed with humility; for God resisteth the proud, and giveth grace to the humble. Humble yourselves therefore under the mighty hand of God, that He may exalt you in due time. 1 *Peter* v. 5, 6.

WIDOWS.

She that is a widow indeed, and desolate, trusteth in God, and continueth in supplications and prayers night and day; but she that liveth in pleasure is dead while she liveth. 1 *Tim.* v. 5, 6.

CHRISTIANS, IN GENERAL.

Thou shalt love thy neighbor as thyself Herein are comprehended all the commandments. *Rom.* xiii. 9, 10. And persevere in prayer for all men. 1 *Tim.* ii. 1, 2.

Happy the house where every one learns and does his duty.

GREGORIAN TONES.

These Tones may be sung to any of the Canticles or Psalms.

First Tone.

Second Tone.

Third Tone.

Fourth Tone.

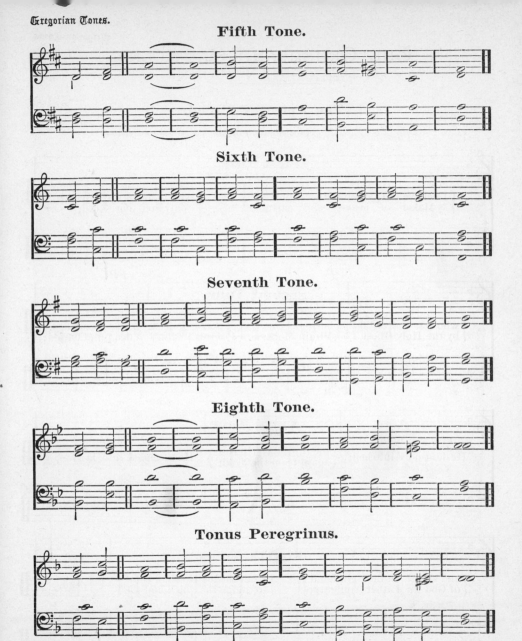

Fifth Tone.

Sixth Tone.

Seventh Tone.

Eighth Tone.

Tonus Peregrinus.

THE CREED AND CANTICLES.

The Apostles' Creed.

(*With harmony.*)

{ I believe in God the Father Almighty, }
{ Maker of heaven and earth. }

{ And in Jesus Christ His }
{ only Son, our Lord; }

p *dim.* *pp*

{ who was conceived }
{ by the Holy Ghost, }

{ born of the }
{ Virgin Mary; }

{ suffered under }
{ Pontius Pilate, }

{ was crucified, }
{ dead, and buried; }

cres - - - cen - - -

He descended into hell;

{ the third day He rose }
{ again from the dead; }

He ascended into heaven,

- do.

{ and sitteth on the right hand }
{ of God the Father Almighty; }

{ from thence He shall come }
{ to judge the quick and the }

dead.

32

f Voices in harmony.

I believe in the Holy Ghost; the holy Christian Church, the Communion of

Ped.

saints; the forgiveness of sins; the Resurrection of the

ff

body; and the Life ev-er-last-ing. A men.

Or this:

The Apostles' Creed.

I believe in God, etc. I believe in the Holy { Ghost; the } { Church, the } holy Christian } { Communion of }

{ saints; the for- } { sins; the Res- } body; and the Life ev-er-last-ing. A-men.
{ giveness of } { urrection of the }

No. 1. Gloria in Excelsis.

OLD CHANT.

Glory be to God on high, and on earth peace, good will towards men.
{ We praise Thee, we bless Thee, we } worship Thee, { we glorify Thee, we give thanks to } Thee for Thy great glory,

O Lord God, heavenly King, God the Fath-er Al - mighty.
{ O Lord, the only begotten Son, } Je - sus Christ; { O Lord God, Lamb of God, } Son of the Father,

That takest away the sin of the world, have mercy up - on us.
Thou that takest away the sin of the world, re - ceive our prayer.
{ Thou that sittest at the right hand of } God the Father, have mercy up - on us.

For Thou only art holy; Thou on - ly art the Lord;
{ Thou only, O Christ, with the } Ho - ly Ghost, { art most high in the } glory of God the Father. A - men.

34

No. 2. Gloria in Excelsis.

Glory be..to God on high, and on earth peace, good will towards men.

{ We praise Thee, we bless Thee, we } worship Thee, { we glorify Thee, we give thanks to } Thee for Thy great glory,

O Lord God, heavenly King, God the Fa-ther Al - mighty.

{ O Lord, the only begotten Son, } Je - sus Christ; { O Lord God, Lamb of God, } Son of the Father,

That takest away..the sin of the world, have mer - cy up - on us.
Thou that takest away..the sin of the world, re - ceive our prayer.

{ Thou that sittest at the right hand..of } God the Father, have mer - cy up - on us.

For Thou on-ly art holy; Thou on - ly art the Lord;

{ Thou only, O Christ, with..the } Ho-ly Ghost, { art most high..in the } glory of God the Father. A-men, A - men.

No. 3. Nunc Dimittis.

ALFRED BENNETT.

CHARLES FRYE.

CROFT.

FIRST TONE.

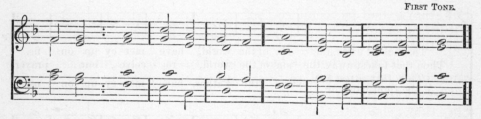

LORD, NOW **:** lettest Thou Thy servant de- | part in | peace: ‖
Ac- | cording | to Thy | Word;
　FOR MINE **:** eyes have seen | Thy sal- | vation ‖
Which Thou hast prepared before the | face of | all | people;
　† A **:** light to | lighten . the | Gentiles ‖
And the glory | of Thy | people | Israel.
　GLORY **:** be to the Father, and | to the | Son, ‖
And | to the | Holy | Ghost,
　As IT **:** was in the beginning, is now, and | ever | shall be, ‖
World | without | end.　A- | men.

　† Repeat second half of double chant in singing this verse.

No. 4. The Beatitudes.

J. Turle.

E. J. Hopkins.   Pring.

Blessed are the | poor in | spirit; ||
For | theirs . is the | kingdom . of | heaven.
Blessed are | they that | mourn, ||
For | they . shall be | comfort- | ed.
Blessed | are the | meek, ||
For | they . shall in- | herit . the | earth.
Blessed are they which do hunger and thirst after | righteous-|ness; ||
For | they . | shall be | filled.
Blessed are the | merci- | ful; ||
For | they . shall ob- | tain | mercy.
Blessed are the | pure in | heart; ||
For | they . shall | see | God.
Blessed are the | peace- | makers; ||
For they . shall be called the | children | of | God.
Blessed are they which are persecuted for | righteous-.ness' | sake; ||
For | theirs . is the | kingdom of | heaven.
Blessed are ye, when men shall revile you, and | perse-cute | you ||
And shall say all manner of evil against you | falsely | for My | sake.
Rejoice and be ex- | ceeding | glad ||
For great is | your re- | ward in | heaven.

No. 5. Te Deum Laudamus.

a) We praise | Thee, O | God ||
We acknowledge | Thee to | be the | Lord.
  All the earth doth | worship | Thee ||
The Father | ever- | last- | ing.
  To Thee all angels | cry a- | loud ||
The heavens, and | all the | powers there- | in.
  To Thee Cherubim and | Sera- | phim ||
Con- | tinual- | ly do | cry,
  Holy, | Holy, | Holy ||
Lord | God of | Saba- | oth;
  Heaven and earth are full of the | Majes- | ty ||
Of | Thy | Glo- | ry.

The glorious company of the Apostles | praise | Thee ||
The goodly fellowship of the | Prophets | praise | Thee.
   The noble army of Martyrs | praise | Thee ||
The holy Church throughout all the world | doth ac- | knowledge | Thee.
   The Father of an infinite | Majes- | ty; ||
Thine adorable, | true and | only | Son.
   Also the | Holy | Ghost ||
The | Com- | . fort- | er.
   b) Thou art the King of Glory | O | Christ. ||
Thou art the everlasting Son | of the | Fa- | ther.
   When Thou tookest upon Thee to de- | liver | man ||
Thou didst humble Thyself to be | born | of a | Virgin.
   When Thou hadst overcome the | sharpness . of | death ||
Thou didst open the kingdom of heaven to | all be- | liev- | ers.
   Thou sittest at the right | hand of | God ||
In the | glory | of the | Father.
   We believe that Thou shalt come to | be our | Judge ||
We therefore pray Thee, help Thy servants whom Thou hast re-
deemed | with Thy | precious | blood.
   Make them to be numbered | with Thy | saints ||
In glory | ever- | last- | ing.
   O Lord, | save Thy | people ||
And | bless Thine | herit- | age.
   Gov- | ern | them ||
And lift them | up for | ev- | er.
   c) Day | by | day ||
We | magni- | fy | Thee.
   And we | worship . Thy | Name ||
Ever, | world with- | out | end.
   Vouch- | safe, O | Lord ||
To keep us this | day with- | out | sin.
   O Lord, have | mercy . up- | on us ||
Have | mercy . up- | on | us.
   O Lord, let Thy mercy | be up- | on us ||
As our | trust | is in | Thee.
   O Lord, in Thee | have I | trusted ||
Let me never | be con- | found- | ed. | Amen.

No. 6. Benedicite, Omnia Opera.

S. MATTHEWS.

ISAAC BARROW.

H. C. BANISTER.

EIGHTH TONE.

O ALL : ye works of the Lord, | bless . ye the | Lord ||
Praise Him and | magni - fy | Him for | ever.
  O ye Angels of the Lord, | bless . ye the | Lord ||

O ye Heavens, | bless | ye the | Lord.
O ye Waters that be above the firmament, | bless . ye the | Lord ||
O ye Powers of the Lord, | bless | ye the | Lord.
O ye Sun and Moon, | bless . ye the | Lord ||
O ye Stars of heaven, | bless | ye the | Lord.
O ye Showers and Dew, | bless . ye the | Lord ||
O ye Winds of God, | bless | ye the | Lord.
O ye Fire and Heat, | bless . ye the | Lord ||
O ye Winter and Summer, | bless | ye the | Lord.
O ye Dews and Frosts, | bless . ye the | Lord ||
O ye Frost and Cold, | bless | ye the | Lord.
O ye Ice and Snow, | bless . ye the | Lord ||
O ye Nights and Days, | bless | ye the | Lord.
O ye Light and Darkness, | bless . ye the | Lord ||
O ye Lightnings and Clouds, | bless | ye the | Lord.
O let the Earth | bless the | Lord ||
Yea, let it praise Him, and | magni - fy | Him for | ever.
O ye Mountains and Hills, | bless . ye the | Lord ||
O all ye Green Things upon the earth, | bless | ye the | Lord.
O ye Wells, | bless . ye the | Lord ||
O ye Seas and Floods, | bless | ye the | Lord.
O ye Whales and all that move in the waters, | bless . ye the | Lord ||
O all ye Fowls of the air, | bless | ye the | Lord.
O all ye Beasts and Cattle, | bless . ye the | Lord ||
O ye Children of Men, | bless | ye the | Lord.
O let Israel | bless the | Lord ||
Praise Him and | magni - fy | Him for | ever.
O ye Priests of the Lord, | bless . ye the | Lord ||
O ye servants of the Lord, | bless | ye the | Lord.
O ye Spirits and Souls of the Righteous, | bless . ye the | Lord. ||
O ye holy and humble Men of heart, | bless | ye the | Lord.
Bless we the Father, and the Son, and the | Holy | Ghost ||
Let us praise Him and | magni - fy | Him for | ever.
GLORY : be to the Father, and | to the | Son, ||
And | to the | Holy | Ghost,
As IT : was in the beginning, is now, and | ever | shall be: ||
World | without | end.   A- | men.

41

Psalms and Chants.
(Festival and General.)

Advent.

(MATINS.)

No. 1. Benedixisti, Domine. Psalm 85.

J. S. SMITH.

HAGER.

W. SAVAGE.

LORD, THOU : hast been favorable | unto . Thy | land ||
Thou hast brought back the cap- | tivi- | ty of | Jacob.
Thou hast forgiven the iniquity | of Thy | people ||
Thou hast | covered | all their | sin.
Thou hast taken away | all Thy | wrath ||
Thou hast turned Thyself from the | fierceness | of Thine | anger.
Turn us, O God of | our sal- | vation ||
And cause Thine | anger . toward | us to | cease.
Wilt Thou be angry with | us for | ever? ||
Wilt Thou draw out Thine anger to | all | gener- | ations?
Wilt Thou not re- | vive us . a- | gain ||
That Thy people | may re- | joice in | Thee?
Shew us Thy | mercy, O | Lord ||
And | grant us | Thy sal- | vation.

I will hear what God the | Lord will | speak ||
For He will speak peace unto His people, and to His saints;   but let
them not | turn a- | gain to | folly.

Surely His salvation is nigh | them that | fear Him ||
That glory may | dwell | in our | land.

Mercy and truth are | met to- | gether ||
Righteousness and | peace have | kissed each | other.

Truth shall spring | out . of the | earth ||
And righteousness | shall look | down from | heaven.

Yea, the Lord shall give | that . which is | good ||
And our | land shall | yield her | increase.

† Righteousness shall | go be- | fore Him ||
And shall set us in the | way of | His | steps.

† Repeat the second half of double chant in singing this verse.

(VESPERS.)

No. 2.   Confitebor tibi.   Psalm 111.

GIBBONS.

ANON.   HINE.

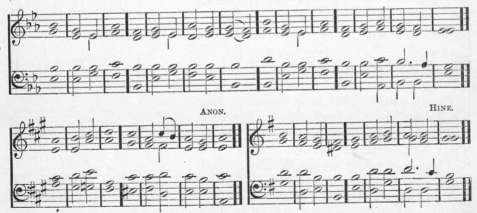

PRAISE YE : the Lord. I will praise the Lord with | my whole | heart ||
In the assembly of the upright, and | in the | congre- | gation.

The works of the | Lord are | great ||
Sought out of all | them . that have | pleasure . there- | in.

His work is honorable and | glor- | ious ||
And His righteous- | ness en- | dureth . for | ever.

43

He hath made His wonderful works to | be re- | membered ||
The Lord is gracious and | full | of com- | passion.
He hath given meat unto | them that | fear Him ||
He will ever be | mindful | of His | covenant.
He hath shewed His people the power | of His | works ||
That He may give them the | herit- . age | of the | heathen.
The works of His hands are verity and | judg- | ment ||
All His com- | mandments | are | sure.
They stand fast for | ever . and | ever. ||
And are done in | truth and | upright- | ness.
He sent redemption | unto . His | people ||
He hath commanded His covenant for ever: holy and | rever- . end
is His | Name.
The fear of the Lord is the be- | ginning . of | wisdom ||
A good understanding have all they that do His commandments;
His | praise en- | dureth . for | ever.

Christmas.

(MATINS.)

No. 3.   Memento, Domine.   Psalm 132.

LORD, RE- : member | Da- | vid ||
And | all | his af- | flictions;
How he sware | unto . the | Lord ||

And vowed unto the | mighty | God of | Jacob;
  Surely I will not come into the tabernacle | of my | house ||
Nor | go up | into my | bed;
  I will not give sleep | to mine | eyes ||
Or | slumber | to mine | eyelids,
  Until I find out a place | for the | Lord ||
An habitation for the | mighty | God of | Jacob.
  Lo, we heard of it at | Ephra- | tah ||
We found it in the | fields | of the | wood.
  We will go into His | taber- | nacles ||
We will | worship | at His | footstool.
  Arise, O Lord, | into . Thy | rest ||
Thou, and the | ark of | Thy | strength.
  Let Thy priests be clothed with | righteous- | ness ||
And let Thy | saints | shout for | joy.
  For Thy servant | David's | sake ||
Turn not away the | face of | Thine A- | nointed.
  The Lord hath sworn in truth | unto | David ||
He | will not | turn from | it;
  Of the fruit of | thy | body ||
Will I | set up- | on thy | throne.
  If thy children will keep My covenant and My testimony that I
shall | teach | them ||
Their children shall also sit upon thy | throne for | ever- | more.
  For the Lord hath | chosen | Zion ||
He hath desired it | for His | habi- | tation.
  This is My | rest for | ever ||
Here will I dwell; for | I . have de- | sired | it.
  I will abundantly | bless . her pro- | vision ||
I will satis- | fy her | poor with | bread.
  I will also clothe her priests | with sal- | vation ||
And her saints shall | shout a- | loud for | joy.
  There will I make the horn of | David . to | bud ||
I have ordained a | lamp for | Mine A- | nointed.
  † His enemies will I | clothe with | shame ||
But upon himself | shall his | crown | flourish.

  † Repeat second half of double chant in singing this verse.

(VESPERS.)

No. 4. Quare fremuerunt gentes. Psalm 2.

J. RANDALL.

GOSS.   OUSELEY.

WHY : do the | heathen | rage ||
And the people im- | agine . a | vain | thing?
The kings of the earth set themselves, and the rulers take | counsel .
to- | gether ||
Against the Lord, and against | His A- | nointed, | saying,
Let us break their | bands a- | sunder ||
And cast a- | way their | cords from | us.
He that sitteth in the | heavens . shall | laugh ||
The Lord shall | have them | in de- | rision.
Then shall He speak unto them | in His | wrath ||
And vex them | in His | sore dis- | pleasure.
Yet have I | set My | King ||
Upon My | holy | hill of | Zion.
I will | declare . the de- | cree ||
The Lord hath said unto Me, Thou art My Son; this day have | I
be- | gotten | Thee.
Ask of Me, and I shall give Thee the heathen for Thine in- | herit- | ance ||
And the uttermost parts of the | earth for | Thy pos- | session.
Thou shalt break them with a | rod of | iron ||
Thou shalt dash them in pieces | like a | potter's | vessel.

Be wise now therefore, | O ye | kings ||
Be instructed, ye | judges | of the | earth.
   Serve the | Lord with | fear ||
And re- | joice | . with | trembling.
   Kiss the Son, lest He be angry, and ye perish from the way, when
His wrath is kindled | but a | little ||
Blessed are all they that | put their | trust in | Him.

Epiphany.

(MATINS.)

No. 5. Deus, judicium. Psalm 72.

HIGGINS.

OUSELEY. ELVEY.

GIVE THE **:** king Thy judgments, | O | God ||
And Thy righteousness | unto . the | King's | Son.
   He shall judge Thy people with | righteous- | ness ||
And | Thy | poor with | judgment.
   The mountains shall bring peace | to the | people ||
And the little | hills, by | righteous- | ness.
   He shall judge the poor of the people, He shall save the children |
of the | needy ||
And shall break in | pieces | the op- | pressor.

They shall fear Thee as long as the sun and | moon en- | dure ||
Through- | out all | gener- | ations.

He shall come down like rain upon the | mown | grass ||
As | showers . that | water . the | earth.

In His days shall the | righteous | flourish ||
And abundance of peace so | long . as the | moon en- | dureth.

He shall have dominion also from | sea to | sea ||
And from the river unto the | ends | of the | earth.

They that dwell in the wilderness shall | bow be- | fore Him ||
And His | enemies . shall | lick the | dust.

The kings of Tarshish and of the isles | shall bring | presents ||
The kings of Sheba and | Seba . shall | offer | gifts.

Yea, all the kings shall fall | down be- | fore Him ||
All | nations . shall | serve | Him.

For He shall deliver the needy | when he | crieth ||
The poor also, and | him that | hath no | helper.

He shall spare the | poor and | needy ||
And shall save the | souls | of the | needy.

He shall redeem their soul from deceit and | vio- | lence ||
And precious shall their | blood be | in His | sight.

And He shall live, and to Him shall be given of the | gold of |
Sheba ||
Prayer also shall be made for Him continually, and | daily . shall | He
be | praised.

There shall be a handful of corn in the earth upon the top of the
mountains: the fruit thereof shall | shake like | Lebanon ||
And they of the city shall | flourish . like | grass . of the | earth.

His Name shall endure for ever; His Name shall be continued
as | long as . the | sun ||
And men shall be blessed in Him; all | nations . shall | call Him |
blessed.

Blessed be the Lord God, the | God of | Israel ||
Who only | doeth | wondrous | things.

† And blessed be His glorious | Name for | ever ||
And let the whole earth be filled with His glory.   A- | men, and |
A- | men.

† Repeat second half of double chant in singing this verse.

48

(VESPERS.)

No. 6. Domine, Dominus Noster. Psalm 8.

LEMON.

STAINER.

O : Lord, our Lord, how excellent is Thy Name in | all the | earth ||
Who hast set Thy | glory . a- | bove the | heavens.

Out of the mouth of babes and sucklings hast Thou ordained
strength because of | Thine | enemies ||
That Thou mightest still the enemy | and . the a- | ven- | ger.

When I consider Thy heavens, the | work of . Thy | fingers ||
The moon and the stars, which Thou | hast or- | dain- | ed ;

What is man, that Thou art | mindful . of | him ||
And the son of man, | that Thou | visit-est | him ?

For Thou hast made him a little lower | than the | angels ||
And hast crowned him with | glory . and | hon- | or.

Thou madest him to have dominion over the | works of . Thy | hands ||
Thou hast put | all things | under . his | feet ;

All | sheep and | oxen ||
Yea, and the | beasts | of the | field ;

The fowl of the air, and the | fish of . the | sea ||
And whatsoever passeth through the | paths | of the | seas.

† O | Lord, our | Lord ||
How excellent is Thy | Name in | all the | earth !

† Repeat second half of double chant in singing this verse.

Lent.

(MATINS.)

No. 7. Miserere mei Deus, secundam. Psalm 51.

LANGDON.

RANDALL.

CROTCH.

W. FELTON.

HAVE : mercy upon me, O God, according to Thy | loving | kindness ||
According unto the multitude of Thy tender mercies, | blot out | my
trans- | gressions.

Wash me thoroughly from | mine in- | iquity ||
And | cleanse me | from my | sin.

For I acknowledge | my trans- | gressions ||
And my | sin is | ever . be- | for me.

Against Thee, Thee only, have I sinned, and done this evil | in Thy | sight ||
That Thou mightest be justified when Thou speakest, and be | clear | when Thou | judgest.

Behold, I was shapen | in in- | iquity ||
And in | sin . did my | mother . con- | ceive me.

Behold, Thou desirest truth in the | inward | parts ||
And in the hidden part Thou shalt | make . me to | know | wisdom.

♦ Purge me with hyssop, and | I . shall be | clean ||
Wash me, and | I . shall be | whiter . than | snow.

Make me to hear | joy and | gladness ||
That the bones which Thou hast | broken | may re- | joice.

Hide Thy face | from my | sins ||
And blot out | all . mine in- | iqui- | ties.

Create in me a clean | heart, O | God ||
And re- | new a . right | spirit . with- | in me.

Cast me not a- | way from . Thy | presence ||
And take not Thy | Holy | Spirit | from me.

Restore unto me the joy of | Thy sal- | vation ||
And uphold | me with | Thy free | Spirit.

Then will I teach trans- | gressors . Thy | ways ||
And sinners shall be con- | verted | unto | Thee.

Deliver me from blood-guiltiness, O God, Thou God of | my sal- | vation ||
And my tongue shall sing aloud | of Thy | righteous- | ness.

O Lord, open | Thou my | lips ||
And my mouth shall | show forth | Thy | praise.

For Thou desirest not sacrifice, else | would I | give it ||
Thou delightest | not in | burnt | offering.

The sacrifices of God are a | broken | spirit ||
A broken and a contrite heart, O God, | Thou wilt | not de- | spise.

Do good in Thy good pleasure | unto | Zion ||
Build Thou the | walls . of Je- | rusa- | lem.

† Then shalt Thou be pleased with the sacrifices of righteousness, with burnt offering and | whole burnt | offering ||
Then shall they offer bullocks up- | on Thine | Al- | tar.

† Repeat second half of double chant in singing this verse.

No. 8. Domine, exaudi. Psalm 143.

R. COOKE.

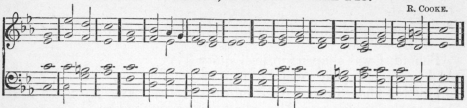

HEAR MY : prayer, O Lord, give ear to my | suppli- | cations ||
In Thy faithfulness answer me, and | in Thy | righteous- | ness.

And enter not into judgment | with Thy | servant ||
For in Thy sight shall no man | living . be | justi- | fied.

For the enemy hath persecuted my soul; he hath smitten my life |
down . to the | ground ||
He hath made me to dwell in darkness, as | those . that have | been
long | dead.

Therefore is my spirit over- | whelmèd . with- | in me ||
My heart with- | in me . is | deso- | late.

I remember the days of old; I meditate on | all Thy | works ||
I muse on the | work | of Thy | hands.

I stretch forth my hands | unto | Thee ||
My soul thirsteth after | Thee, . as a | thirsty | land.

Hear me speedily, O Lord; my | spirit | faileth ||
Hide not Thy face from me, lest I be like unto them that | go down |
into . the | pit.

Cause me to hear Thy lovingkindness in the morning; for in |
Thee . do I | trust ||
Cause me to know the way wherein I shall walk; for I | lift . up
my | soul unto | Thee.

Deliver me, O Lord, | from mine | enemies ||
I flee unto | Thee to | hide | me.

Teach me to do Thy will; for | Thou art . my | God ||
Thy Spirit is good; lead me into the | land | of up- | rightness.

Quicken me, O Lord, for Thy | Name's | sake ||
For Thy righteousness' sake | bring my | soul . out of | trouble.

And of Thy mercy cut | off mine | enemies ||
And destroy all them that afflict my soul; for | I am | Thy | servant.

Easter.

(MATINS.)

No. 9.   Conserva me, Domine.   Psalm 16.

C. H. STEWART.

PRE- : serve | me, O | God ||
For in Thee | do I | put my | trust.

O my soul, thou hast said unto the Lord, Thou | art my | Lord ||
My goodness ex- | tendeth | not to | Thee;

But to the saints that are in the earth, and | to the | excellent ||
In whom is | all | my de- | light.

Their sorrows shall be | multi- | plied ||
That hasten | after . an- | other | god.

Their drink offerings of blood will | I not | offer ||
Nor take up their | names | into . my | lips.

The Lord is the portion of mine inheritance and | of my | cup ||
Thou main- | tainest | my | lot.

The lines are fallen unto me in | pleasant | places ||
Yea, I have a | goodly | herit- | age.

I will bless the Lord, Who hath | given . me | counsel ||
My reins also instruct me | in the | night- | seasons.

I have set the Lord | always . be- | fore me ||
Because He is at my right hand, I | shall not | be | moved.

Therefore my heart is glad, and my | glory . re- | joiceth ||
My flesh also shall | rest | . in | hope.

For Thou wilt not leave my | soul in | hell ||
Neither wilt Thou suffer Thine Holy | One to | see cor- | ruption.

Thou wilt shew me the | path of | life ||
In Thy presence is fullness of joy; at Thy right hand there are |
pleasures . for | ever- | more.

(VESPERS.)

No. 10. Confitemini Domino. Psalm 118.

O GIVE **:** thanks unto the Lord, for | He is | good ||
Because His | mercy **.** en- | dureth **.** for | ever.

   Let Israel | now | say ||
That His | mercy **.** en- | dureth **.** for | ever.

   Let the house of Aaron | now | say ||
That His | mercy **.** en- | dureth **.** for | ever.

   Let them now that fear the | Lord | say ||
That His | mercy **.** en- | dureth **.** for | ever.

   I called upon the | Lord **.** in dis- | tress ||
The Lord answered me, and set me | in a | large | place.

   The Lord is on my side; I | will not | fear ||
What can | man do | unto | me?

   The Lord taketh my part with | them that | help me ||
Therefore shall I see my desire upon | them that | hate | me.

   It is better to | trust **.** in the | Lord ||
Than to put | confi- | dence in | man.

   It is better to | trust **.** in the | Lord ||
Than to put | confi- | dence in | princes.

   All nations compassed | me a- | bout ||
But in the Name of the | Lord will | I de- | stroy them.

   They compassed me about; yea, they compassed | me a- | bóut ||
But in the Name of the | Lord I | will de- | stroy them.

   They compassed me about like bees; they are quenched as the ⟩
fire of | thorns ||

For in the Name of the | Lord I | will de- | stroy them.

Thou hast thrust sore at me that | I might | fall ||

But the | Lord | helped | me.

The Lord is my | strength and | song ||

And is be- | come | my sal- | vation.

The voice of rejoicing and salvation is in the tabernacles | of the
righteous ||

The right hand of the Lord | doeth | valiant- | ly.

The right hand of the Lord | is ex- | alted ||

The right hand of the Lord | doeth | valiant- | ly.

I shall not | die, but | live ||

And de- | clare the | works . of the | Lord.

The Lord hath chastened . me | sore ||

But He hath not given me | over | unto | death.

Open to me the gates of | righteous- | ness ||

I will go into them, and | I will | praise the | Lord.

This | gate . of the | Lord ||

Into which the | righteous | shall | enter.

I will praise Thee, for | Thou hast | heard me ||

And art be- | come | my sal- | vation.

The stone which the | builders . re- | fused ||

Is become the | head stone | of the | corner.

This is the | Lord's | doing ||

It is | marvel- . lous | in our | eyes.

This is the day which the | Lord hath | made ||

We will rejoice | and be | glad in | it.

Save now, I beseech Thee, | O | Lord ||

O Lord, I beseech Thee, | send | now pros- | perity.

Blessed be He that cometh in the | Name . of the | Lord ||

We have blessed you out of the | house | of the | Lord.

God is the Lord, which hath | showed . us | light ||

Bind the sacrifice with cords, even unto the | horns | of the | altar.

Thou art my God, and I will | praise | Thee ||

Thou art my God, | I . will ex- | alt | Thee.

† O give thanks unto the Lord; for | He is | good ||

For His | mercy . en- | dureth . for | ever.

† Repeat the second half of double chant in singing this verse.

Ascension.

(MATINS.)

No. 11. Domini est terra. Psalm 24.

PRATT.

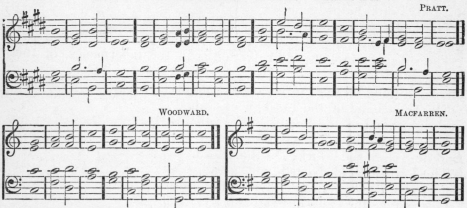

WOODWARD.

MACFARREN.

THE : earth is the Lord's, and the | fulness . there- | of ||
The world, and | they that | dwell there- | in.

For He hath founded it up- | on the | seas ||
And established | it up- | on the | floods.

Who shall ascend into the | hill . of the | Lord ||
Or who shall stand | in His | holy | place?

He that hath clean hands, and a | pure | heart ||
Who hath not lifted up his soul unto vanity, nor) sworn de- | ceitful- | ly.

He shall receive the blessing | from the | Lord ||
And righteousness from the | God of | his sal- | vation.

This is the generation of | them that | seek Him ||
That | seek thy | face, O | Jacob.

Lift up your heads, O ye gates; and be ye lift up, ye ever- |
lasting | doors ||
And the King of | glory | shall come | in.

Who is this | King of | glory? ||
The Lord strong and mighty, the | Lord | mighty . in | battle.

Lift up your heads, O ye gates; even lift them up, ye ever- |
lasting | doors ||
And the King of | glory | shall come | in.

Who is this | King of | glory? ||
The Lord of hosts, | He . is the | King of | glory.

(VESPERS.)

No. 12. Dixit Dominus. Psalm 110.

JACOB.

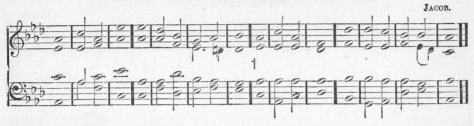

OUSELEY.　　　　　　　　W. S. HOYTE.

THE LORD : said | unto . my | Lord ||
Sit Thou at My right hand, until I make Thine | ene - mies | Thy |
footstool.

The Lord shall send the rod of Thy strength | out of | Zion ||
Rule Thou in the | midst | of Thine | enemies.

Thy people shall be willing in the day of Thy power, in the beau-
ties of holiness from the | womb . of the | morning ||
Thou hast the | dew | of Thy | youth.

The Lord hath sworn, and will | not re- | pent ||
Thou art a priest for ever after the order | of Mel- | chize- | dek.

The Lord at | Thy right | hand ||
Shall strike through kings in the | day | of His | wrath.

He shall judge among the heathen, He shall fill the places with
the | dead | bodies ||
He shall wound the heads | over | many | countries.

† He shall drink of the | brook . in the | way ||
Therefore shall He | lift | up the | head.

† Repeat second half of double chant in singing this verse.

57

Pentecost.

(MATINS.)

No. 13.   Exaltabo Te.   Psalm 145.

I WILL : extol Thee, my | God, O | King ||
And I will bless Thy | Name for | ever . and | ever.
　Every day will I | bless | Thee ||
And I will praise Thy | Name for | ever . and | ever.
　Great is the Lord, and greatly | to be | praised ||
And His greatness | is un- | searcha- | ble.
　One generation shall praise Thy | works . to an- | other ||
And shall de- | clare Thy | mighty | acts.

I will speak of the glorious honor of Thy | majes- | ty ||
And | of Thy | wondrous | works.

And men shall speak of the might of Thy | terri- . ble | acts ||
And I will de- | clare Thy | great- | ness.

They shall abundantly utter the memory of | Thy great |
goodness ||
And shall sing of | Thy | righteous- | ness.

The Lord is gracious, and | full of . com- | passion ||
Slow to anger, | and of | great | mercy.

The Lord is | good to | all ||
And His tender mercies are | over | all His | works.

All Thy works shall praise Thee, | O | Lord ||
And Thy | saints shall | bless | Thee.

They shall speak of the glory | of Thy | kingdom ||
And | talk | of Thy | power;

To make known to the sons of men His | mighty | acts ||
And the glorious | majes- . ty | of His | kingdom.

Thy kingdom is an ever- | lasting | kingdom ||
And Thy dominion endureth through- | out all | gener- | ations.

The Lord upholdeth | all that | fall ||
And raiseth up all those | that be | bowed | down.

The eyes of all | wait up- . on | Thee ||
And Thou givest them their | meat in | due | season.

Thou | openest . Thine | hand ||
And satisfiest the desire of | every | living | thing.

The Lord is righteous in | all His | ways ||
And | holy . in | all His | works.

The Lord is nigh unto all them that | call up- | on Him ||
To all that call | up- on | Him in | truth.

He will fulfil the desire of | them that | fear Him ||
He also will hear their cry, | and will | save | them.

The Lord preserveth all | them that | love Him ||
But all the | wicked . will | He de- | stroy.

† My mouth shall speak the | praise . of the | Lord ||
And let all flesh bless His holy | Name for | ever . and | ever.

† Repeat second half of double chant in singing this verse.

59

(VESPERS.)

No. 14. Benedic, Anima mea. Psalm 104.

R. COOKE, OR RUSSELL.

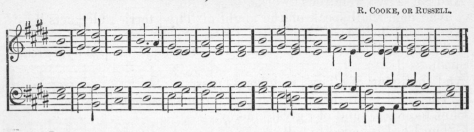

TURLE.   G. A. MACFARREN.

BLESS THE : Lord, | O my | soul ||
O Lord my God, Thou art very great; Thou art clothed with | honor.
and | majes- | ty.

Who coverest Thyself with light as | with a | garment ||
Who stretchest out the | heavens | like a | curtain.

Who maketh His | angels | spirits ||
His | ministers . a | flaming | fire.

O Lord, how manifold | are Thy | works ||
In wisdom hast Thou made them all; the earth is | full of | Thy | riches.

Thou sendest forth Thy Spirit, they | are cre- | ated ||
And Thou renewest the | face | of the | earth.

The glory of the Lord shall en- | dure for | ever ||
The Lord shall re- | joice | in His | works.

I will sing unto the Lord as | long . as I | live ||
I will sing praise to my God | while I | have my | being.

My meditation of Him | shall be | sweet ||
I will be | glad | in the | Lord.

Trinity.

(MATINS.)

No. 15. Deus misereatur nostri. Psalm 67.

FLINTOFF.

GARRETT.

GOSS.

GOD BE : merciful unto | us, and | bless us ||
And cause His | face to | shine up- | on us.

That Thy way may be | known . upon | earth ||
Thy saving | health a- | mong all | nations.

Let the people praise | Thee, O | God ||
Let | all the | people | praise Thee.

O let the nations be glad and | sing for | joy ||
For Thou shalt judge the people righteously, and govern the | nations |
upon | earth.

Let the people praise | Thee, O | God ||
Let | all the | people | praise Thee.

Then shall the earth | yield her | increase ||
And God, even our own | God, shall | bless | us.

† God |. shall | bless us ||
And all the | ends . of the | earth shall | fear Him.

† Repeat second half of double chant in singing this verse.

61

(VESPERS.)

No. 16. Lauda, anima mea. Psalm 146.

RANDALL.

GADSBY.

FELTON.

PRAISE : | ye the | Lord ||
Praise the | Lord, | O my | soul.

While I live will I | praise the | Lord ||
I will sing praises unto my God | while I | have any | being.

Put not your | trust in | princes ||
Nor in the son of man, in | whom there | is no | help.

His breath goeth forth, he returneth | to his | earth ||
In that very | day his | thoughts | perish.

Happy is he that hath the God of Jacob | for his | help ||
Whose hope is in the | Lord | his | God;

Which made heaven and earth, the sea, and all that | therein | is ||
Which | keepeth | truth for | ever:

Which executeth judgment | for the . op- | pressed ||
Which giveth | food | to the | hungry.

The Lord | looseth . the | prisoners ||
The Lord openeth the | eyes | of the | blind.

The Lord raiseth them that are | bowed | down ||
The Lord | loveth . the | right- | eous.

The Lord preserveth the strangers; He relieveth the father- | less
and | widow ||
But the way of the wicked He | turneth | upside | down.

† The Lord shall reign for ever, even thy God, O Zion, unto |
all gener- | ations ||
Praise | ye | . the | Lord.   † Repeat second half of double chant in singing this verse.

Reformation.
(MATINS.)
No. 17. Deus noster refugium. Psalm 46.

LUTHER.

W. H. HAVERGAL.

TALLIS.

GOD IS : our | Refuge . and | Strength ||
A very | present | help in | trouble.
    Therefore will not we fear, though the | earth . be re- | moved ||
And though the mountains be carried into the | midst | of the | sea;
    Though the waters thereof | roar . and be | troubled ||
Though the mountains | shake . with the | swelling . there- | of.
    There is a river, the streams whereof shall make glad the | city . of | God ||
The holy place of the tabernacles | of the | Most | High.
    God is in the midst of her; she shall | not be | moved ||
God shall help her, and | that right | ear- | ly.
    The heathen raged, the | kingdoms . were | moved ||
He uttered His | voice, the | earth | melted.
    The Lord of | hosts is | with us ||
The God of | Jacob | is our | Refuge.
    Come, behold the | works . of the | Lord ||
What desolations | He hath | made . in the | earth.
    He maketh wars to cease unto the | end . of the | earth ||
He breaketh the bow, and cutteth the spear in sunder; He burneth
the | chari - ot | in the | fire.
    Be still, and know that | I am | God ||
I will be exalted among the heathen, I will be ex- | alted | in the | earth.
    † The Lord of | hosts is | with us ||
The God of | Jacob | is our | Refuge.

† Repeat second half of double chant in singing this verse.   63

(VESPERS.)

No. 18. In Convertendo. Psalm 126.

WHEN THE : Lord turned again the captivity of | Zi- | on, ||
We | were like | them that | dream.
Then was our mouth | filled . with | laughter, ||
And our | tongue with | sing- | ing;
Then said they a- | mong the | heathen, ||
The Lord hath | done great | things for | them.
The Lord hath done | great things | for us; ||
Where- | of | we are | glad.
Turn again our captivity, | O | Lord, ||
As the | streams | in the | south.
They that | sow in | tears ||
Shall | reap | . in | joy.
He that goeth forth and | weep- | eth, ||
Bearing | pre- | . cious | seed,
Shall doubtless come again with re- | joic- | ing, ||
Bring- | ing his | sheaves with | him.

General.

No. 19. Dominus Regit Me. Psalm 23.

HAWES.

J. PEARCE.

C. BRADLEY.

THE **:** Lord | is my | shepherd; ||
I | shall | not | want.

He maketh me to lie down in | green | pastures: ||
He leadeth me be- | side the | still | waters.

He re- | storeth **.** my | soul: ||
He leadeth me in the paths of righteousness | for His | Name's | sake ||

Yea, though I walk through the valley of the shadow of death,
I will | fear no | evil: ||
For Thou art with me; Thy rod, and Thy | staff they | comfort | me.

Thou preparest a table before me in the presence | of mine |
enemies: ||
Thou anointest my head with oil; my | cup | run - neth | over.

Surely goodness and mercy shall follow me all the | days of my |
life: ||
And I will dwell in the | house **.** of the | Lord for | ever.

No. 20. Dominus illuminatio. Psalm 27.

W. B. GILBERT.

WOODWARD.

FISHER.

ATTWOOD.

LANGDON.

OUSELEY.

THE LORD : is my Light and | my Sal- | vation ||
Whom | shall |. I | fear?

The Lord is the | strength . of my | life; ||
Of | whom shall | I. be a- | fraid?

66

When the wicked, even mine enemies and my foes, came upon me io | eat up . my | flesh ||
They | stumbled | and | fell.

Though a host should encamp against me, my | heart . shall not | fear ||
Though war should rise against me, in | this will | I be | confident.

One thing have I desired of the Lord, that | will I . seek | after ||
That I may dwell in the house of the Lord | all the | days . of my | life.

To behold the beauty | of the | Lord, ||
And to in- | quire | in His | temple.

For in the time of trouble He shall hide me in | His pa- | vilion ||
In the secret of His tabernacle shall He hide me; He shall set me | up up- | on a | rock.

And now shall mine head be | lifted | up; ||
Above mine | ene - mies | round a- | bout me.

Therefore will I offer in His tabernacle sacri- | fices . of | joy ||
I will sing, yea, I will sing | praises | unto . the | Lord.

Hear, O Lord, when I | cry . with my | voice: ||
Have mercy also upon | me, and | answer | me.

When Thou saidst, Seek | ye My | face ||
My heart said unto Thee, Thy | face, Lord, | will I | seek.

Hide not Thy | face far | from me ||
Put not Thy | servant . a- | way in | anger.

Thou hast | been my | help; ||
Leave me not, neither forsake me, O | God of | my sal- | vation.

When my father and my | mother . for- | sake me ||
Then the | Lord will | take me | up.

Teach me Thy | way, O | Lord; ||
And lead me in a plain path, be- | cause | of mine | enemies.

Deliver me not over unto the | will . of mine | enemies ||
For false witnesses are risen up against me, and | such as | breathe out | cruelty.

I | had | fainted ||
Unless I had believed to see the goodness of the Lord in the | land | of the | living.

Wait | on the | Lord ||
Be of good courage, and He shall strengthen thine heart; | wait, I | say, . on the | Lord.

No. 21. Quam dilecta tabernacula. Psalm 84.

J. L. ROGERS.

HACKETT.   W. H. HAVERGAL.

How : amiable are Thy | taber- | nacles ||
O | Lord | of | hosts!
My soul longeth, yea, even fainteth for the | courts . of the | Lord ||
My heart and my flesh crieth | out . for the | living | God.
    Yea, the sparrow hath found an house, and the swallow a nest for
herself, where she may | lay her | young ||
Even Thine altars, O Lord of hosts, my | King | and my | God.
    Blessed are they that | dwell in . Thy | house ||
They will be | still | praising | Thee.
    Blessed is the man whose | strength . is in | Thee ||
In whose heart | are the | ways of | them,
    Who, passing through the valley of Baca | make . it a | well ||
The rain | also | filleth . the | pools.
    They go from | strength to | strength ||
Every one of them in Zion ap- | peareth . be- | fore | God.
    O Lord God of hosts, | hear my | prayer ||
Give | ear, O | God of | Jacob.
    Behold, O | God our | Shield ||
And look upon the | face of | Thine A- | nointed.
    For a day in Thy courts is better | than a | thousand ||
I had rather be a doorkeeper in the house of my God, than to | dwell
in the | tents of | wickedness.

For the Lord God is a | Sun and | Shield ||
The Lord will | give | grace and | glory.

No good thing will He withhold from them that | walk up- | rightly ||
O Lord of hosts, blessed is the | man that | trusteth . in | Thee.

No. 22. Venite Exultemus Domino. Psalm 95.

BOYCE.

TALLIS.

W. MACFARREN.

O : come, let us sing | unto . the | Lord: ||
Let us make a joyful noise to the | Rock of | our sal- | vation.

Let us come before His presence | with thanks- | giving, ||
And make a joyful | noise . unto | Him with | psalms.

For the Lord is a | great | God, ||
And a great | King a- | bove all | gods.

In His hand are the deep places | of the | earth: ||
The strength of the | hills is | His | also.

The sea is His, and | He | made it: ||
And His hands | form- . ed the | dry | land.

O come, let us worship | and bow | down: ||
Let us kneel be- | fore the | Lord our | Maker.

† For He | is our | God; ||
And we are the people of His pasture, | and the l sheep of . His | hand.

† Repeat second half of double chant in singing this verse.

69

No. 23. Cantate Domino. Psalm 98.

CROTCH.

DUPUIS.   GOSS.

O : sing unto the Lord a | new | song; ||
For He | hath done | marvel - lous | things.
His right hand, and His | holy | arm, ||
Hath | gotten | Him the | victory.

The Lord hath made known | His sal- | vation: ||
His righteousness hath He openly showed in the | sight | of the | heathen.

He hath remembered His mercy and His truth toward the | house of | Israel: ||
All the ends of the earth have seen the sal- | vation | of our | God.

Make a joyful noise unto the Lord, | all the | earth: ||
Make a loud noise, and re- | joice, | and sing | praise.

Sing unto the Lord | with the | harp; ||
With the harp, and the | voice | of a | psalm.

With trumpets and | sound of | cornet ||
Make a joyful noise be- | fore the | Lord, the | King.

Let the sea roar, and the | fulness . there- | of: ||
The world, and | they that | dwell there- | in.

Let the floods clap their hands; let the hills be joyful together be- | fore the | Lord; ||
For He | cometh . to | judge the | earth;
With righteousness shall He | judge the | world, ||
And the | people . with | equi- | ty.

No. 24. Jubilate Deo. Psalm 100.

J. TURLE.

GARRETT.

RUSSELL.

MAKE A : joyful noise unto the Lord, | all ye | lands. ||
Serve the Lord with gladness; come before His | presence | with | singing.
Know ye that the Lord | He is | God; ||
It is He that hath made us, and not we ourselves: we are His people, and the | sheep of | His | pasture.
Enter into His gates with thanksgiving, and into His | courts with | praise: ||
Be thankful unto | Him, and | bless His | Name.
For the Lord is good; His mercy is | ever- | lasting; ||
And His truth endureth to | all | gener- | ations.

No. 25. Qui habitat. Psalm 91.

J. PEARCE.

BARNBY.

B. SMITH.

ALFRED BENNETT.

H. PURCELL.

HE THAT : dwelleth in the secret place of the | Most | High ‖
Shall abide under the shadow | of the | Al- | mighty.

I will say of the Lord, He is my Refuge | and my | Fortress ‖
My God; in | Him | will I | trust.

Surely He shall deliver thee from the | snare . of the | fowler ‖
And from the | noisome | pesti- | lence.

He shall cover thee with His feathers, and under His wings | shalt
thou | trust ‖
His truth shall | be thy | shield and | buckler.

Thou shalt not be afraid for the | terror . by | night ‖
Nor for the | arrow . that | flieth . by | day;
Nor for the pestilence that | walketh . in | darkness ‖
Nor for the de- | struction . that | wasteth . at | noonday.

A thousand shall fall at thy side, and ten thousand at | thy
right | hand ‖
But it | shall not | come nigh | thee.

Only with thine eyes shalt | thou be- | hold ‖
And | see . the re- | ward . of the | wicked.

Because thou hast made the Lord, which | is my | Refuge ‖
Even the Most | High, thy | habi- | tation:
There shall no | evil . be- | fall thee ‖
Neither shall any | plague come | nigh thy | dwelling.

For He shall give His angels charge | over | thee ‖
To | keep . thee in | all thy | ways.

They shall bear thee up | in their | hands ‖
Lest thou dash thy | foot a- | gainst a | stone.

Thou shalt tread upon the | lion and | adder ‖
The young lion and the dragon shalt thou | trample | under | feet.

Because he hath set his love upon Me, therefore will I de- | liver |
him: ‖
I will set him on high, because | he hath | known My | Name.

He shall call upon Me, and I will | answer | him ‖
I will be with him in trouble; I will deliver | him, and | honor | him,
With long life will I | satis- . fy | him ‖
And | show him | My sal- | vation.

No. 26. Bonum est confiteri. Psalm 92.

It is : a good thing to give thanks | unto . the | Lord ||
And to sing praises unto Thy | Name, | O Most | High;
　To show forth Thy lovingkindness | in the | morning ||
And Thy | faithful -. ness | every | night,
　Upon an instrument of ten strings, and up- | on the | psaltery ||
Upon the harp | with a | solemn | sound.
　For Thou, Lord, hast made me glad | through Thy | work ||
I will triumph in the | works | of Thy | hands.
　O Lord, how great | are Thy | works ||
And Thy | thoughts are | very | deep.
　A brutish man | knoweth | not ||
Neither doth a | fool . under- | stand | this.
　When the wicked spring as the grass, and when all the workers of
in- | iquity . do | flourish ||
It is that they shall be destroyed for ever; but Thou, Lord, art most |
high for | ever- | more.
　For, lo, Thine enemies, O Lord, for, lo, Thine | enemies . shall | perish ||
All the workers of in- | iqui-. ty | shall be | scattered.
　But my horn shalt Thou exalt like the horn of an | uni- | corn ||
I shall be a- | nointed | with fresh | oil.
　Mine eye also shall see my desire | on mine | enemies ||
And mine ears shall hear my desire of the wicked that | rise | up
a- | gainst me.

The righteous shall flourish | like the | palm tree ||
He shall grow like a | cedar . in | Leba- | non.
Those that be planted in the | house . of the | Lord ||
Shall flourish in the | courts | of our | God.
They shall still bring forth fruit | in old | age ||
They shall be | fat and | flourish- | ing;
To show that the | Lord is | upright ||
He is my Rock: and there is no un- | righteous- | ness in | **Him.**

No. 27.   Levavi Oculos.   Psalm 121.

H. LOWER.

J. TURLE.   J. PURCELL.

I WILL : lift up mine eyes | unto . the | hills, ||
From | whence | cometh . my | help.
My help cometh | from the | Lord, ||
Which | made | heaven . and | earth.
He will not suffer thy | foot . to be | moved: ||
He that | keepeth . thee | will not | slumber.
Behold, He that | keepeth | Israel ||
Shall | neither | slumber . nor | sleep.
The Lord ι is thy | keeper: ||
The Lord is thy | shade . upon | thy right | **hand.**
The sun shall not | smite thee . by | day, ||
Nor the | moon | by | night.
The Lord shall preserve thee | from all | evil: ||
He | shall pre- | serve thy | soul.
The Lord shall preserve thy going out and thy | coming | in ||
From this time forth, and | even . for | ever | more.

No. 28. Domine, refugium. Psalm 90.

HANDEL.

H. ROUND.   E. J. HOPKINS.

MORNINGTON.

C. A. BARRY.   CHARD.

LORD, THOU : hast been our | dwelling- | place ||
In | all | gener- | ations.

Before the mountains were brought forth, or ever Thou hadst formed the earth | and the | world ||

Even from everlasting to ever- | lasting, | Thou art | God.
Thou turnest man | to de- | struction ||
And sayest, Re- | turn, ye | children . of | men.
For a thousand years in Thy sight are but as yesterday when | it is | past ||
And as a | watch | in the | night.
Thou carriest them away as with a flood; they | are . as a | sleep ||
In the morning they are like | grass which | groweth | up.
In the morning it flourisheth, and | groweth | up: ||
In the evening it | is cut | down, and | withereth.
For we are consumed | by Thine | anger ||
And by Thy | wrath | are we | troubled.
Thou hast set our iniquities be- | fore | Thee ||
Our secret sins in the | light of | Thy | countenance.
For all our days are passed away | in Thy | wrath ||
We spend our years | as a | tale . that is | told.
The days of our years are threescore years and ten; and if by reason of strength they be | fourscore | years ||
Yet is their strength labor and sorrow; for it is soon cut off | and we | fly a- | way.
Who knoweth the power | of Thine | anger ||
Even according to Thy fear, | so is | Thy | wrath.
So teach us to | number . our | days ||
That we may apply our | hearts | unto | wisdom.
Return, O | Lord, how | long ||
And let it repent Thee con- | cerning | Thy | servants.
O satisfy us early | with Thy | mercy ||
That we may rejoice and be | glad | all our | days.
Make us glad according to the days wherein Thou hast af- | flicted | us ||
And the years wherein | we have | seen | evil.
Let Thy work appear | unto . Thy | servants ||
And Thy | glory | unto . their | children.
And let the beauty of the Lord our God | be up- | on us ||
And establish Thou the work of our | hands up- | on | us;
Yea, the | work of . our | hands ||
Es- | tablish | Thou | it.

No. 29. Benedic, anima mea. Psalm 103.

CAMIDGE.

W. H. MONK.

G. J. ELVEY.

H. LESLIE.

W. H. MONK.

C. I. JEKYLL.

BLESS THE : Lord, | O my | soul ||
And all that is within me, | bless His | holy | Name.
   Bless the Lord, | O my | soul ||
And for- | get not | all His | benefits;
   Who forgiveth all | thine in- | iquities ||
Who healeth | all | thy dis- | eases;
   Who redeemeth thy | life . from de- | struction ||
Who crowneth thee with loving- | kindness . and | tender | mercies;

Who satisfieth thy mouth with | good | things ||
So that thy youth is re- | newed | like the | eagle's.
The Lord executeth righteous- | ness and | judgment ||
For | all that | are op- | pressed.
He made known His | ways . unto | Moses ||
His acts | unto . the | children . of | Israel.
The Lord is merciful and | gra- | cious ||
Slow to anger, and | plen- | teous in | mercy.
He will not | always | chide ||
Neither will He | keep His | anger . for | ever.
He hath not dealt with us | after . our | sins ||
Nor rewarded us ac- | cording . to | our in- | iquities.
For as the heaven is high a- | bove the | earth ||
So great is His mercy toward | them that | fear | Him.
As far as the east is | from the | west ||
So far hath He removed | our trans- | gressions | from **us.**
Like as a father | pitieth . his children ||
So the Lord | piti - eth | them that | fear Him.
For He | knoweth . our | frame ||
He re- | membereth that | we are | dust.
As for man, his | days . are as | grass ||
As a flower of the field, | so he | flourisheth.
For the wind passeth over it, and | it is | gone ||
And the place thereof shall | know it | no | more.
But the mercy of the Lord is from everlasting to everlasting
upon | them that | fear Him ||
And His righteousness | unto | children's | children;
To such as | keep His | covenant ||
And to those that remember His com- | mand- . ments to | do | them.
The Lord hath prepared His throne | in the | heavens ||
And His kingdom | ruleth | over | all.
Bless the Lord, ye His angels, that ex- | cel in | strength ||
That do His commandments, hearkening unto the | voice | of His | Word.
Bless ye the Lord, all | ye His | hosts ||
Ye ministers of | His, that | do His | pleasure.
Bless the Lord, all His works in all places of | His do- | minion ||
Bless the | Lord, | O my | soul.

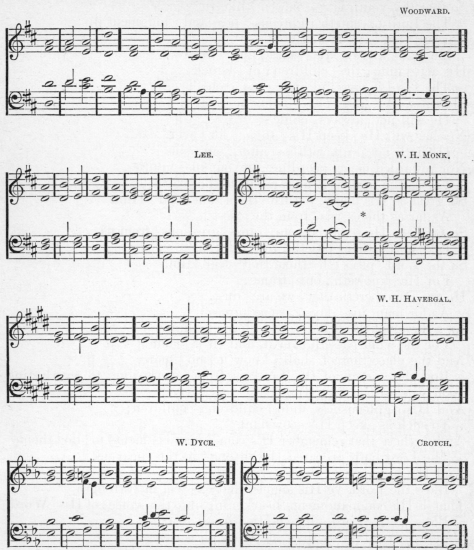

No. 30. Non nobis, Domine. Psalm 115.

WOODWARD.

LEE.

W. H. MONK.

W. H. HAVERGAL.

W. DYCE.

CROTCH.

* Small notes for organ only : the vocal parts are in unison.

Not unto : us, O Lord, not unto us, but unto Thy | Name give | glory ‖
For Thy mercy, and | for Thy | truth's | sake.

Wherefore should the | heathen | say : ‖
Where is | now | their | God?

But our God is | in the | heavens ‖
He hath done whatso- | ever | He hath | pleased.

Their idols are | silver . and | gold ‖
The | work of | men's | hands.

They have mouths, but they | speak | not ‖
Eyes have they, | but they | see | not;

They have ears, but they | hear | not ‖
Noses have they, | but they | smell | not;

They have hands, but they handle not; feet have they, but they | walk | not ‖
Neither | speak they | through their | throat.

They that make them are | like . unto | them ‖
So is every | one that | trusteth | in them.

O Israel, trust | thou . in the | Lord ‖
He is their | help | and their | shield.

O house of Aaron | trust . in the | Lord ‖
He is their | help | and their | shield.

Ye that fear the Lord, | trust . in the | Lord ‖
He is their | help | and their | shield.

The Lord hath been mindful of us; | He will | bless us ‖
He will bless the house of Israel; He will | bless the | house of | Aaron.

He will bless them that | fear the | Lord ‖
Both | small | and | great.

The Lord shall increase you | more and | more ‖
You | and | your | children.

Ye are blessed | of the | Lord ‖
Which | made | heaven . and | earth.

The heaven, even the heavens, | are the | Lord's ‖
But the earth hath He given | to the | children . of | men.

The dead | praise . not the | Lord ‖
Neither any that | go down | into | silence.

But we will | bless the | Lord ‖
From this time forth and for evermore. | Praise | . the | Lord.

81

No. 31. Laudate Dominum. Psalm 147.

H. SMYTH.

EDWARDS.

OXFORD CHANT.

J. SOAPER.

E. G. MONK.

ALDRICH.

PRAISE YE : the Lord, for it is good to sing praises | unto . our | God ||
For it is pleasant; and | praise is | come- | ly.
The Lord doth build up Je- | rusa- | lem ||
He gathereth together the | outcasts . of | Isra- | el.

He healeth the | broken . in | heart ||
And | bindeth | up their | wounds.

He telleth the number | of the | stars ||
He calleth them | all | by their | names.

Great is our Lord, and of | great | power ||
His under- | standing . is | infi- | nite.

The Lord lifteth | up the | meek ||
He casteth the | wicked | down to the | ground.

Sing unto the Lord | with thanks- | giving ||
Sing praise upon the | harp | unto . our | God;

Who covereth the heaven with clouds, Who prepareth | rain . for
the | earth ||
Who maketh grass to | grow up- | on the | mountains.

He giveth to the | beast his | food ||
And to the young | ra- | vens which | cry.

He delighteth not in the | strength . of the | horse ||
He taketh not pleasure in the | legs | of a | man.

The Lord taketh pleasure in | them that | fear Him ||
In those that | hope in | His | mercy.

Praise the Lord, O Je- | rusa- | lem ||
Praise thy | God, | O | Zion.

For He hath strengthened the bars | of thy | gates ||
He hath | blessed . thy | children . with- | in thee.

He maketh peace | in thy | borders ||
And filleth thee with the | finest | of the | wheat.

He sendeth forth His commandment | upon | earth ||
His word | runneth | very | swiftly.

He giveth | snow like | wool ||
He scattereth the | hoar | frost like | ashes.

He casteth forth His | ice like | morsels ||
Who can | stand be- | fore His | cold?

He sendeth out His word, and | melteth | them ||
He causeth His wind to blow, | and the | waters | flow.

He sheweth His word | unto | Jacob ||
His statutes and His | judgments | unto | Israel.

He hath not dealt so with | any | nation ||
And as for His judgments, they have not known them. | Praise | ye
the | Lord.

No. 32. Beati immaculati. Psalm 119.

E. J. Hopkins.

I.   R. Farrant.   II.   W. Macfarren.

I. BLESSED **:** are the undefiled | in the | way ||
Who walk in the | law | of the | Lord.
    Blessed are they that keep His | testi- | monies ||
And that seek Him | with the | whole | heart.
    They also do | no in- | iquity ||
They | walk | in His | ways.
    Thou hast com- | manded | us ||
To keep Thy | precepts | dili- | gently.
    O that my ways | were di- | rected ||
To | keep | Thy | statutes!
    Then shall I | not **.** be a- | shamed ||
When I have respect unto | all | Thy com- | mandments.
    I will praise Thee with up- | rightness **.** of | heart ||
When I shall have | learned **.** Thy | righteous | judgments.
    I will keep | Thy | statutes ||
O forsake me | not | utter- | ly.

In quo corrigit?

II. WHEREWITHAL **:** shall a young man | cleanse his | way ||
By taking heed thereto ac- | cording | to Thy | word.
    With my whole heart | have I | sought Thee ||
O let me not wander | from | Thy com- | mandments.

Thy word have I hid | in **mine** | **heart** ||
That I | might not | sin a- | gainst **Thee.**

Blessed art | Thou, O | **Lord** ||
Teach | me | Thy | statutes.

With my lips have | I de- | clared ||
All the | judgments | of Thy | mouth.

I have rejoiced in the way of Thy | testi- | **monies** ||
As | much as | in all | riches.

I will meditate in | Thy | precepts ||
And have re- | spect | unto . Thy | ways.

I will delight myself in | Thy | statutes ||
I will | not for- | get Thy | word.

III.

E. W. Bullinger.

In æternum, Domine.

III. For : ever, | O | Lord ||
Thy | Word is | settled . in | heaven.

Thy faithfulness is unto | all gener- | ations ||
Thou hast established the | earth, and | it a- | bideth.

They continue this day according to Thine | ordi- | nances ||
For | all are | Thy | servants.

Unless Thy law had been | my de- | lights ||
I should then have | perished . in | mine af- | fliction.

I will never for- | get Thy | precepts ||
For with them | Thou hast | quickened | me.

I am Thine, | save | me ||
For | I have | sought Thy | precepts.

The wicked have waited for me | to de- | stroy **me** ||
But I will con- | sider . Thy | testi- | monies.

I have seen an end of | all per- | fection ||
But Thy commandment | is ex- | ceeding | broad.

IV.

W. H. MONK.

Lucerna pedibus meis.

IV. THY WORD : is a lamp | unto my | feet ||
And a | light | unto . my | path.
  I have sworn, and I | will per- | form it ||
That I will | keep Thy | righteous | judgments.
  I am afflicted | very | much ||
Quicken me, O Lord, ac- | cording | unto . Thy | word.
  Accept, I beseech Thee, the freewill offerings of my | mouth, O | Lord ||
And | teach me | Thy | judgments.
  My soul is continually | in my | hand ||
Yet do I | not for- | get Thy | law.
  The wicked have laid a | snare for | me ||
Yet I | erred not | from Thy | precepts.
  Thy testimonies have I taken as an herit- | age for | ever ||
For they are the re- | joicing | of my | heart.
  I have inclined mine heart to perform Thy | statutes | always ||
Even | unto | the | end.

V.

A. H. BROWN.

Iniquos odio habui.

V. I : hate | vain | thoughts ||
But Thy | law | do I | love.
  Thou art my hiding place | and my | shield ||
I | hope in | Thy | word.

Depart from me, ye | evil | doers ||
For I will keep the com- | mandments | of my | God.

Uphold me according unto Thy word; that | I may | live ||
And let me not be a- | shamed | of my | hope.

Hold Thou me up, and I | shall be | safe ||
And I will have respect unto Thy | statutes . con- | tinual- | ly.

Thou hast trodden down all them that err from | Thy | statutes ||
For | their de- | ceit is | falsehood.

Thou puttest away all the wicked of the | earth like | dross ||
Therefore I | love Thy | testi- | monies.

My flesh trembleth for | fear of | Thee ||
And I am a- | fraid | of Thy | judgments.

No. 33. Laudate Dominum. Psalm 117.

H. GADSBY.

C. A. BARRY.

O : praise the Lord, | all ye | nations; ||
Praise Him | all | . ye | people.

For His merciful kindness is | great . toward | us; ||
And the truth of the Lord endureth for ever. | Praise | ye the | Lord.

No. 34. Laudate Dominum. Psalm 148.

HENRY SMART.

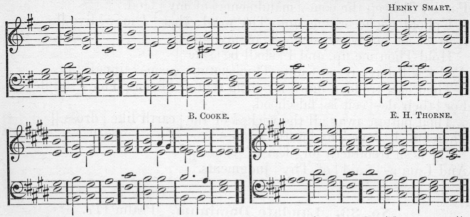

B. COOKE.

E. H. THORNE.

PRAISE YE : the Lord: praise ye the Lord | from the | heavens: ||
Praise | . Him | in the | heights.
 Praise ye Him, | all His | angels: ||
Praise | ye Him, | all His | hosts.
 Praise ye Him, | sun and | moon: ||
Praise Him, | all ye | stars of | light.
 Praise Him, ye | heavens . of | heavens: ||
And ye waters that | be a- | bove the | heavens.
 Let them praise the Name | of the | Lord: ||
For He commanded, | and they | were cre- | ated.
 He hath also established them for- | ever . and | ever: ||
He hath made a de- | cree which | shall not | pass.
 Praise the Lord | from the | earth: ||
Ye | dragons | and all | deeps.
 Fire, and hail; | snow, and | vapors: ||
Stormy | wind ful- | filling . His | word.
 Mountains, and | all | hills: ||
Fruitful | trees, and | all | cedars;
 Beasts, and | all | cattle: ||
Creeping | things, and | flying | fowl;
 Kings of the earth, and | all | people: ||
Princes, and all | judges | of the | earth;
 Both young men, and | maid- | ens:||
Old | men, | . and | children; 88

Let them praise the | Name . of the | Lord: ||
For His Name alone is excellent; His glory is a- | bove the | earth
and | heaven.

He also exalteth the horn of His people, the praise of | all His | saints: ||
Even of the children of Israel, a people near unto Him. | Praise | ye
the | Lord.

No. 35. De Profundis. Psalm 130.

H. PURCELL.

MACFARREN.

H. KEETON.

OUT OF THE : depths | have I | cried ||
Unto | Thee, | . O | Lord.

Lord, | hear my | voice: ||
Let Thine ears be attentive to the | voice . of my | suppli- | cations.

If Thou, Lord, shouldest mark in- | iqui- | ties, ||
O | Lord, | who shall | stand?

But there is for- | giveness . with | Thee, ||
That | Thou | mayest . be | feared.

I wait for the Lord, my | soul doth | wait, ||
And in His | word | do I | hope.

My soul waiteth for the Lord more than they that | watch . for the |
morning ||
I say, more than they that | watch | for the | morning.

Let Israel hope in the Lord, for with the | Lord . there is | mercy ||
And with | Him is | plenteous . re- | demption.

And He shall re- | deem | Israel ||
From | all . his in- | iqui- | ties.

No. 36. Benedicam Dominum. Psalm 34.

J. JONES.

TOURS.

C. I. JEKYLL.

R. P. GOODENOUGH.

NOVELLO.

BATTISHILL.

I WILL : bless the Lord at | all | times: ||
His praise shall con- | tinual- . ly | be . in my | mouth.
    My soul shall make her | boast . in the | Lord; ||
The humble shall | hear there- . of, | and be | glad.
    O magnify the | Lord with | me; ||
And let us ex- | alt His | Name to- | gether.
    I sought the Lord, | and He | heard me ||
And delivered | me from | all my | fears.

They looked unto Him, | and were | lightened: ||
And their | faces . were | not a- | shamed.

This poor man cried, and the | Lord | heard him, ||
And saved him | out of | all his | troubles.

The angel of the Lord encampeth round about | them that | fear Him; ||
And | . de- | liver- . eth | them.

O taste and see that the | Lord is | good; ||
Blessed is the | man that | trusteth . in | Him.

O fear the Lord, | ye His | saints; ||
For there is no want to | them that | fear | Him.

The young lions do lack, and | suffer | hunger: ||
But they that seek the Lord shall not | want | any . good | thing.

Come, ye children, hearken | unto | me: ||
I will teach you the | fear | of the | Lord.

What man is he that de- | sireth | life; ||
And loveth many | days, that | he may . see | good?

Keep thy | tongue from | evil: ||
And thy | lips from | speaking | guile.

Depart from evil, | and do | good; ||
Seek | peace, | and pur- | sue it.

The eyes of the Lord are up- | on the | righteous; ||
And His ears are | open | unto . their | cry.

The face of the Lord is against | them . that do | evil; ||
To cut off the remembrance | of them | from the | earth.

The righteous cry, and the | Lord | heareth : ||
And delivereth them | out of | all their | troubles.

The Lord is nigh unto them that are of a | broken | heart; ||
And saveth such as be | of a | contrite | spirit.

Many are the afflictions | of the | righteous : ||
But the Lord delivereth him | out | of them | all.

He keepeth | all his | bones ; ||
Not | one of | them is | broken.

Evil shall | slay the | wicked, ||
And they that hate the righteous | shall be | deso- | late.

The Lord redeemeth the soul | of His | servants; ||
And none of them that trust in | Him . shall be | deso- | late.

No. 37. Laudate Dominum. Psalm 150.

ALFRED BENNETT.

P. HUMPHREYS.   H. W. BAKER.

PRAISE YE : the Lord.   Praise God in His | sanctu- | ary; ||
Praise Him in the | firma- . ment | of His | power.
　Praise Him for His | mighty | acts; ||
Praise Him according | to His | excel- . lent | greatness.
　Praise Him with the | sound . of the | trumpet; ||
Praise Him with the | psalter- | y and | harp.
　Praise Him with | timbrel . and | dance; ||
Praise Him with stringed | instru- | ments and | organ.
　Praise Him upon the | loud | cymbals; ||
Praise Him upon the | high | sounding | cymbals.
　Let everything that hath breath | praise the | Lord; ||
Praise | ye | . the | Lord.

HYMNS AND TUNES.

WORSHIP: PRAISE AND THANKSGIVING.

1

From all that Dwell Below the Skies.

WELLS. L. M.

1. From all that dwell be - low the skies Let the Cre -
2. E - ter - nal are Thy mer - cies, Lord, E - ter - nal

- a - tor's praise a - rise; Let the Re - deem - er's Name be sung
truth at - tends Thy Word. Thy praise shall sound from shore to shore,

Through ev - 'ry land, by ev - 'ry tongue.
Till suns shall rise and set no more. A - men.

Watts, 1719.

2

Before Jehovah's Awful Throne.

OLD HUNDRED. L. M. *(Rhythmic form.)*　　　　　　　　　GENEVA, 1551.

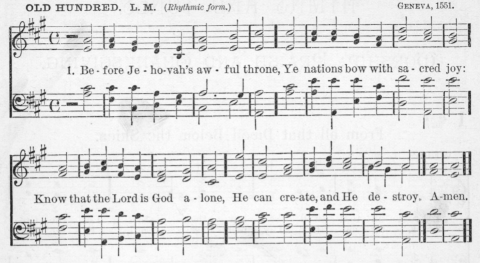

1. Be - fore Je - ho-vah's aw - ful throne, Ye nations bow with sa - cred joy:

Know that the Lord is God a - lone, He can cre-ate, and He de - stroy. A-men.

2 His sovereign power, without our aid,
　Made us of clay, and formed us men;
And when like wandering sheep we
　　strayed,
He brought us to His fold again.

3 We are His people, we His care,
　Our souls and all our mortal frame.
What lasting honors shall we rear,
　Almighty Maker, to Thy Name?

4 We'll crowd Thy gates with thankful
　　songs,
　High as the heavens our voices raise;
And earth, with her ten thousand tongues,
　Shall fill Thy courts with sounding
　　praise.

5 Wide as the world is Thy command,
　Vast as eternity Thy love;
Firm as a rock Thy truth must stand,
　When rolling years shall cease to move.

Watts, 1719. a.

Before Jehovah's Awful Throne.

OLD HUNDRED. L. M. *(Modern form.)*　　　　　　　　GENEVA, 1551.

1. Be - fore Je - ho-vah's aw - ful throne, Ye　nations bow with sa - cred joy:

Before Jehovah's Awful Throne.—Concluded.

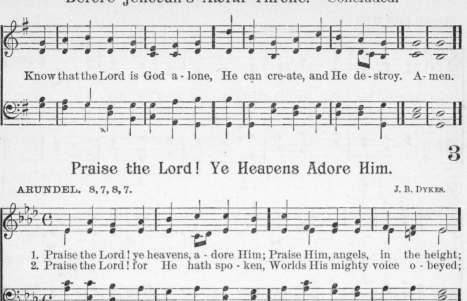

Know that the Lord is God a - lone, He can cre-ate, and He de - stroy. A - men.

Praise the Lord! Ye Heavens Adore Him.

3

ARUNDEL. 8, 7, 8, 7.   J. B. DYKES.

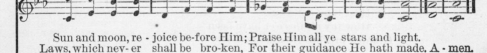

1. Praise the Lord! ye heavens, a - dore Him; Praise Him, angels, in the height;
2. Praise the Lord! for He hath spo - ken, Worlds His mighty voice o - beyed;

Sun and moon, re - joice be-fore Him; Praise Him all ye stars and light.
Laws, which nev- er shall be bro-ken, For their guidance He hath made. A - men.

3 Praise the Lord! for He is glorious;
    Never shall His promise fail;
    God hath made His grace victorious,
    Sin and death shall not prevail.

4 Praise the God of our salvation;
    Hosts on high, His power proclaim;
    Heaven and earth, and all creation,
    Laud and magnify His Name!

Hymns for the Foundling Hospital, 1809;
Ascribed to John Kempthorne, (1775–1838.)

4

Praise to the Lord.

LOBE DEN HERREN.

STRALSUND, 1665.

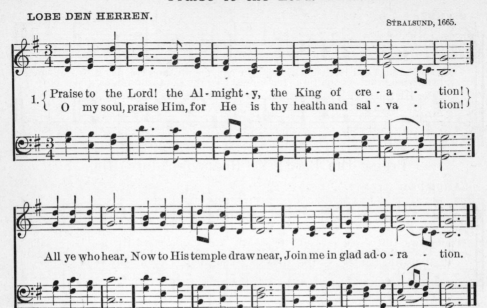

1. { Praise to the Lord! the Al-might-y, the King of cre-a - tion!
   { O my soul, praise Him, for He is thy health and sal-va - tion!

All ye who hear, Now to His temple draw near, Join me in glad ad-o-ra - tion.

2 Praise to the Lord! who o'er all things so wondrously reigneth,
Shelters thee under His wings, yea, so gently sustaineth;
    Hast thou not seen
    How thy desires e'er have been
Granted in what He ordaineth?

3 Praise to the Lord! who doth prosper thy work and defend thee;
Surely His goodness and mercy here daily attend thee.
    Ponder anew
    What the Almighty can do,
If with His love He befriend thee!

4 Praise to the Lord! Oh let all that is in me adore Him!
All that hath life and breath, come now with praises before Him!
    Let the Amen
    Sound from His people again;
Gladly for aye we adore Him.

Joachim Neander (1640–1680) 1679.
Tr. Miss Winkworth (1829–1878), 1863. *Abridged.*

Oh, What Praises Shall we Render.

RIPLEY. 8, 7, 8, 7. D.

GREGORIAN.

1. { Oh, what prais - es shall we ren - der To the Lord who reigns a - bove,
   { For His mer - cies, constant, ten - der, For His con - de-scend-ing love!

Though we oft - en have of - fend - ed, And transgressed His ho - ly will,

Still has He our souls be-friend-ed; We may call Him Father still. A - men.

2 Heavenly Father, Thou hast taught us
   Thus to seek Thee in our youth;
Hitherto Thy grace hath brought us,
   Lead us onward in Thy truth.
We are weak, do Thou uphold us,
   And from every snare defend;
Let Thy mighty arms enfold us,
   Save us, keep us, to the end.

3 Oh, our Father, great and glorious!
   Draw our youthful hearts to Thee;
Let Thy grace be there victorious,
   Let Thy love our portion be.
May we know Thy great salvation,
   Serve and love Thee all our days;
Then in heaven, Thy habitation,
   Join to sing Thine endless praise.

Jno. Burton, Jr.

6

Mighty God, While Angels Bless Thee.

PRAISE. 8, 7, 8, 7. (*With Chorus.*)   ALBERT LOWE.

1. Might-y God, while an-gels bless Thee, May a mor-tal lisp Thy Name?
2. Lord of ev-'ry land and na-tion, An-cient of e-ter-nal days!

Lord of men, as well as an-gels, Thou art ev-'ry creature's theme.
Sounded through the wide cre-a-tion Be Thy just and law-ful praise.

CHORUS.

Al-le-lu-ia, Al-le-lu-ia, Al-le-lu-ia. A-men.

3 For the grandeur of Thy nature,
  Grand beyond a seraph's thought;
For created works of power,
  Works with skill and kindness wrought:

4 For Thy Providence, that governs
  Through Thine empire's wide domain
Wings an angel, guides a sparrow:
  Blessed be Thy gentle reign.

5 But Thy rich, Thy free Redemption,
  Dark through brightness all along—
Thought is poor, and poor expression:
  Who dare sing that awful song!

6 From the highest throne in glory
  To the Cross of deepest woe!
All to ransom guilty captives!
  Flow, my praise, for ever flow.

Robert Robinson, **1774.**

Lord, With Glowing Heart I'd Praise Thee.

7

AUTUMN. 8, 7, 8, 7. D.

A Spanish Melody.

1. Lord, with glow-ing heart I'd praise Thee For the bliss Thy love be-stows,

For the pardoning grace that saves me, And the peace that from it flows.

Help, O God, my weak en-deav-or; This dull soul to rapture raise:

Thou must light the flame, or nev-er Can my love be warmed to praise. A-men.

2 Praise, my soul, the God that sought thee,
  Wretched wanderer, far astray;
Found thee lost, and kindly brought thee
  From the paths of death away.
Praise, with love's devoutest feeling,
  Him who saw thy guilt-born fear,
And the light of hope revealing,
  Bade the blood-stained Cross appear.

3 Lord, this bosom's ardent feeling
  Vainly would my lips express:
Low before Thy footstool kneeling,
  Deign Thy suppliant's prayer to bless.
Let Thy grace, my soul's chief treasure,
  Love's pure flame within me raise:
And, since words can never measure,
  Let my life show forth Thy praise.

Francis Scott Key, 1826.

8

O Bless the Lord, my Soul.

ETERNITY. S. M. (*First tune.*)

H. J. GAUNTLETT.

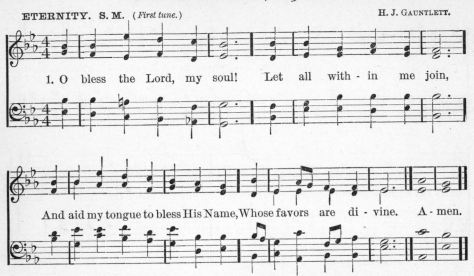

1. O bless the Lord, my soul! Let all with-in me join,

And aid my tongue to bless His Name, Whose favors are di-vine. A-men.

2 O bless the Lord, my soul!
  Nor let His mercies lie
Forgotten in unthankfulness,
  And without praises die.

3 'Tis He forgives thy sins;
  'Tis He relieves thy pain;
'Tis He that heals thy sicknesses,
  And gives thee strength again.

4 He crowns thy life with Love,
  When ransomed from the grave;

He that redeemed my soul from death
  Hath sovereign power to save.

5 He fills the poor with good;
  He gives the sufferers rest:
The Lord hath judgments for the proud,
  And justice for the opprest.

6 His wondrous works and ways
  He made by Moses known;
But sent the world His truth and grace
  By His beloved Son.

Watts, 1719. *a.*

O Bless the Lord, my Soul.

OLNEY. S. M. (*Second tune.*)

LOWELL MASON.

1. O bless the Lord, my soul! Let all with-in me join,

O Bless the Lord, my Soul.—Concluded.

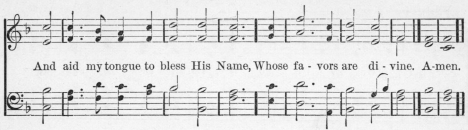

And aid my tongue to bless His Name, Whose fa - vors are di - vine. A-men.

9

Come, Sound His Praise Abroad.

SILVER STREET. S. M.

Isaac Smith, 1770.

1. Come, sound His praise a - broad, And hymns of glo - ry sing!

Je - ho - vah is the sov - 'reign God, The u - ni - ver - sal King. A-men.

2 He formed the deeps unknown;
  He gave the seas their bound;
The watery worlds are all His own,
  And all the solid ground.

3 Come, worship at His throne;
  Come, bow before the Lord:
We are His works and not our own,
  He formed us by His word.

4 To-day attend His voice,
  Nor dare provoke His rod;
Come, like the people of His choice,
  And own your gracious God!

Watts, 1719.

101

10

Holy, Holy, Holy, Lord.

WEBER. 7, 7, 7, 7.

C. M. Von Weber.

1. Ho - ly, ho - ly, ho - ly Lord! Be Thy glo - rious Name a - dored. Lord, Thy mer - cies nev - er fail: Hail, ce - les - tial Good - ness, hail! A - men.

2 Though unworthy, Lord, Thine ear
Deign our humble songs to hear.
Purer praise we hope to bring,
When around Thy throne we sing.

3 There no tongue shall silent be;
All shall join in harmony;
That through heaven's capacious round
Praise to Thee may ever sound.

4 Lord, Thy mercies never fail:
Hail, celestial Goodness, hail!
Holy, holy, holy Lord!
Be Thy glorious Name adored.

Benjamin Williams, 1778. a.

When All Thy Mercies, O My God.

ST. MARTIN. C. M.

Wm. Tansur, 1753.

1. When all Thy mer - cies, O my God, My ris - ing soul sur - veys, Trans - port - ed with the view, I'm lost In won - der, love, and praise. A - men.

2 Ten thousand thousand precious gifts
  My daily thanks employ;
  Nor is the least a cheerful heart
  That tastes those gifts with joy.

3 Through every period of my life
  Thy goodness I'll pursue;
  And after death, in distant worlds,
  The glorious theme renew.

4 When nature fails, and day and night
  Divide Thy works no more,
  My ever grateful heart, O Lord,
  Thy mercy shall adore.

5 Through all eternity to Thee
  A joyful song I'll raise:
  But oh! eternity's too short
  To utter all Thy praise.

Joseph Addison, 1712.

12

Praise ye the Lord.

LOBT FROH DEN HERRN. P. M.

H. G. NÄGELI, 1836.

1. Praise ye the Lord In sim-ple joy-ous meas-ure;
He hears each word Of chil-dren's praise with pleas-ure;
Praise ye the Lord, praise ye the Lord. A - men.

2 Though children, we   Thy glorious praise are telling;
Attentive be,   From heaven, Thy holy dwelling,
Thou calledst little ones to Thee.

3 Thy praise alone   Our hearts would render ever;
Up to Thy throne   Ascends our weak endeavor;
Our outpoured song accept and own.

4 Our stammering,   Our feeble voice Thou hearest;
O gracious King,   E'en for our praise Thou carest;
Triumphant then, to Thee we sing.

5 In glory we,   Our heavenly Father praising,
Shall happy be,   New songs unnumbered raising;
Unceasing through eternity.

G. Gessner, † 1843.
Tr. Harriett R. Spaeth, 1895.

Angel Voices Ever Singing.

ANGEL VOICES. 8, 5, 8, 5, 8, 7.   A. S. Sullivan, 1871.

1. An - gel voi - ces, ev - er sing - ing, Round Thy throne of light,

An - gel harps for ev - er ring - ing, Rest not day nor night;

Thousands on - ly live to bless Thee, And con - fess Thee, Lord of might! A - men.

2 Thou, who art beyond the farthest
    Mortal eye can scan,
  Can it be that Thou regardest
    Songs of sinful man?
  Can we feel that Thou art near us,
    And wilt hear us? Yea, we can!

3 Here, great God, to-day we offer
    Of Thine own to Thee;
  And for Thine acceptance proffer,
    All unworthily,
  Hearts and minds, and hands and voices,
    In our choicest melody.

4 Honor, glory, might, and merit,
    Thine shall ever be,
  Father, Son, and Holy Spirit,
    Blessèd Trinity!
  Of the best that Thou hast given,
    Earth and heaven render Thee!

Francis Pott, 1861.

14

Now Thank we all our God.

NUN DANKET ALLE GOTT. 6, 7, 6, 7, 6, 6, 6, 6. (*Modern form.*) J. CRÜGER, 1649.

1. { Now thank we all our God, With heart and hands and voi - ces,
    { Who wondrous things hath done, In whom His earth re - joi - ces;

Who from our moth - er's arms Hath bless'd us on our way

With count-less gifts of love, And still is ours to - day. A - men.

2 O may this bounteous God,
   Through all our life be near us,
With ever joyful hearts,
   And blessed peace to cheer us;
And keep us in His grace,
   And guide us when perplexed,
And free us from all ills,
   In this world and the next.

3 All praise and thanks to God
   The Father, now be given,
The Son and Him who reigns
   With them in highest heaven;
The One eternal God,
   Whom earth and heaven adore;
For thus it was, is now,
   And shall be evermore!

Martin Rinkart, 1644.
Tr. Miss Winkworth, 1858. a.

15

Praise, my Soul, the King of Heaven.

LAUDA, ANIMA MEA. 8, 7, 8, 7, 8, 7.　　　　　　　JOHN GOSS, (1800–1880), 1867.

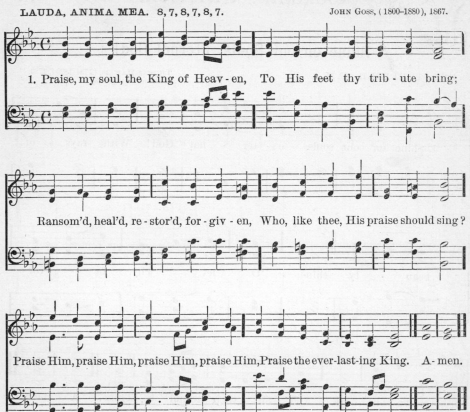

1. Praise, my soul, the King of Heav-en, To His feet thy trib-ute bring;

Ransom'd, heal'd, re-stor'd, for-giv-en, Who, like thee, His praise should sing?

Praise Him, praise Him, praise Him, praise Him, Praise the ever-last-ing King.　A-men.

2 Praise Him for His grace and favor
　To our fathers in distress;
Praise Him, still the same as ever,
　Slow to chide, and swift to bless;
　‖: Praise Him, praise Him, :‖
Glorious in His faithfulness.

3 Father-like, He tends and spares us,
　Well our feeble frame He knows;
In His hands He gently bears us,
　Rescues us from all our foes;
　‖: Praise Him, praise Him, :‖
Widely as His mercy flows.

4 Angels, in the height adore Him!
　Who behold Him face to face;
Sun and moon bow down before Him,
　Dwellers all in time and space,
　‖: Praise Him, praise Him, :‖
Praise with us the God of grace.

Henry Francis Lyte, (1793–1847), 1834.

WORSHIP: PETITION.

16

Shine on our Souls, Eternal God!

CHESTERFIELD. C. M.

THOMAS HAWEIS, (1734–1820), 1780.
HAR. BY GAUNTLETT.

1. Shine on our souls, e-ter-nal God! With rays of beau-ty shine; O let Thy fa-vor crown our days, And all their round be Thine. A-men.

2 Did we not raise our hands to Thee,
   Our hands might toil in vain:
   Small joy success itself could give,
   If Thou Thy love restrain.

3 With Thee let every week begin,
   With Thee each day be spent,
   For Thee each fleeting hour improved,
   Since each by Thee is lent.

4 Thus cheer us through this toilsome road,
   Till all our labors cease;
   And heaven refresh our weary souls
   With everlasting peace.

Doddridge, 1755. *a.*

17

Saviour, Who Thy Flock art Feeding.

BROCKLESBURY. 8, 7, 8, 7.

CLARIBEL.

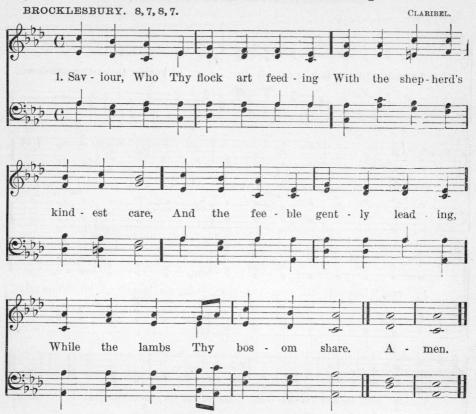

1. Sav - iour, Who Thy flock art feed - ing With the shep - herd's kind - est care, And the fee - ble gent - ly lead - ing, While the lambs Thy bos - om share. A - men.

2 Now, these little ones receiving,
   Fold them in Thy gracious arm!
   There, we know, Thy word believing,
   Only there secure from harm!

3 Never, from Thy pasture roving,
   Let them be the lion's prey;
   Let Thy tenderness, so loving,
   Keep them all life's dangerous way.

4 Then, within Thy fold eternal,
   Let them find a resting-place,
   Feed in pastures ever vernal,
   Drink the rivers of Thy grace.

Wm. Augustus Muhlenberg, 1826.

18

Love Divine, All Love Excelling.

ADVENT. 8, 7, 8, 7. D. (*First tune.*)

BERTHOLD TOURS.

1. Love di-vine, all love ex-cell-ing, Joy of heav'n, to earth come down!

Fix in us Thy hum-ble dwell-ing, All Thy faith-ful mer-cies crown.

Je-sus, Thou art all com-pas-sion, Pure, un-bound-ed love Thou art;

Vis-it us with Thy sal-va-tion, En-ter ev-'ry trembling heart. A-men.

2 Breathe, O breathe Thy loving Spirit
    Into every troubled breast!
Let us all in Thee inherit,
    Let us find Thy promised rest.
Take away the love of sinning,
    Alpha and Omega be;
End of faith, as its beginning,
    Set our hearts at liberty.

3 Come, Almighty to deliver,
    Let us all Thy life receive;
Graciously return, and never,
    Never more Thy temples leave!

Thee we would be always blessing,
    Serve Thee as Thy hosts above,
Pray and praise Thee without ceasing,
    Glory in Thy precious love.

4 Finish then Thy new creation,
    Pure and spotless let us be;
Let us see Thy great salvation
    Perfectly restored in Thee!
Changed from glory into glory,
    Till in heaven we take our place,
Till we cast our crowns before Thee,
    Lost in wonder, love, and praise.

C. Wesley, 1746. a.

Love Divine, All Love Excelling.

DJUP ÄR ÄNNU VINTERM DVOLA. 8, 7, 8, 7. D. *(Second tune.)*

SWEDISH MELODY.
(MISSIONSSÄNGER.)

1. Love di - vine, all love ex-cell-ing, Joy of heav'n, to earth come down!

Fix in us Thy hum-ble dwell-ing, All Thy faith-ful mer-cies crown.

Je - sus, Thou art all com-pas-sion, Pure, un-bound-ed love Thou art;

Vis - it us with Thy sal-va-tion, En-ter ev-'ry trembling heart. A-men.

19

Open now thy Gates of Beauty.

NEANDER. 8, 7, 8, 7, 7, 7.   JOACHIM NEANDER, 1680.

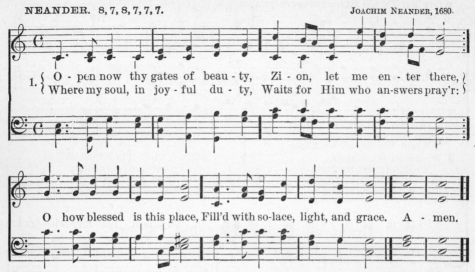

1. O - pen now thy gates of beau - ty, Zi - on, let me en - ter there,
Where my soul, in joy - ful du - ty, Waits for Him who an-swers pray'r:

O how blessed is this place, Fill'd with so-lace, light, and grace. A - men.

2 Yes, my God, I come before Thee,
Come Thou also down to me;
Where we find Thee and adore Thee
There a heaven on earth must be.
To my heart O enter Thou,
Let it be Thy temple now.

3 Here Thy praise is gladly chanted,
Here Thy seed is duly sown:
Let my soul, where it is planted,
Bring forth precious sheaves alone.
So that all I hear may be
Fruitful unto life in me.

4 Thou my faith increase and quicken,
Let me keep Thy gift divine,
Howsoe'er temptations thicken,
May Thy Word still o'er me shine;
As my pole-star through my life,
As my comfort in my strife.

5 Speak, O God, and I will hear Thee,
Let Thy will be done indeed;
May I undisturbed draw near Thee
While Thou dost Thy people feed;
Here of life the fountain flows,
Here is balm for all our woes.

Benjamin Schmolk, 1704.
Tr. Miss Winkworth, 1862.

20

Jesus, High in Glory.

ST. WYSTAN. 6, 5, 6, 5.   LORD T. BUTLER.

1. Je - sus, high in glo - ry, Lend a list - 'ning ear;

Jesus, High in Glory.—Concluded.

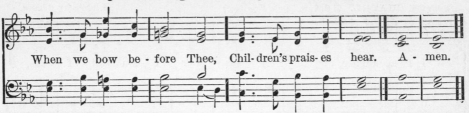

When we bow be-fore Thee, Chil-dren's prais-es hear. A-men.

2 Though Thou art so holy,
　Heaven's Almighty King,
Thou wilt stoop to listen,
　When Thy praise we sing.

3 We are little children,
　Weak and apt to stray;
Saviour, guide and keep us
　In the heavenly way.

4 Save us, Lord, from sinning;
　Watch us day by day;
Help us now to love Thee;
　Take our sins away.

5 Then when Thou dost call us
　To our heavenly home,
We shall gladly answer,
　Saviour, Lord, we come.

J. E. Clark.

Grant us, O our Heavenly Father.

21

OXFORD. 8, 7, 8, 7.　　　　　　　　　　JOHN STAINER, (1840).

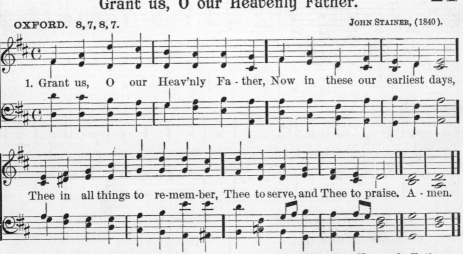

1. Grant us, O our Heav'nly Fa-ther, Now in these our earliest days,

Thee in all things to re-mem-ber, Thee to serve, and Thee to praise. A-men.

2 Drawing nearer still and nearer,
　May we close and closer cling
To our Lord, and to His altar
　There ourselves an offering bring.

3 Blest in joy, upheld in sorrow,
　At our work as in His sight,
May His presence still be with us,
　As we do it with our might.

4 Serving Thee, our Heavenly Father,
　From the dawn to set of sun,
Serving Thee in life's young morning,
　Till our work on earth is done,—

5 Till the shadows of the evening
　Shall for ever pass away,
And the Resurrection morning
　Kindle into perfect day.

Godfrey Thring, 1881.

22

I Need Thee, Precious Jesus.

SAVOY CHAPEL. 7, 6, 7, 6. D. (*First tune.*)

J. BAPTISTE CALKIN.

1. I need Thee, pre-cious Je-sus, For I am full of sin;

My soul is dark and guilt-y, My heart is dead with-in.

I need the cleans-ing fount-ain Where I can al-ways flee,

The Blood of Christ most pre-cious, The sinner's per-fect plea. A-men.

2 I need Thee, precious Jesus,
    For I am very poor;
A stranger and a pilgrim,
    I have no earthly store.
I need the love of Jesus
    To cheer me on my way,
To guide my doubting footsteps,
    To be my strength and stay.

3 I need Thee, precious Jesus,
    I need a friend like Thee,
A friend to soothe and pity,
    A friend to care for me.

I need the heart of Jesus
    To feel each anxious care,
To tell my every trial,
    And all my sorrows share.

4 I need Thee, precious Jesus,
    And hope to see Thee soon,
Encircled with the rainbow
    And seated on Thy throne:
There, with Thy blood-bought children,
    My joy shall ever be,
To sing my Jesus' praises,
    To gaze, O Lord, on Thee.

F. Whitfield, 1855.

I Need Thee, Precious Jesus.

ST. CHRISTOPHER. 7, 6, 7, 6. D. (*Second tune.*)

F. C. MAKER.

1. I need Thee, pre - cious Je - sus, For I am full of sin;

My soul is dark and guilt - y, My heart is dead with - in.

I need the cleans-ing fount - ain Where I can al - ways flee,

The blood of Christ most pre - cious, The sin - ner's per - fect plea. A - men.

Worship: The Lord's Day.

23

O Day of Rest and Gladness!

ICH FREU MICH IN DEM HERREN. 7, 6, 7, 6. D.   BARTHOLOMÄUS HELDER, 1646.

1. O day of rest and glad-ness! O day of joy and light!
O balm of care and sad-ness, Most beau-ti-ful, most bright,

On thee the high and low-ly, Through a-ges join'd in tune,

Sing, ho-ly, ho-ly, ho-ly, To God the great Tri-une.   A-men.

2 On thee, at the creation,
  The light first had its birth;
On thee, for our salvation,
  Christ rose from depths of earth;
On thee, our Lord, victorious,
  The Spirit sent from heaven;
And thus on thee most glorious,
  A triple light was given.

3 To-day, on weary nations,
  The heavenly manna falls;
To holy convocations
  The silver trumpet calls,

Where gospel light is glowing
  With pure and radiant beams,
And living water flowing
  With soul-refreshing streams.

4 New graces ever gaining
  From this one day of rest,
We reach the rest remaining
  To spirits of the blest;
To Holy Ghost be praises,
  To Father and to Son,
The Church her voice upraises
  To Thee, blest Three in One.

Wordsworth, 1862.

Safely Through Another Week.

24

DEJLIG ER DEN HIMMEL BLAA! 7, 7, 7, 7, 7, 7.   FROM DANISH CHORALBOG.

1. Safe-ly through an-oth-er week, God has brought us on our way:
Let us now a bless-ing seek, Wait-ing in His courts to-day;
Day of all the week the best, Em-blem of e-ter-nal rest. A-men.

2 Mercies multiplied each hour
  Through the week, our praise demand;
Guarded by Thy mighty power,
  Fed and guided by Thy hand;
Though ungrateful we have been,
  Only made returns of sin.

3 While we pray for pardoning grace,
  Through the dear Redeemer's Name,
Show Thy reconciling face,
  Take away our sin and shame:
From our worldly cares set free,
  May we rest this day in Thee.

4 Here we're come, Thy Name to praise;
  Let us feel Thy presence near:
May Thy glory meet our eyes,
  While we in Thy house appear:
Here afford us, Lord, a taste
Of our everlasting feast.

5 May the Gospel's joyful sound
  Conquer sinners, comfort saints;
Make the fruits of grace abound,
  Bring relief for all complaints.
Thus may all our Sabbaths prove,
Till we join the Church above.

John Newton, 1779. a.

25

Again the Morn of Gladness.

CLEETHORPES. 7, 6, 7, 6. D. (*With Chorus.*)   T. R. MATTHEWS, (1826 ——).

1. A-gain the morn of glad-ness, The morn of light is here; And earth it-self looks fair-er, And heav'n it-self more near: The bells, like an-gel voi-ces, Speak peace to ev-'ry breast, And all the land lies qui-et To keep the day of rest.

CHORUS.

Glo-ry be to Je-sus, Let all the chil-dren say; He rose a-gain, He rose a-gain, On this glad day! A-men.

Again the Morn of Gladness.—Concluded.

2 Again, O loving Saviour,
    The children of Thy grace
Prepare themselves to seek Thee
    Within Thy chosen place.
Our song shall rise to greet Thee,
    If Thou our hearts wilt raise;
If Thou our lips wilt open
    Our mouth shall show Thy praise.
      Glory be to Jesus, etc.

3 The shining choir of angels
    That rest not day or night,
The crowned and palm-decked martyrs,
    The saints arrayed in white,
The happy lambs of Jesus
    In pastures fair above,—
These all adore and praise Him
    Whom we, too, praise and love.
      Glory be to Jesus, etc.

4 The Church on earth rejoices
    To join with these to-day;
In every tongue and nation
    She calls her sons to pray:
Across the Northern snow-fields,
    Beneath the Indian palms,
She makes the same pure offering,
    And sings the same sweet psalms.
      Glory be to Jesus, etc.

5 Toll out, sweet bells, His praises!
    Sing, children, sing His Name!
Still louder and still farther
    His mighty deeds proclaim!
Till all whom He redeemèd
    Shall own Him Lord and King,
Till every knee shall worship,
    And every tongue shall sing!
      Glory be to Jesus, etc.

John Ellerton, (1826 ———).

This is the Day of Light.

26

DOMENICA. S. M.

HERBERT S. OAKELEY, 1889.

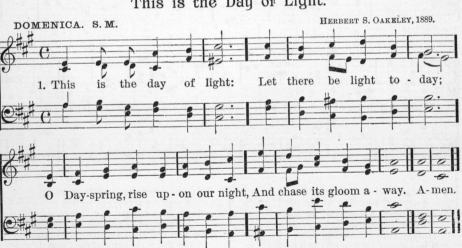

1. This is the day of light: Let there be light to-day;
O Day-spring, rise up-on our night, And chase its gloom a-way. A-men.

2 This is the day of rest:
    Our failing strength renew!
On weary brain and troubled breast
    Shed Thou Thy freshening dew.

3 This is the day of peace:
    Thy peace our spirits fill;
Bid Thou all ill and discord cease,
    The waves of strife be still.

4 This is the day of prayer:
    Let earth to heaven draw near:
Lift up our hearts to seek Thee there;
    Come down to meet us here.

5 This is the first of days:
    Send forth Thy quickening breath,
And wake dead souls to love and praise,
    O Vanquisher of death!

John Ellerton, 1867.

27

Alleluia! Fairest Morning!

HER VIL TIES, HER VIL TIES. 8, 7, 8, 7, 7, 7.

J. C. GEBAUER.

1. Al - le - lu - ia! Fair-est morn-ing! Fair - er than our words can say!

Down we lay the heav- y bur-den Of life's toil and care to - day:

While this morn of joy and love Brings fresh vig- or from a - bove. A - men.

2 Sunday, full of holy glory!
  Sweetest rest-day of the soul!
Light upon a world of darkness
  From thy blessèd moments roll!
Holy, happy, heavenly day,
Thou canst charm our grief away.

3 In the gladness of His worship
  I will seek my joy to-day:
It is then I learn the fulness
  Of the grace for which I pray,
When the Word of life is given,
Like the Saviour's voice from heaven

4 Let the day with Thee be ended,
  As with Thee it has begun;
And Thy blessing, Lord, be granted,
  Till earth's days and weeks are done:
That at last Thy servant may
Keep eternal Sabbath-day.

Jonathan Krause, 1732.
Tr. Jane Borthwick. a.

WORSHIP: OPENING.

28

Lord Jesus Christ, Be Present Now!

HERR JESU CHRIST, DICH ZU UNS WEND. L. M

CANTIONALE SACRUM.
GOTHA, 1651.

1. Lord Je - sus Christ, be pres - ent now! And let Thy Ho - ly Spir - it bow All hearts in love and fear to - day, To hear the truth and keep Thy way. A - men.

2 Open our lips to sing Thy praise,
 Our hearts in true devotion raise,
 Strengthen our faith, increase our light,
 That we may know Thy Name aright:

3 Until we join the host that cry
 "Holy art Thou, O Lord most High!"
 And 'mid the light of that blest place
 Shall gaze upon Thee face to face.

4 Glory to God, the Father, Son,
 And Holy Spirit, Three in One!
 To Thee, O blessed Trinity,
 Be praise throughout eternity!

William II., Duke of Saxe-Weimar, 1638.
Tr. Miss Winkworth, 1862.

29

Shepherd of Tender Youth.

HEMANS. 6, 6, 4, 6, 6, 6, 4.

1. Shep - herd of ten - der youth, Guid - ing in love and truth Through devious ways; Christ, our tri-umph-ant King, We come Thy Name to sing, And here our chil - dren bring, To join Thy praise. A - men.

2 Thou art our holy Lord,
  O all-subduing Word,
    Healer of strife:
  Thou didst Thyself abase,
  That from sin's deep disgrace
  Thou mightest save our race,
    And give us life.

3 O wisdom's great High Priest!
  Thou hast prepared the feast
    Of holy love;
  And in our mortal pain
  None calls on Thee in vain:
  Help Thou dost not disdain,
    Help from above.

4 Ever be near our side,
  Our Shepherd and our Guide,
    Our staff and song:
  Jesus, Thou Christ of God,
  By Thine enduring Word,
  Lead us where Thou hast trod;
    Make our faith strong.

5 So now, and till we die,
  Sound we Thy praises high,
    And joyful sing:
  Let all the holy throng
  Who to Thy Church belong,
  Unite and swell the song
    To Christ our King!

From Clement of Alexandria, ab. 200.
Tr. Henry Martyn Dexter, 1846.

When Little Samuel Woke.

ST. GODRIC. 6, 6, 6, 6, 8, 8, or H. M.

J. B. DYKES, 1862.

1. When lit-tle Sam-uel woke, And heard his Mak-er's voice, At ev-'ry word He spoke, How much did he re-joice! O blessed, hap-py, child to find The God of heav'n so near and kind. A-men.

2 If God would speak to me,
  And say He is my Friend,
How happy I should be!
  O, how I would attend!
The smallest sin I then would fear,
If God Almighty were so near.

3 And does He never speak?
  O yes; for in His Word
He bids me come and seek
  The God that Samuel heard.
And every sin I well may fear,
Since God Almighty is so near.

4 Like Samuel let me say,
  Whene'er I read His Word,
"Speak, Lord, I would obey"
  The voice that Samuel heard;
And when I in Thy house appear,
"Speak, for Thy servant waits to hear."

Jane Taylor, 1809.

31

Lord, a Little Band and Lowly.

LUCERNE. 8, 7, 8, 7.

T. A. WILLIS.

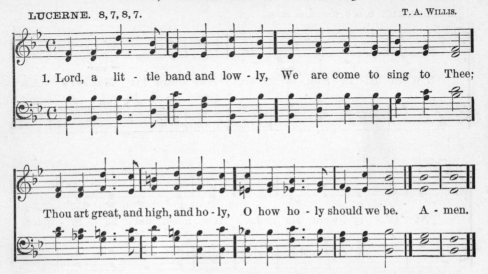

1. Lord, a lit-tle band and low-ly, We are come to sing to Thee;

Thou art great, and high, and ho-ly, O how ho-ly should we be. A-men.

2 Fill our hearts with thoughts of Jesus,
  And of heaven where He is gone;
And let nothing ever please us
  He would grieve to look upon.

3 For we know the Lord of Glory
  Always sees what children do,

And is writing now the story
  Of our thoughts and actions too.

4 Let our sins be all forgiven,
  Make us fear whate'er is wrong;
Lead us on our way to heaven,
  There to sing a nobler song.

Mrs. Skelley, 1844.

32

Blessed Jesus, at Thy Word.

LIEBSTER JESU, WIR SIND HIER. 7, 8, 7, 8, 8, 8.

JOHANN RUDOLPH AHLE, (1625–1673), 1664.

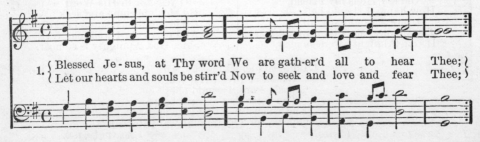

1. { Blessed Je-sus, at Thy word We are gath-er'd all to hear Thee;
   { Let our hearts and souls be stirr'd Now to seek and love and fear Thee;

Blessed Jesus, at Thy Word.—Concluded.

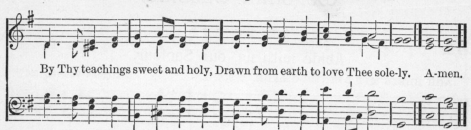

By Thy teachings sweet and holy, Drawn from earth to love Thee sole-ly. A-men.

2 All our knowledge, sense, and sight
  Lie in deepest darkness shrouded,
Till Thy Spirit breaks our night
  With the beams of truth unclouded.
Thou alone to God canst win us,
Thou must work all good within us.

3 Glorious Lord, Thyself impart!
  Light of light, from God proceeding,
Open Thou our ears and heart,
  Help us by Thy Spirit's pleading,
Hear the cry Thy people raises,
Hear, and bless our prayers and praises.

Tobias Clausnitzer, 1671.
Tr. Miss Winkworth, 1853.

Father, Bless our School To-day. 33

GOTT SEI DANK DURCH ALLE WELT. 7, 7, 7, 7.

FREYLINGHAUSEN'S GESANGBUCH. HALLE, 1704.

1. Fa-ther, bless our school to-day; Be in all we do and say;

Be in ev-'ry song we sing, Ev-'ry pray'r to Thee we bring. A-men.

2 Jesus, well-beloved Son,
  May Thy will by us be done;
Come and meet with us to-day;
Teach us, Lord, Thyself, we pray.

3 Holy Spirit, Mighty power,
  Consecrate this Lord's day hour;
Unto us Thine unction give;
Touch our souls that we may live.

125

Worship: Closing.

34

Abide with us, our Saviour.

ACH BLEIB MIT DEINER GNADE. 7, 6, 7, 6.

MELCHIOR VULPIUS, 1609.

1. A - bide with us, our Sav - iour, Nor let Thy mer - cy cease; From Sa - tan's might de - fend us, And grant our souls re - lease. A - men.

2 Abide with us, our Saviour,
　Sustain us by Thy Word;
That we with all Thy people
　To life may be restored.

3 Abide with us, our Saviour,
　Thou Light of endless light;
Increase to us Thy blessings,
　And save us by Thy might.

Joshua Stegmann, 1630.
Tr. Unknown, 1848.

126

On What Has Now Been Sown.

CHRISTCHURCH. 6, 6, 6, 6, 8, 8, or H. M.   CHARLES STEGGALL, 1865.

1. On what has now been sown, Thy bless-ing, Lord, be-stow;

The pow'r is Thine a-lone To make it spring and grow:

Do Thou the gracious harvest raise, And Thou a-lone shalt have the praise. A-men.

2 To Thee our wants are known,
From Thee are all our powers,
Accept what is Thine own,
And pardon what is ours:
Our praises, Lord, and prayers receive,
And to Thy Word a blessing give.

3 O grant that each of us,
Who meet before Thee here,
May meet together thus,
When Thou and Thine appear,
And follow Thee to heaven our home;
Even so, Amen, Lord Jesus, come!

John Newton, 1779.

36

For a Season Called to Part.

SOLITUDE. 7, 7, 7, 7.   L. T. DOWNES.

1. For a sea-son call'd to part, Let us now our-selves com-mend

To the gracious eye and heart Of our ev-er-pres-ent Friend. A - men.

2 Jesus, hear our humble prayer:
   Tender Shepherd of Thy sheep,
Let Thy mercy and Thy care
   All our souls in safety keep.

3 What we each have now been taught,
   Let our memories retain:

May we, if we live, be brought
   Here to meet in peace again.

4 Then, if Thou instruction bless,
   Songs of praises shall be given;
We'll our thankfulness express,
   Here on earth and when in heaven.

John Newton, 1776. a.

37

Lord, Dismiss us with Thy Blessing.

SICILIAN HYMN. 8, 7, 8, 7, 4, 7.

1. { Lord, dis - miss us with Thy blessing, Fill our hearts with joy and peace! }
   { Let us each, Thy love pos-sess-ing, Tri-umph in re - deem-ing grace. }

Lord, Dismiss us with Thy Blessing.—Concluded.

O re-fresh us, O re-fresh us, Trav'lling thro' this wil-der-ness. A-men.

2 Thanks we give and adoration
  For Thy Gospel's joyful sound.
May the fruits of Thy salvation
  In our hearts and lives abound:
‖: May Thy presence :‖
With us evermore be found.

3 So, whene'er the signal's given
  Us from earth to call away,
Borne on angels' wings to heaven,
  Glad the summons to obey,
‖: May we, ready, :‖
Rise and reign in endless day.

Walter Shirley, 1774. a.

The Lord be with us as we Bend. 38

KEITH. C. M.

O. B. KEITH.

1. The Lord be with us as we bend His bless-ing to re-ceive;

His gift of peace up-on us send, Be-fore His courts we leave. A-men.

2 The Lord be with us as we walk
  Along our homeward road;
In silent thought or friendly talk
  Our hearts be still with God.

3 The Lord be with us till the night
  Shall close the day of rest;

Be He of every heart the Light,
  Of every home the Guest.

4 And when our nightly prayers we say,
  His watch He still shall keep,
Crown with His grace His own blest day,
  And guard His people's sleep.

John Ellerton, 1870.

39

Heavenly Father, Send Thy Blessing.

NEWTON FERNS. 8, 7, 8, 7. (*First tune.*) SAMUEL SMITH, (1804–1873.)

1. Heav'n - ly Fa - ther, send Thy bless - ing
On Thy chil - dren gath - er'd here, May they all Thy
Name con - fess - ing, Be to Thee for ev - er dear. A - men.

2 May they be like Joseph, loving,
    Dutiful, and chaste, and pure;
And their faith, like David, proving,
    Steadfast unto death endure.

3 Holy Saviour, Who in meekness
    Didst vouchsafe a child to be,
Guide their steps and help their weakness,
    Bless and make them like to Thee.

4 Temples of the Holy Spirit,
    May they with Thy glory shine,
And immortal bliss inherit,
    And for evermore be Thine.

C. Wordsworth, 1863.

Heavenly Father, Send Thy Blessing.

BETHANY. 8, 7, 8, 7. D. (*Second tune.*)   HENRY SMART, 1867.

1. Heav'n-ly Fa-ther, send Thy bless-ing On Thy chil-dren gather'd here,

May they all Thy name con-fess-ing, Be to Thee for ev-er dear.

2. May they be like Jo-seph, lov-ing, Du-ti-ful, and chaste, and pure;

And their faith, like Da-vid, proving, Steadfast un-to death en-dure. A-men.

40

Saviour, Again to Thy Dear Name.

ELLERS. 10, 10, 10, 10.

EDWARD J. HOPKINS, 1866.

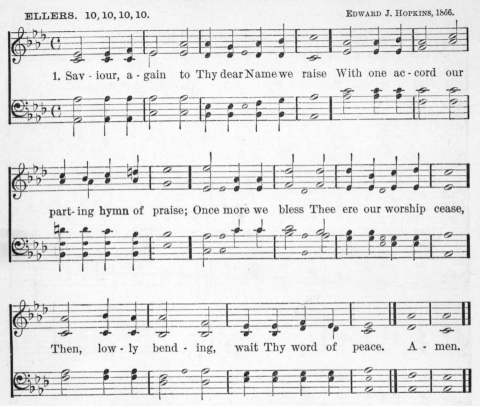

1. Sav-iour, a-gain to Thy dear Name we raise With one ac-cord our part-ing hymn of praise; Once more we bless Thee ere our worship cease, Then, low-ly bend-ing, wait Thy word of peace. A-men.

2 Grant us Thy peace upon our homeward way;
With Thee began, with Thee shall end the day;
Guard Thou the lips from sin, the hearts from shame,
That in this house have called upon Thy Name.

3 Grant us Thy peace, Lord, through the coming night,
Turn Thou for us its darkness into light;
From harm and danger keep Thy children free,
For dark and light are both alike to Thee.

4 Grant us Thy peace throughout our daily life,
Our balm in sorrow, and our stay in strife;
Then, when Thy voice shall bid our conflict cease,
Call us, O Lord, to Thine eternal peace.

John Ellerton, 1866.

GOD AND HIS WORKS: GOD.

Hail, Father, Son, and Holy Ghost.

41

ST. OSWIN. C. M.

J. B. DYKES, (1823–1876.)

1. Hail, Fa - ther, Son, and Ho - ly Ghost, One God in Per - sons Three; Of Thee we make our joy - ful boast, Our songs we make of Thee. A - men.

2 Present alike in every place,
   Thy Godhead we adore:
Beyond the bounds of time and space,
   Thou dwell'st for evermore.

3 In wisdom infinite Thou art,
   Thine eye doth all things see;
And every thought of every heart
   Is fully known to Thee.

4 Whate'er Thou wilt, in earth below
   Thou dost in heaven above;
But chiefly we rejoice to know
   The Almighty God is Love.

5 Thou lov'st whate'er Thy hands have made;
   Thy goodness we rehearse,
In shining characters displayed
   Throughout our universe.

6 Mercy, with love, and endless grace,
   O'er all Thy works doth reign:
But mostly Thou delight'st to bless
   Thy favorite creature, man.

7 Wherefore let every creature give
   To Thee the praise designed;
But chiefly, Lord, the thanks receive,
   The hearts of all mankind.

C. Wesley, 1763.

42

God is Love: His Mercy Brightens.

STUTTGART. 8, 7, 8, 7.

1. God is Love: His mer - cy bright - ens
All the path in which we rove; Bliss He wakes, and
woe He light - ens: God is Wis - dom, God is Love. A - men.

2 Chance and change are busy ever;
    Man decays, and ages move:
    But His mercy waneth never;
    God is Wisdom, God is Love.

3 Even the hour that darkest seemeth
    Will His changeless goodness prove;
    From the gloom His brightness streameth
    God is Wisdom, God is Love.

4 He with earthly cares entwineth
    Hope and comfort from above:
    Everywhere His glory shineth;
    God is Wisdom, God is Love.

John Bowring, 1825. a.

GOD AND HIS WORKS: CREATION.

43

Heaven and Earth, and Sea and Air.

EVER FAITHFUL, EVER SURE. 7, 7, 7, 7.

1. Heav'n and earth, and sea and air, All their Mak - er's praise de - clare: Wake, my soul, a - wake and sing, Now thy grate - ful prais - es bring. A - men.

2 See the glorious orb of day
Breaking through the clouds his way:
Moon and stars with silvery light
Praise Him through the silent night.

3 See how He hath everywhere
Made this earth so rich and fair;
Hill and vale and fruitful land,
All things living, show His hand.

4 See how through the boundless sky
Fresh and free the birds do fly;
Fire and wind and storm are still
Servants of His royal Will.

5 See the water's ceaseless flow,
Ever circling to and fro:
From the sources to the sea,
Still it rolls in praise to Thee.

6 Lord, great wonders workest Thou!
To Thy sway all creatures bow:
Write Thou deeply in my heart
What I am, and what Thou art!

Joachim Neander, 1677.
Tr. Miss Winkworth, 1853. a.

44

All Things Bright and Beautiful.

ALL THINGS BRIGHT. 7, 6, 7, 6. D. *(With Refrain.)*   JOHN HULLAH.

:S: CHORUS. *Unison.*

All things bright and beau - ti - ful, All creatures great and small,

Harmony.

All things wise and won - der - ful, The Lord God made them all!

Duet.   *Trio.*

1. Each lit - tle flow'r that o - pens, Each lit - tle. bird that

Duet.   *Trio.*

sings,   He made their glow - ing col - ors,   He

All Things Bright and Beautiful.—Concluded.

Harmony.

made their ti - ny wings. The rich man in his cas - tle, The poor man at his gate, God made them high or low - ly, And or - der'd their es - tate. A - men.

Chorus. :S: *After 3rd Verse and Chorus.*

2 The purple-headed mountain,
  The river running by,
The sunset and the morning
  That brighten up the sky,
The cold wind in the winter,
  The pleasant summer sun,
The ripe fruit in the garden,
  He made them every one.

3 The tall trees in the greenwood,
  The meadows where we play,
The rushes by the water,
  We gather every day;
He gave us eyes to see them,
  And lips that we might tell
How great is God Almighty,
  Who doeth all things well.

Cecil F. Alexander, (1823 ——).

137

GOD AND HIS WORKS: PROVIDENCE.

45

God, Who Made the Earth.

5, 6, 6, 4.

ADAPTED FROM J. E. ROE.

1. God, who made the earth, The air, the sky, the sea,

Who gave the light its birth, Car - eth for me. A - men.

2 God, who made the grass,
   The flower, the fruit, the tree,
The day and night to pass,
   Careth for me.

3 God, who made the sun,
   The moon, and stars, is He
Who, when life's clouds come on,
   Careth for me.

4 God, who made all things
   On earth, in air, in sea,
Who changing seasons brings,
   Careth for me.

5 God, who gave me health,
   Be this my prayer to Thee,
That when I sink in death
   Thou care for me.

6 God, who sent His Son
   To die on Calvary,
He, if I lean on Him,
   Will care for me.

7 When in heaven's bright land
   I all His loved ones see,
I'll sing with that blest band,
   God cared for me.

Sarah B. Rhodes, 1870.

46

Guide me, O Thou Great Jehovah.

EPSOM COLLEGE, 8, 7, 8, 7, 4, 7.

S. J. ROWTON.

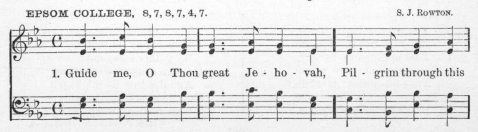

1. Guide me, O Thou great Je - ho - vah, Pil - grim through this

Guide me, O Thou Great Jehovah.—Concluded.

bar - ren land; I am weak, but Thou art might - y,
Hold me with Thy pow'r - ful hand; Bread of heav - en,
Bread of heav - en, Feed me till I want no more. A - men.

2 Open now the crystal fountain,
    Whence the healing streams do flow;
  Let the fiery, cloudy pillar,
    Lead me all my journey through:
      ‖: Strong Deliverer, :‖
    Be Thou still my Strength and Shield!

3 When I tread the verge of Jordan,
    Bid my anxious fears subside:
  Death of death and hell's destruction,
    Land me safe on Canaan's side:
      ‖: Songs of praises :‖
    I will ever give to Thee.

William Williams, 1773.

139

47

Father, Whate'er of Earthly Bliss.

NAOMI. C. M.

ARRANGED FROM JOHANN G. NÄGELI.
BY LOWELL MASON, 1836.

1. Fa - ther, what - e'er of earth - ly bliss Thy sov - 'reign
hand de - nies, Ac - cept - ed at Thy throne of grace,
Let this pe - ti - tion rise... A - men.

2 Give me a calm, a thankful heart,
   From every murmur free;
The blessings of Thy grace impart,
   And let me live to Thee.

3 Let the sweet hope that Thou art mine
   My path of life attend;
Thy presence through my journey shine,
   And crown my journey's end.

Anne Steele, 1760. **a.**

GOD AND HIS WORKS: ANGELS.

Up Above the Bright Blue Sky.

48

ANGELI. 7, 6, 7, 7, 6.

GEO. C. F. HAAS.

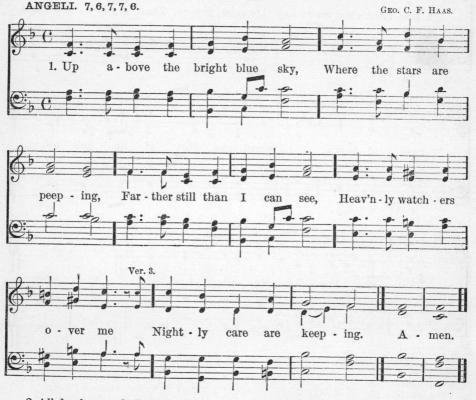

1. Up a-bove the bright blue sky, Where the stars are peep-ing, Far-ther still than I can see, Heav'n-ly watch-ers o-ver me Night-ly care are keep-ing. A-men.

2 All day long and all night, too,
  While I'm safely sleeping,
Busy on their task of love
They are sent from heaven above,
  Faithful vigil keeping.

3 And while us, from evil things,
  Angels are defending,
Little children, robed in white,
Sing before the throne of light
  In daylight never ending.

4 Jesus took them for His own,
  Made them pure and holy,
And on earth His gentle love
Trained them for their home above,
  Safe from sin and folly.

5 Blessed Jesus, take me, too,
  Though I'm weak and lowly,
Let Thy gentle grace within
Make my garments white and clean,
  And my spirit holy.

141

49

Our Thanks and Praise to Thee be Given.

ST. CLEMENT. L. M.

C. C. SCHOLEFIELD.

1. Our thanks and praise to Thee be giv-en, Thou Lord of earth and Lord of heav'n, For count-less hosts of an-gels bright, That serve Thy Son in cloud-less light. A - men.

2 Pure in their nature, good, and true,
'Tis their delight Thy will to do;
From heaven they come the souls to guard
That trust in Thy most holy Word.

3 They joy when but one sinner turns;
Their zeal for Jesus ever burns;
They serve His people night and day,
And turn full many an ill away.

4 All little ones, awake, asleep,
And every child of Thine they keep;
O'er all Thy kingdom, far and near,
They give their kind and loving care.

5 When death approaches, then they come,
To soften pain, and guide us home;
And when the spirit leaves the clay,
To waft us to the realms of day.

6 Give us, O Lord, the grace and power
To serve Thee well each day and hour;
Grant us the zeal and fervent love
To serve as angels serve above.

7 Let these good spirits with us be,
When in Thy house we worship Thee;
And bid them all our path defend
Till this our life on earth shall end.

From the Latin of Philip Melanchthon, (1497-1560).
Tr. Jos. A. Seiss, 1890.

God Doth Send His Angels.

EVERSLEY. 11, 11, 11, 11.

J. W. ELLIOTT.

1. God doth send His An - gels, help - ing, at His word,
All His faith - ful chil - dren, like their faith - ful Lord;
Sooth - ing them in sor - row, arm - ing them in strife,
Op'n - ing wide the tomb-doors, lead-ing in - to Life. A - men.

2 Father, send Thine Angels unto us, we pray;
Leave us not to wander, all along our way.
Let them guard and guide us, whereso'er we be,
Till our resurrection brings us home to Thee.

THE CHURCH YEAR: ADVENT.

51

Come, Thou Long-expected Jesus.

ST. HILARY. 8, 7, 8, 7. D.

GANTHER.

1. Come, Thou long-ex-pect-ed Je-sus, Born to set Thy peo-ple free;

From our fears and sins re-lease us, Let us find our rest in Thee.

Is-rael's Strength and Con-so-la-tion, Hope of all the earth Thou art;

Dear De-sire of ev-'ry na-tion, Joy of ev-'ry long-ing heart. A-men.

2 Born Thy people to deliver;
  Born a Child, and yet a King;
Born to reign in us for ever,
  Now Thy gracious kingdom bring.

By Thine own eternal Spirit,
  Rule in all our hearts alone;
By Thine all-sufficient merit,
  Raise us to Thy glorious Throne.

C. Wesley, 1745.

O How Shall I Receive Thee?

ST. THEODULPH. 7, 6, 7, 6. D.   MELCHIOR TESCHNER, AB. 1613.

1. { O how shall I re - ceive Thee, How greet Thee, Lord, a - right? }
   { All na - tions long to see Thee, My hope, my heart's de - light! }

O kin - dle, Lord, most ho - ly, Thy lamp with - in my breast,

To do in spir - it low - ly All that may please Thee best. A - men.

2 Thy Zion palms is strewing,
   And branches fresh and fair;
My heart, its powers renewing,
   An anthem shall prepare.
My soul puts off her sadness
   Thy glories to proclaim;
With all her strength and gladness
   She fain would serve Thy Name.

3 I lay in fetters groaning,
   Thou comest to set me free!
I stood, my shame bemoaning,
   Thou comest to honor me!
A glory Thou dost give me,
   A treasure safe on high,
That will not fail nor leave me
   As earthly riches fly.

4 Love caused Thy Incarnation,
   Love brought Thee down to me.
Thy thirst for my salvation
   Procured my liberty.
O Love beyond all telling,
   That led Thee to embrace,
In love all love excelling,
   Our lost and fallen race!

5 Rejoice then, ye sad-hearted,
   Who sit in deepest gloom,
Who mourn o'er joys departed,
   And tremble at your doom:
He who alone can cheer you,
   Is standing at the door;
He brings His pity near you,
   And bids you weep no more.

Paul Gerhardt, 1653.
Tr. Seaton's Leeds Church H. B., 1859.

53

Hark, the Glad Sound, the Saviour Comes.

DIE HELLE SONN IST NUN DAHIN. C. M. (*First tune.*)   S. H. STADE, 1644.

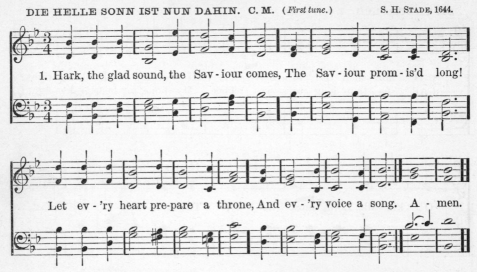

1. Hark, the glad sound, the Saviour comes, The Saviour prom-is'd long!

Let ev-'ry heart pre-pare a throne, And ev-'ry voice a song. A-men.

2 On Him the Spirit, largely poured,
    Exerts His sacred fire;
Wisdom and might, and zeal and love,
    His holy breast inspire.

3 He comes the prisoners to release,
    In Satan's bondage held:
The gates of brass before Him burst,
    The iron fetters yield.

4 He comes from thickest films of vice
    To clear the mental ray,

And on the eyeballs of the blind
    To pour celestial day.

5 He comes the broken heart to bind,
    The bleeding soul to cure,
And with the treasures of His grace
    To enrich the humble poor.

6 Our glad hosannas, Prince of Peace!
    Thy welcome shall proclaim;
And heaven's eternal arches ring
    With Thy beloved Name.

Doddridge, 1755.

Hark, the Glad Sound, the Saviour Comes.

HENRY. C. M. (*Second tune.*)   S. B. POND.

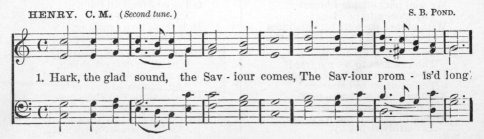

1. Hark, the glad sound, the Saviour comes, The Saviour prom - is'd long

Hark, the Glad Sound, the Saviour Comes.—Concluded.

Let ev - 'ry heart pre- pare a throne, And ev - 'ry voice a song. A · men.

54

On Jordan's Banks the Herald's Cry.

ALSTONE. L. M.

CHARLES EDWARD WILLING.

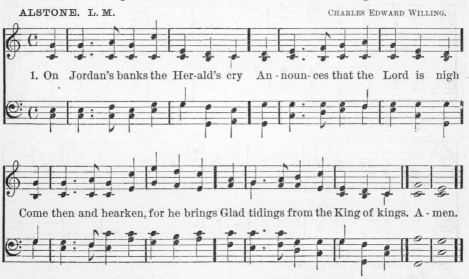

1. On Jordan's banks the Her-ald's cry An - noun- ces that the Lord is nigh

Come then and hearken, for he brings Glad tidings from the King of kings. A - men.

2 Then cleansed be every breast from sin,
Make straight the way for God within,
And let us all our hearts prepare
For Christ to come and enter there.

3 For Thou art our Salvation, Lord,
Our Refuge and our great Reward.
Without Thy grace our life must fade,
And wither like a flower decayed.

4 Stretch forth Thy hand, to health restore,
And make us rise to fall no more:
Once more upon Thy people shine,
And fill the world with love divine.

5 To Him who left the throne of heaven
To save mankind, all praise be given:
Like praise be to the Father done,
And Holy Spirit Three in One.

John Chandler, 1837. *a.*

55

Rejoice, all ye Believers.

IHR CHRISTEN AUSERKOREN. 7, 6, 7, 6. D.

J. Crüger, 1653.

1. { Re - joice, all ye be - liev - ers, And let your lights ap - pear!
   The eve - ning is ad - vanc - ing, And dark - er night is near. }

The Bridegroom is a - ris - ing, And soon He draw - eth nigh.

Up, pray, and watch and wres- tle; At midnight comes the cry! A - men.

2 The watchers on the mountain
   Proclaim the Bridegroom near;
Go meet Him as He cometh,
   With hallelujahs clear.
The marriage-feast is waiting,
   The gates wide open stand;
Up, up, ye heirs of glory;
   The Bridegroom is at hand!

3 Ye saints, who here in patience
   Your cross and sufferings bore,
Shall live and reign for ever,
   When sorrow is no more.

Around the throne of glory
   The Lamb ye shall behold,
In triumph cast before Him
   Your diadems of gold!

4 Our Hope and Expectation,
   O Jesus, now appear;
Arise, Thou Sun so longed for,
   O'er this benighted sphere!
With hearts and hands uplifted,
   We plead, O Lord, to see
The day of earth's redemption,
   That brings us unto Thee!

Laurentius Laurenti, 1700.
Tr. Jane Borthwick, 1853.

O Come, let us Raise.

SIEBOTH. 5, 5, 5, 5. D.

J. SIEBOTH.

1. O come, let us raise Our trib-ute of song; Thanks-giv-ing and praise

To Je-sus be-long; He comes from a-bove Our bliss to be-gin,

Make per-fect in love, And free us from sin. A-men.

2 The old and the young,
   His people by choice,
With heart, soul and tongue,
   In Him may rejoice;
We meet Him to-day
   Triumphantly crowned,
And welcome His way,
   In chorus around.

3 Hosanna!—that word
   To children is dear;
To Jesus our Lord,
   We'll echo it here;

Let worldlings despise,
   And enemies rail,
Hosannas shall rise,
   Hosannas prevail.

4 God's temple shall ring,
   While under His eye,
Hosanna we sing,
   For Jesus draws nigh:
Hosanna! our breath
   Through life shall proclaim;
Hosanna! in death,
   In glory the same!

J. Montgomery.

57

Lift up Your Heads, ye Mighty Gates!

MACHT HOCH DIE THÜR. 8, 8, 8, 8, 8, 8, 6, 6.   HALLE, 1704.

1. Lift up your heads, ye might-y gates! Be-hold the King of glo-ry waits;

The King of kings is draw-ing near, The Sav-iour of the world is here;

Life and sal-va-tion He doth bring, Wherefore re-joice, and glad-ly sing:

We praise Thee, Fa-ther, now, Cre-a-tor, wise art Thou! A-men.

Lift up Your Heads, ye Mighty Gates.—Concluded.

2 The Lord is just, a Helper tried,
Mercy is ever at His side;
His kingly crown is holiness,
His sceptre, pity in distress,
The end of all our woe He brings;
Wherefore the earth is glad and sings:
  We praise Thee, Saviour, now,
  Mighty in deed art Thou!

3 O blest the land, the city blest,
Where Christ the Ruler is confest!
O happy hearts and happy homes
To whom this King in triumph comes!
The cloudless Sun of joy He is,
Who bringeth pure delight and bliss:
  O Comforter Divine,
  What boundless grace is Thine!

4 Fling wide the portals of your heart;
Make it a temple, set apart
From earthly use for heaven's employ,
Adorned with prayer, and love, and joy;
So shall your Sovereign enter in,
And new and nobler life begin:
  To Thee, O God, be praise,
  For word and deed and grace!

5 Redeemer, come! I open wide
My heart to Thee; here, Lord, abide!
Let me Thy inner presence feel,
Thy grace and love in me reveal;
Thy Holy Spirit guide us on,
Until our glorious goal be won!
  Eternal praise and fame
  We offer to Thy Name.

George Weissel, 1630.
Tr. Miss Winkworth, 1855. a.

58

Give to our God Immortal Praise.

PRIMA LUX. L. M.

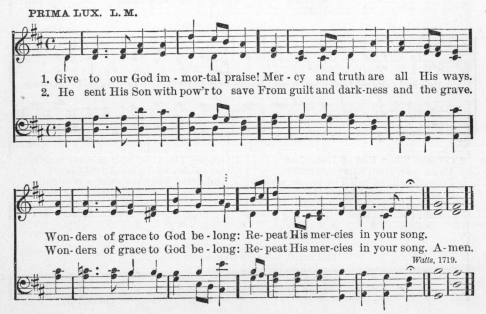

1. Give to our God im-mor-tal praise! Mer-cy and truth are all His ways.
2. He sent His Son with pow'r to save From guilt and dark-ness and the grave.

Won-ders of grace to God be-long: Re-peat His mer-cies in your song.
Won-ders of grace to God be-long: Re-peat His mer-cies in your song. A-men.

Watts, 1719.

59

O Come, O Come, Emmanuel.

BENISON. 8, 8, 8, 8, 8, 8.

JOHN HULLAH.

1. O come, O come, Em-man-u-el, And ran-som cap-tive Is-ra-el,

That mourns in lone-ly ex-ile here, Un-til the Son of God ap-pear.

Rejoice! rejoice! Em-man-u-el Shall come to thee, O Is-ra-el! A-men.

2 O come, Thou Rod of Jesse, free
Thine own from Satan's tyranny;
From depths of hell Thy people save
And give them victory o'er the grave.
Rejoice! rejoice! Emmanuel
Shall come to thee, O Israel!

3 O come, Thou Day-Spring, come and cheer
Our spirits by Thine Advent here:
And drive away the shades of night,
And pierce the clouds, and bring us light
Rejoice! rejoice! Emmanuel
Shall come to thee, O Israel!

4 O come, Thou Key of David, come,
And open wide, our heavenly home:
Make safe the way that leads on high,
And close the path to misery.
Rejoice! rejoice! Emmanuel
Shall come to thee, O Israel!

From " Greater Antiphons," ab. 12th Century.
Tr. John Mason Neale, 1851.

O'er the Distant Mountains Breaking.

HER VIL TIES, HER VIL TIES. 8, 7, 8, 7, 4, 7.　　　　　　A. P. BERGGREN.

1. O'er the dis - tant mountains breaking Comes the reddening dawn of day;

Rise, my soul, from sleep a - wak - ing, Rise, and sing, and watch, and pray;

'Tis thy Saviour, 'tis thy Saviour, On His bright re-turn-ing way. A - men.

2 O Thou long-expected! Weary
　Waits my anxious soul for Thee;
Life is dark, and earth is dreary,
　Where Thy light I do not see;
　‖: O my Saviour, :‖
When wilt Thou return to me?

3 Nearer is my soul's salvation,
　Spent the night, the day at hand;
Keep me in my lowly station,
　Watching for Thee, till I stand,
　‖: O my Saviour, :‖
In Thy bright, Thy promised land.

4 With my lamp, well trimmed and burning,
　Swift to hear and slow to roam,
Watching for Thy glad returning,
　To restore me to my home.
　‖: Come, my Saviour, :‖
Thou hast promised; quickly come.

J. S. B. Monsell, 1862.

61

Wake, Awake, for Night is Flying.

WACHET AUF RUFT UNS DIE STIMME. PHILIP NICOLAI, (1556–1608), 1599.

1. Wake, a-wake, for night is fly - - ing, The watchmen
Mid - night hears the wel - come voi - - ces, And at the

on the height are cry - ing; A-wake Je - ru - sa - lem at last!
thrilling cry re - joi - ces: Come forth, ye vir-gins, night is . . . past!

The Bridegroom comes, a-wake, Your lamps with gladness take, Hal-le-lu-jah!

And for His marriage feast prepare, For ye must go to meet Him there. A-men.

Wake, Awake, for Night is Flying.—Concluded.

2 Zion hears the watchman singing,
  And all her heart with joy is springing,
    She wakes, she rises from her gloom;
  For her Lord comes down all glorious,
  The strong in grace, in truth victorious,
    Her Star is risen, her Light is come!
      Ah come, Thou blessed Lord,
        O Jesus, Son of God,
          Hallelujah!
  We follow till the halls we see
  Where Thou hast bid us sup with Thee.

3 Now let all the heavens adore Thee,
  And men and angels sing before Thee,
    With harp and cymbal's clearest tone:
  Of one pearl each shining portal,
  Where we are with the choir immortal,
    Of angels round Thy dazzling throne;
      Nor eye hath seen, nor ear
        Hath yet attained to hear
          What there is ours,
  But we rejoice, and sing to Thee
  Our hymns of joy eternally.

Philip Nicolai, (1556–1608), 1599.
Tr. Miss Winkworth, (1827–1878), 1858.

O That I Had an Angel's Tongue.

62

NUN DANKET ALL. C. M.

J. CRÜGER, 1656.

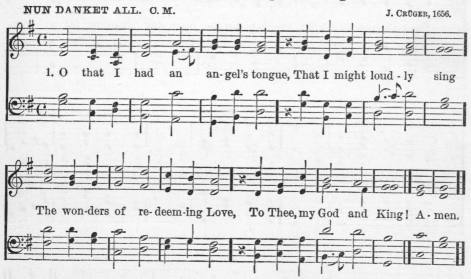

1. O that I had an angel's tongue, That I might loud-ly sing
The won-ders of re-deem-ing Love, To Thee, my God and King! A-men.

2 Let the redeemèd of the Lord
  Their thankful voices raise:
  Can we be dumb while angels sing
  Our great Redeemer's praise?

3 O sing aloud in boundless grace
  Which thus hath set us free;
  Extol with songs, my savèd soul,
  Thy Saviour's Love to thee.

4 Give endless thanks to God, and say,
  What Love was this in Thee,
  That Thou hast not withheld Thy Son,
  Thine only Son, from me!

John Mason.

63

Long the Nations Waited.

VEXILLUM. 6, 5, 6, 5, 12 lines.   HENRY SMART, 1868.

1. Long the na-tions wait-ed, Thro' the troubled night, Looking, longing, yearning,

For the promis'd light. Prophets saw the morn-ing Breaking far a - way,

Minstrels sing the splendor Of that op'ning day. While in re - gal glo-ry,

'Mid e - ter- nal light, Reign'd the King Immortal, Ho-ly, In - fi - nite. A - men.

Long the Nations Waited.—Concluded.

2 Brightly dawned the Advent
  Of the new-born King,
Joyously the watchers
  Heard the angels sing.
Sadly closed the evening
  Of His hallowed life,
As the noontide darkness
  Veiled the last dread strife
Lo! again in glory,
  'Mid eternal light,
Reigns the King Immortal,
  Holy, Infinite.

3 Lo! again He cometh,
  Robed in clouds of light,
As the Judge Eternal,
  Armed with power and might.
Nations to His footstool
  Gathered then shall be;

Earth shall yield her treasures,
  And her dead the sea.
Till the trumpet soundeth,
  'Mid eternal light
Reign, Thou King Immortal,
  Holy, Infinite.

4 Jesus, Lord and Master,
  Prophet, Priest and King.
To Thy feet triumphant,
  Hallowed praise we bring.
Thine the pain and weeping,
  Thine the victory;
Power, and praise, and honor,
  Be, O Lord, to Thee.
High in regal glory,
  'Mid eternal light,
Reign, O King Immortal,
  Holy, Infinite.

John Julian, 1882. a.

Lo, the Lamb, so Long Expected. 64

ARUNDEL. 8, 7, 8, 7.

J. B. DYKES.

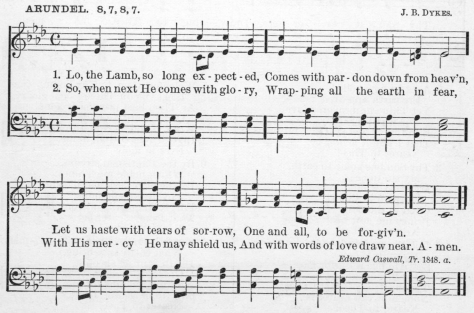

1. Lo, the Lamb, so long ex-pect-ed, Comes with par-don down from heav'n,
2. So, when next He comes with glo-ry, Wrap-ping all the earth in fear,

Let us haste with tears of sor-row, One and all, to be for-giv'n.
With His mer-cy He may shield us, And with words of love draw near. A-men.

Edward Caswall, Tr. 1848. a.

65

Nearer, my God, to Thee!

KEDRON. 6, 4, 6, 4, 6, 6, 4.

A. B. SPRATT.

1. Near - er, my God to Thee! Near - er to Thee! Through Word and Sac - ra- ment, Thou com'st to me. Thy grace is ev - er near, Thy Spir - it ev - er here, Draw - ing to Thee. A - men.

2 Ages on ages rolled,
    Ere earth appeared,
Yet Thine unmeasured love
    The way prepared;
E'en then Thou yearndst for me
That I might nearer be,
    Nearer to Thee!

3 Thy Son has come to earth,
    My sin to bear,
My every wound to heal,
    My pain to share.
"God in the flesh" for me,
Brings me now nearer Thee,
    Nearer to Thee!

4 Lo! all my debt is paid,
    My guilt is gone.
See! He has risen for me,
    My throne is won.
Thanks, O my God, to Thee!
None now can nearer be.
    Nearer to Thee!

5 Welcome, then, to Thy home,
    Blest One in Three!
As Thou hast promised, come!
    Come, Lord, to me!
Work, Thou, O God, through me,
Live, Thou, O God, in me,
    Ever in me!

6 By the Baptismal stream,
    Which made me Thine,
By the dear flesh and blood,
    Thy love made mine,
Purge, Thou, all sin from me,
That I may nearer be,
    Nearer to Thee!

7 Surely it matters not
    What earth may bring,
Death is of no account,
    Grace will I sing.
Nothing remains for me,
Save to be nearer Thee,
    Nearer to Thee!

H. E. Jacobs, 1887.

The Church Year: Christmas.

Silent Night! Holy Night!

66

SILENT NIGHT. 6, 6, 8, 9, 6.   FRANZ GRUBER, Dec. 24th, 1818.

1. Si - lent night! Ho - ly night! All is calm, all is bright,

Round yon Vir - gin Mother and Child! Ho - ly In - fant, so ten-der and mild,

Sleep in heav-en-ly peace, Sleep in heav-en-ly peace. A - men.

2 Silent night! Holy night!
Shepherds quake at the sight!
Glories stream from Heaven afar,
Heavenly hosts sing Alleluia,
‖: Christ, the Saviour, is born! :‖

3 Silent night! Holy night!
Son of God, love's pure light
Radiant beams from Thy holy Face,
With the dawn of redeeming grace,
‖: Jesus, Lord, at Thy birth. :‖

From the German of Joseph Mohr, 1818.

67

Hark! What Mean Those Holy Voices.

TRUST. 8, 7, 8. 7. (*First tune.*) MENDELSSOHN.

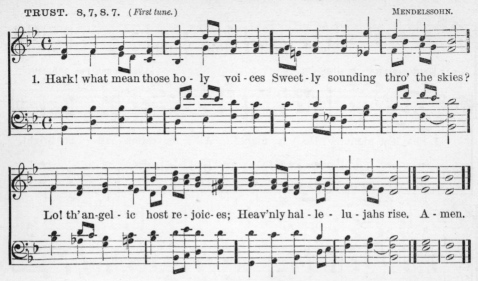

1. Hark! what mean those ho - ly voi - ces Sweet - ly sounding thro' the skies?

Lo! th'an-gel - ic host re - joic- es; Heav'nly hal - le - lu - jahs rise. A - men.

2 Listen to the wondrous story,
  Which they chant in hymns of joy:
  "Glory in the highest, glory!
  Glory be to God most high!"

3 "Peace on earth, good-will from heaven,
  Reaching far as man is found;
  Souls redeemed, and sins forgiven;
  Loud our golden harps shall sound."

4 "Christ is born, the great Anointed;
  Heaven and earth His praises sing!

O receive whom God appointed
  For your Prophet, Priest, and King."

5 "Hasten, mortals, to adore Him;
  Learn His Name, and taste His joy;
  Till in heaven ye sing before Him,
  Glory be to God most high!"

6 Let us learn the wondrous story
  Of our great Redeemer's birth;
  Spread the brightness of His glory,
  Till it cover all the earth.

John Cawood, 1814. *a.*

Hark! What Mean Those Holy Voices.

HOLY VOICES. 8, 7, 8, 7. (*Second tune.*) G. H. GEER.

1. Hark! what mean those ho - ly voi - ces Sweet- ly sounding thro' the skies?

Hark! What Mean Those Holy Voices.—Concluded.

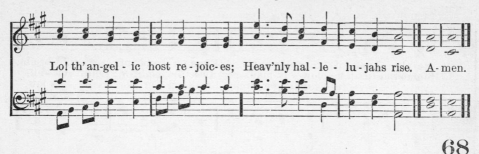

Lo! th'an-gel-ic host re-joic-es; Heav'nly hal-le-lu-jahs rise. A-men.

68

A Babe is Born in Bethlehem.

PUER NATUS IN BETHLEHEM. 8, 8, 8.   A PRE-REFORMATION MELODY IN DENMARK.

1. A Babe is born in Beth-le-hem, Beth-le-hem, There-fore re-joice Je-
2. With-in a man-ger He doth lie, He doth lie, Whose throne is set a-

ru-sa-lem.   Hal-le-lu-jah! Hal-le-lu-jah!
bove the sky.   Hal-le-lu-jah! Hal-le-lu-jah! A-men.

3 Stillness was all the ‖: manger round, :‖
The creature its Creator found.
Hallelujah! Hallelujah!

4 The wise men came, led ‖: by the star, :‖
Gold, myrrh, and incense brought from far.
Hallelujah! Hallelujah!

5 His mother is the ‖: Virgin mild, :‖
And He the Father's only Child.
Hallelujah! Hallelujah!

6 The serpent's wound He ‖: beareth not, :‖
Yet takes our blood, and shares our lot.
Hallelujah! Hallelujah!

7 Our human flesh He ‖: enters in, :‖
But bears no single taint of sin.
Hallelujah! Hallelujah!

8 To fallen man Him-‖: self He bowed, :‖
That He might lift us up to God.
Hallelujah! Hallelujah!

9 On this most blessed ‖: Jubilee, :‖
All glory be, O God, to Thee.
Hallelujah! Hallelujah!

10 O Holy Three, we ‖: Thee adore, :‖
This day, henceforth, for evermore.
Hallelujah! Hallelujah!

From the Latin, by C. P. Krauth, 1867.

69

Hark! A Burst of Heavenly Music.

JOYFUL SONG. 8, 7, 8, 7. D. (*With Refrain.*)

C. A. MARKS.

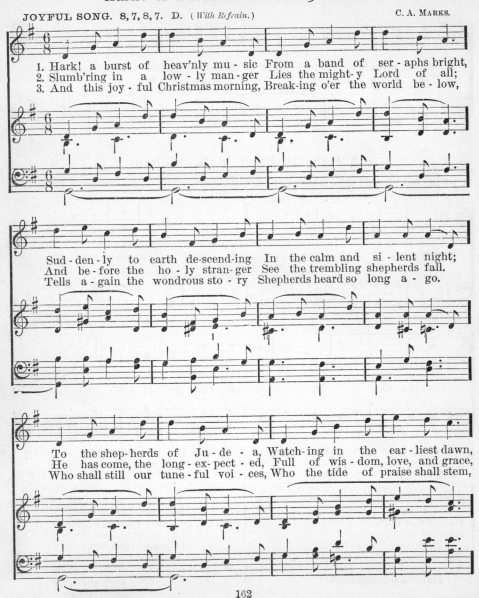

1. Hark! a burst of heav'nly mu - sic From a band of ser - aphs bright,
2. Slumb'ring in a low - ly man - ger Lies the might- y Lord of all;
3. And this joy - ful Christmas morning, Break-ing o'er the world be - low,

Sud - den - ly to earth de-scend-ing In the calm and si - lent night;
And be - fore the ho - ly stran - ger See the trembling shepherds fall.
Tells a - gain the wondrous sto - ry Shepherds heard so long a - go.

To the shep-herds of Ju - de - a, Watch-ing in the ear - liest dawn,
He has come, the long - ex - pect - ed, Full of wis - dom, love, and grace,
Who shall still our tune - ful voi - ces, Who the tide of praise shall stem,

Hark! A Burst of Heavenly Music.—Concluded.

Lo! they hear the joy-ful tid-ings, "Je-sus, Prince of Peace is born!"
To re-deem His ru-ined creatures, To re-store our fall-en race.
Which the bless-ed an-gels taught us, In the fields of Beth-le-hem?

REFRAIN.

Sweet and clear those an-gel voi-ces, Echoing through the star-ry sky,
So let an-gels wake the cho-rus! So let ran-som'd men re-ply!
Hark! we hear a-gain the cho-rus, Ringing through the star-ry sky,

cres.   *ff*

As they chant the heav'nly chorus, "Glo-ry be to God on high!"
Chanting the ce-les-tial anthem, "Glo-ry be to God on high!"
And we join the heav'nly anthem, "Glo-ry be to God on high!" A-men.

Ped.

From Goodrich's Service and Tune Book.

70

Hark! the Herald Angels Sing.

MENDELSSOHN. 7, 7, 7, 7, D. (*With Refrain.*) MENDELSSOHN.

1. Hark! the her - ald - an - gels sing, "Glo - ry to the new-born King;

Peace on earth, and mer - cy mild, God and sin - ners rec - on - cil'd!"

Joy - ful all ye na - tions, rise, Join the tri - umph of the skies;

U - ni - ver - sal na - ture say, Christ the Lord is born to - day.

REFRAIN.

Hark! the her - ald - an - gels sing Glo - ry to the new-born King. A - men

Hark! the Herald Angels Sing.—Concluded.

2 Christ, by highest heaven adored,
Christ, the everlasting Lord:
Late in time behold Him come,
Offspring of a virgin's womb!
Veiled in flesh, the Godhead see,
Hail the incarnate Deity!
Pleased as Man with men to appear,
Jesus, our Immanuel here!
   Hark! etc.

3 Hail, the heavenly Prince of Peace,
Hail, the Sun of Righteousness!
Light and life to all He brings,
Risen with healing in His wings.

Mild He lays His glory by,
Born that man no more may die;
Born to raise the sons of earth;
Born to give them second birth.
   Hark! etc.

4 Come, Desire of nations, come,
Fix in us Thy humble home;
O, to all Thyself impart,
Formed in each believing heart!
Hark! the herald-angels sing,
"Glory to the new-born King;
Peace on earth, and mercy mild,
God and sinners reconciled!"
   Hark! etc.

Charles Wesley, 1739.

The Happy Christmas Comes Once More. 71

EMMANUEL. L. M.   C. BALLE, 1850.

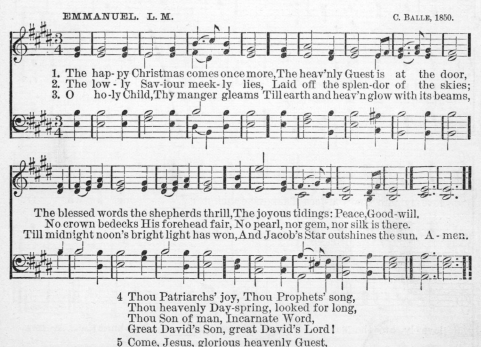

1. The hap-py Christmas comes once more, The heav'nly Guest is at the door,
2. The low-ly Sav-iour meek-ly lies, Laid off the splen-dor of the skies;
3. O ho-ly Child, Thy manger gleams Till earth and heav'n glow with its beams,

The blessed words the shepherds thrill, The joyous tidings: Peace, Good-will.
No crown bedecks His forehead fair, No pearl, nor gem, nor silk is there.
Till midnight noon's bright light has won, And Jacob's Star outshines the sun. A-men.

4 Thou Patriarchs' joy, Thou Prophets' song,
Thou heavenly Day-spring, looked for long,
Thou Son of man, Incarnate Word,
Great David's Son, great David's Lord!

5 Come, Jesus, glorious heavenly Guest,
Keep Thine own Christmas in our breast,
Then David's harp-strings, hushed so long,
Shall swell our Jubilee of song.

C. P. Krauth, sug. by Danish, 1867.

72

Rejoice, Rejoice, ye Christians.

FREUT EUCH, IHR LIEBEN CHRISTEN. 7, 6, 7, 6. D. (*First tune.*)

L. SCHRÖTER, 1587.

1. Re - joice, re - joice, ye Chris - tians, With all your hearts, this morn!
O hear the bless - ed tid - ings, "The Lord, the Christ, is born!" Now
brought us by the an - gels That stand a - bout God's throne; O
love - ly are the voi - ces That make such tid - - ings known, O
love - ly are the voi - ces That make such tid - - ings known. A - men.

Rejoice, Rejoice, ye Christians.—Concluded.

2 O hearken to their singing!
   This Child shall be your Friend;
The Father so hath willed it,
   That thus your woes should end.
The Son is freely given,
   That in Him ye may have
The Father's grace and blessing,
   And know He loves to save.

3 Nor deem the form too lowly
   That clothes Him at this hour;
For know ye what it hideth?
   'Tis God's almighty power.

Though now within the manger
   So poor and weak He lies,
He is the Lord of all things,
   He reigns above the skies.

4 Sin, death, and hell, and Satan
   Have lost the victory;
This Child shall overthrow them,
   As ye shall surely see.
Their wrath shall naught avail them;
   Fear not, their reign is o'er;
This Child shall overthrow them;
   O hear, and doubt no more!

Unknown, 1540.
Tr. Miss Winkworth, 1862.

Rejoice, Rejoice, ye Christians.

GLADNESS. 7, 6, 7, 6. D. (*Second tune.*)　　　　　F. F. BUERMEYER.

1. Rejoice, rejoice, ye Christians, With all your hearts, this morn! O hear the bless-ed

tidings, "The Lord, the Christ is born!" Now brought us by the angels That stand a-

bout God's throne; O lovely are the voices That make such tidings known. A - men.

73

O Little Town of Bethlehem!

ST. LOUIS. 7, 6, 7, 6. D.

LEWIS H. REDNER.

1. O lit-tle town of Beth-le-hem! How still we see thee lie;
A-bove thy deep and dream-less sleep The si-lent stars go by;
Yet in thy dark-ness shin-eth The ev-er-last-ing Light;
The hopes and fears of all the years Are met in thee to-night. A-men.

2 For Christ is born of Mary,
  And gathered all above,
While mortals sleep, the angels keep
  Their watch of wondering love.
O morning stars, together
  Proclaim the holy birth!
And praises sing to God our King,
  And peace to men on earth.

3 How silently, how silently,
  The wondrous gift is given!
So God imparts to human hearts
  The blessings of His heaven.

No ear may hear His coming,
  But in this world of sin,
Where meek souls will receive Him still,
  The dear Christ enters in.

4 O holy Child of Bethlehem!
  Descend to us, we pray;
Cast out our sin, and enter in,
  Be born in us to-day.
We hear the Christmas angels,
  The great glad tidings tell:
O come to us, abide with us,
  Our Lord Emmanuel!

Phillips Brooks, 1880.

All my Heart this Night Rejoices.

WARUM SOLLT ICH MICH DENN GRÆMEN. P. M.

JOHN GEORGE EBELING, 1666.

1. All my heart this night re-joi - ces, As I hear, Far and near, Sweet-est an - gel voi - ces; Christ is born, their choirs are sing -- ing, Till the air Ev - 'ry-where Now with joy is ring - ing. A - men.

2 Come, then, let us hasten yonder;
   Here let all,   Great and small,
Kneel in awe and wonder,
   Love Him who with love is yearning;
Hail the star   That from far
Bright with hope is burning.

3 Ye who pine in weary sadness,
   Weep no more   For the door
Now is found of gladness.
   Cling to Him, for He will guide you
Where no cross,   Pain or loss,
Can again betide you.

4 Hither come, ye poor and wretched,
   Know His will   Is to fill
Every hand outstretched;
   Here are riches without measure,
Here forget   All regret,
Fill your hearts with treasure.

5 Thee, dear Lord, with deed I'll cherish,
   Live to Thee,   And with Thee
Dying, shall not perish;
   But shall dwell with Thee forever,
Far on high,   In the joy
That can alter never.

Paul Gerhardt, 1656.
Tr. Miss Winkworth, 1858.

75

Shout the Glad Tidings, Exultingly Sing.

AVISON. P. M.
CHORUS.

Shout the glad tid - ings, ex - ult - ing - ly sing,.............

Je - ru - sa - lem tri - umphs, Mes - si - ah is King!

1. Si - on, the mar - vel - lous sto - ry be tell - ing, The Son of the Highest, how

low - ly His birth! The brightest arch - an - gel in glo - ry ex - cell - ing,

Shout the Glad Tidings, Exultingly Sing.—Concluded.

Repeat 1st Chorus.

He stoops to re-deem thee, He reigns up-on earth:

Chorus after last verse.

Shout the glad tidings, ex-ult-ing-ly sing,......... Je-ru-salem triumphs, Mes-

si-ah is King, Mes-si-ah is King, Mes-si-ah is King. A-men.

2 Tell how He cometh; from nation to nation,
   The heart-cheering news let the earth echo round;
How free to the faithful He offers salvation,
   How His people with joy everlasting are crowned.

3 Mortals, your homage be gratefully bringing,
   And sweet let the gladsome hosanna arise;
Ye angels, the full Alleluia be singing;
   One chorus resound through the earth and the skies.

W. A. Muhlenberg, 1828.

76
While Shepherds Watched their Flocks by Night.

GABRIEL. C. M. D.

1. While shepherds watched their flocks by night, All seat-ed on the ground,

The an-gel of the Lord came down, And glo-ry shone a-round.

"Fear not," said he, for might-y dread Had seized their trou-bled mind;

"Glad tid-ings of great joy I bring To you and all man-kind." A-men.

2 "To you, in David's town, this day
  Is born, of David's line,
A Saviour, who is Christ the Lord,
  And this shall be the sign:
The heavenly babe you there shall find,
  To human view displayed,
All meanly wrapt in swathing-bands,
  And in a manger laid."

3 Thus spake the seraph, and forthwith
  Appeared a shining throng
Of angels, praising God, who thus
  Addressed their joyful song:—
"All glory be to God on high,
  And to the earth be peace:
Good-will, henceforth, from heaven to
  Begin and never cease."   [men,

Nahum Tate, 1703.

I Love to Hear the Story.

7, 6, 7, 6, D.

1. I love to hear the sto-ry, Which an-gel voi-ces tell,

How once the King of glo-ry Came down on earth to dwell;

I am both weak and sin-ful, But this I sure-ly know,

The Lord came down to save me, Be-cause He loved me so. A-men.

2 I'm glad my blessed Saviour
Was once a child like me,
To show how pure and holy
His little ones might be;
And if I try to follow
His footsteps here below,
He never will forget me,
Because He loves me so.

3 To sing His love and mercy
My sweetest songs I'll raise;
And though I cannot see Him,
I know He hears my praise;
For He has kindly promised
That even I may go
To sing among His angels,
Because He loves me so.

Emily Huntington Miller (1833—), **1867.**

78

Emmanuel! We Sing Thy Praise.

GERMANY. L. M. (*First tune.*)   BEETHOVEN.

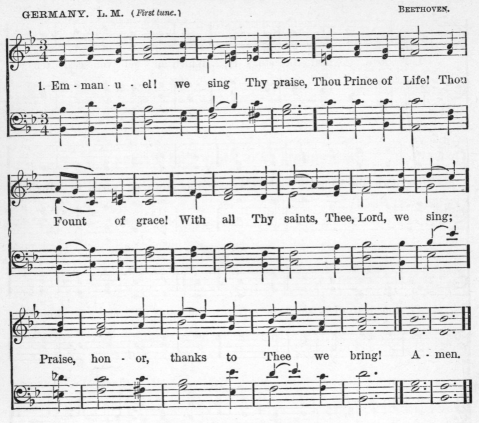

1. Em‑man‑u‑el! we sing Thy praise, Thou Prince of Life! Thou
Fount of grace! With all Thy saints, Thee, Lord, we sing;
Praise, hon‑or, thanks to Thee we bring! A‑men.

2 E'er since the world began to be,
How many a heart hath longed for Thee!
And Thou, O long-expected Guest,
Hast come at last to make us blest!

3 Now art Thou here: we know Thee now;
In lowly manger liest Thou:
A Child, yet makest all things great;
Poor, yet is earth Thy robe of state.

4 Now fearless I can look on Thee:
From sin and grief Thou set'st me free:
Thou bearest wrath, Thou conquerest death,
Fear turns to joy Thy glance beneath.

Emmanuel! We Sing Thy Praise.—Concluded.

5 Thou art my Head, my Lord divine:
I am Thy member, wholly Thine;
And in Thy Spirit's strength would still
Serve Thee according to Thy will.

6 Thus will I sing Thy praises here,
With joyful spirit year by year:
And they shall sound before Thy throne,
Where time nor number more is known.

Paul Gerhardt, 1556.
Tr. Miss Winkworth, 1855.

Emmanuel! We Sing Thy Praise.

GEBORN IST GOTTES SOEHNELEIN. L. M. (*Second tune.*)   M. PRAETORIUS, 1609.

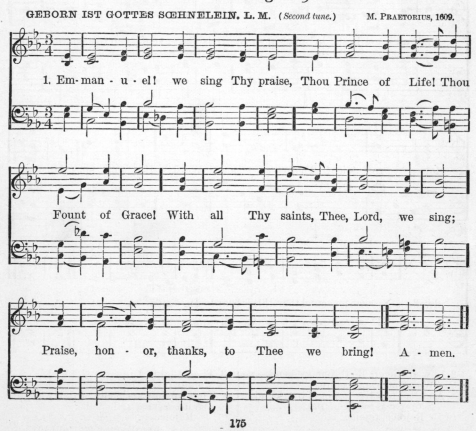

1. Em-man-u-el! we sing Thy praise, Thou Prince of Life! Thou Fount of Grace! With all Thy saints, Thee, Lord, we sing; Praise, hon-or, thanks, to Thee we bring! A-men.

79

Joy Fills Our Inmost Hearts To-day.

GAUDETE. 8, 6, 8, 6, 8, 6, 8, 4.　　　　　　　　　SAMUEL SMITH (1804—1873).

Joy fills our in-most hearts to-day, The Roy-al Child is born: And an-gel hosts, in glad ar-ray, His ad-vent keep this morn. Re-joice, re-joice! Th'In-car-nate Word Has come on earth to dwell; No sweeter sound than this is heard—Im-man-u-el. A-men.

2 Low at the cradle-throne we bend,
　　We wonder and adore;
　And feel no bliss can ours transcend,
　　No joy was sweet before.
　　Rejoice, rejoice! etc.

3 Thou Light of uncreated Light,
　　Shine on us, Holy Child,
　That we may keep Thy birthday bright
　　With service undefiled.
　　Rejoice, rejoice! etc.

Wm. Chatterton Dix (1837—) 1865.

Beside a Manger Lowly.

80

ROTTERDAM. 7, 6, 7, 6, D.

BERTHOLD TOURS, 1875.

1. Be - side a man - ger low - ly, A moth - er, pale and mild,
With eyes se - rene and ho - ly, Is watch - ing o'er her child,
I, too, would gaze and pon - der, Bowed down in hom - age low,
For sight more full of won - der, This earth did nev - er show. A - men.

2 Across the mists of ages,
   That Infant's form divine,
Unchanging still, engages
   The heart before His shrine.
For though in God's Anointed
   The world no charm espies,
Faith reads the signs appointed,
   "'Tis Christ, my Lord," she cries.

3 Behold the "Branch" of David,
   The "Shiloh," famed of old,
The Son of Virgin Mother,
   By prophet's lips foretold,

Behold the seed of woman,
   Repairer of the Fall,
The Child Divine, yet human,
   Emmanuel, Lord of all!

4 Oh, tender plant, upspringing
   Amid the desert dry!
Oh, dawn of promise, flinging
   Thy rays o'er earth and sky!
Oh, glad and gushing river,
   From love's own fountain poured,
Spring up—flow on forever,
   'Till all men know the Lord!

81

Angels from the Realms of Glory.

C. Chr. Hoffman.

HELLIGAAND, VOR SORG DU SLUKKE. 8, 7, 8, 7, 4, 7. (*First tune.*)

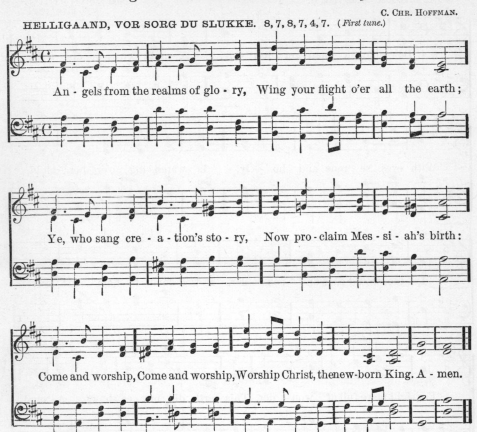

An - gels from the realms of glo - ry, Wing your flight o'er all the earth;

Ye, who sang cre - a - tion's sto - ry, Now pro - claim Mes - si - ah's birth:

Come and worship, Come and worship, Worship Christ, the new-born King. A - men.

2 Shepherds in the field abiding,
    Watching o'er your flocks by night;
God with man is now residing,
    Yonder shines the infant-light:
    ‖: Come and worship, :‖
Worship Christ, the new-born King.

3 Sages, leave your contemplations;
    Brighter visions beam afar;
Seek the great Desire of nations,
    Ye have seen His native star:
    ‖: Come and worship, :‖
Worship Christ, the new-born King.

4 Saints before the altar bending,
    Watching long in hope and fear,
Suddenly the Lord, descending,
    In His temple shall appear:
    ‖: Come and worship, :‖
Worship Christ, the new-born King.

J. Montgomery, 1819.

178

Angels from the Realms of Glory.

(Second tune.)
Voices in Unison.

W. B. GILBERT.

1. An - gels from the realms of glo - ry, Wing your flight o'er all the earth; Ye who sang cre - a - tion's sto - - ry,

Voices in Harmony.

Now pro - claim Mes - si - ah's birth. Come and wor - ship, Come and wor - ship, Wor-ship Christ, the new - born King! A - men.

82

Come Hither, ye Faithful, Triumphantly Sing.

PORTUGUESE HYMN. ADESTE FIDELES. 11, 11, 11, 11.   JOHN READING, 1680.

1. Come hith - er, ye faith - ful, tri - um - phant-ly sing: Come see in the man - ger the an - gels' dread King! To Beth - le - hem has - ten, with joy - ful ac - cord; O come ye, come hith - er; O come ye, come hith - er; O come ye, come hith - er, to wor - ship the Lord! A - men.

Come Hither, ye Faithful, Triumphantly Sing.—Concluded.

2 True Son of the Father, He comes from the skies;
To be born of a Virgin, He does not despise:
To Bethlehem hasten, with joyful accord;
O come ye, come hither, to worship the Lord!

3 Hark, hark to the angels, all singing in heaven,
"To God in the highest all glory be given!"
To Bethlehem hasten, with joyful accord;
O come ye, come hither, to worship the Lord!

4 To Thee, then, O Jesus, this day of Thy birth,
Be glory and honor through heaven and earth.
True Godhead incarnate, omnipotent Word!
O come, let us hasten to worship the Lord!

Edward Caswall, 1848. *a.*

Good News from Heaven the Angels Bring. 83

VOM HIMMEL HOCH DA KOMM ICH HER. L. M.   LEIPZIG, 1539.

1. Good news from heav'n the an-gels bring, Glad tid-ings to the earth they sing:

To us this day a Child is giv'n, To crown us with the joy of heav'n. A-men.

2 This is the Christ, our God and Lord,
Who in all need shall aid afford;
He will Himself our Saviour be,
From all our sins to set us free.

3 To us that blessedness He brings,
Which from the Father's bounty springs:
That in the heavenly realm we may
With Him enjoy eternal day.

4 All hail, Thou noble Guest this morn,
Whose Love did not the sinner scorn:
In my distress Thou comest to me;
What thanks shall I return to Thee?

5 Were earth a thousand times as fair,
Beset with gold and jewels rare,
She yet were far too poor to be
A narrow cradle, Lord, for Thee.

6 Ah, dearest Jesus, holy Child,
Make Thee a bed, soft, undefiled,
Within my heart, that it may be
A quiet chamber kept for Thee.

7 Praise God upon His heavenly throne,
Who gave to us His only Son:
For this His hosts, on joyful wing,
A blest New Year of mercy sing.

Martin Luther, 1535. *Tr. Arthur Tozer Russell*, 1848,
and Miss Winkworth, 1855.

84

It Came Upon the Midnight Clear.

CAROL. C. M. D. (*First tune.*)   R. S. WILLIS.

1. It came up-on the midnight clear, That glo-rious song of old,

From an-gels bend-ing near the earth, To touch their harps of gold:

"Peace on the earth, good-will to men From heaven's all-gra-cious King;"

The world in sol-emn still-ness lay To hear the an-gels sing. A-men.

2 Still through the cloven skies they come,
    With peaceful wings unfurled;
And still their heavenly music floats
    O'er all the weary world.
Above its sad and lowly plains
    They bend on hovering wing,
And ever o'er its Babel sounds
    The blessed angels sing.

3 O ye, beneath life's crushing load,
    Whose forms are bending low,
Who toil along the climbing way
    With painful steps and slow!

Look now, for glad and golden hours
    Come swiftly on the wing;
O rest beside the weary road,
    And hear the angels sing.

4 For lo! the days are hastening on,
    By prophets seen of old,
When with the ever-circling years,
    Shall come the time foretold.
When the new heaven and earth shall own
    The Prince of Peace their King,
And the whole world send back the song
    Which now the angels sing.

Edmund H. Sears, 1860.

182

It Came Upon the Midnight Clear.

PRINCE OF PEACE. C. M. D. (*Second tune.*)   J. B. DYKES, 1873.

1. It came up-on the midnight clear, That glorious song of old, From an-gels bend-ing near the earth, To touch their harps of gold: "Peace on the earth, good-will to men, From heaven's all-gra-cious King;" The world in sol-emn still-ness lay, To hear the an-gels sing, To hear the an - gels sing. A - men.

To hear . . . . . the an - gels sing.

85

The New-Born King, Who Comes To-day.

THE HOLY CITY. C. M. D.   S. A. WARD.

1. The new-born King, who comes to-day, Brings tid-ings of great joy,.......

Which sin can nev-er take a-way, Nor death, nor hell de-stroy;

Re-joice, ye Gen-tile lands, re-joice, And hail this glo-rious dawn;

For God comes down frail man to crown—The Lord of Life is born! A-men.

2 He comes not as a King of earth,
 In pomp and pride to reign;
He seeks a poor and humble birth,
 But free from sinful stain;
Rejoice, ye Gentile lands, rejoice,
 Glad hymns of triumph sing,
The Wonderful, the Counsellor,
 He comes, your God and King!

3 For us He leaves His Father's throne,
 His sapphire throne on high,
And comes to dwell on earth alone,
 For fallen man to die.
Rejoice, ye Gentile lands, rejoice,
 And hail Messiah's dawn;
Our God comes down, earth's joy and
The King of Love is born. [crown,

184

The New-Born King, Who Comes To-day.—Concluded.

4 Glad Gentiles in their eastern home
  His radiant star behold;
To God, their King, they joy to bring
  Sweet incense, myrrh, and gold.
Rejoice, ye Gentile lands, rejoice,
  In heaven your praises sing;
Before Him fall, the Lord of all,
  Your Maker and your King!

5 We join your song, celestial throng,
  Whose anthems never cease;
We tune our lyres, with angel choirs,
  To hail the Prince of Peace!
Rejoice, ye Gentile lands, rejoice,
  And hail Immanuel's morn;
For God comes down frail man to crown,
  To us a Child is born.

Moravian.

86

Sing Ye the Songs of Praise.

6, 4, 6, 4, 6, 6, 6, 4.

MRS. C. FAREBROTHER.

1. Sing ye the songs of praise; Christmas is come! High your glad voices raise; Christmas is come! Cast worldly cares a-way, Wor-ship and hom-age pay, Wel-come the blessed day, Christmas is come! A-men.

2 This day in Bethlehem
    Jesus was born!
  King of Jerusalem
    Jesus was born!
  Sun of all righteousness,
  Shining with blessedness,
  Healing our wretchedness,
    Jesus was born!

3 Cleanse us from all our sin,
    Saviour Divine!
  Make our thoughts pure within,
    Saviour Divine!
  Let not Thy love depart,
  But holy gifts impart,
  Born into every heart,
    Great Prince of Peace!

W. Layng. Abridged.

87

Joy to the World; the Lord is Come!

ANTIOCH. C. M. (*First tune.*)

G. F. HANDEL.

1. Joy to the world; the Lord is come! Let earth re-ceive her King.

Let ev-'ry heart pre-pare Him room, And heav'n and na-ture sing, And
And heav'n and nature

And heav'n and nature

heav'n and na-ture sing, And heav'n, and heav'n and na-ture sing. A-men.
sing, ... And heav'n, etc.

sing, And heav'n and nature sing, And heav'n, etc.

2 Joy to the earth; the Saviour reigns!
   Let men their songs employ;
While fields and floods, rocks, hills, and plains,
   Repeat the sounding joy.

3 No more let sins and sorrows grow,
   Nor thorns infest the ground.
He comes to make His blessings flow
   Far as the curse is found.

4 He rules the world with truth and grace,
   And makes the nations prove
The glories of His righteousness,
   And wonders of His Love.

Watts, 1719.

186

Joy to the World; the Lord is Come!

ICH SAG ES JEDEM DASS ER LEBT. C. M. (*Second tune.*)   SPAZIER.

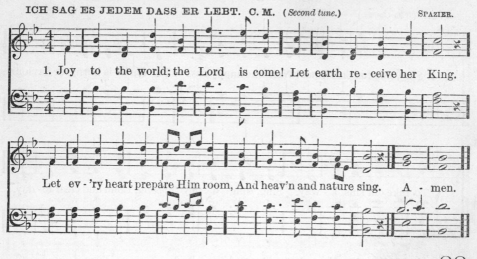

1. Joy to the world; the Lord is come! Let earth re - ceive her King.

Let ev - 'ry heart prepare Him room, And heav'n and nature sing. A - men.

88

As Each Happy Christmas.

ALLE JAHRE WIEDER. 6, 5, 6, 5.   JOH. CHRIST. HEINR. RINK, (1770–1846).

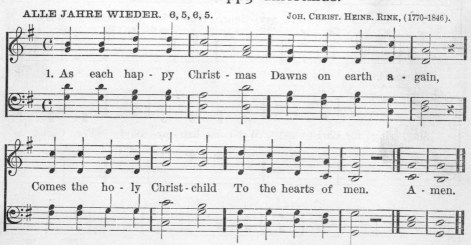

1. As each hap - py Christ - mas Dawns on earth a - gain,

Comes the ho - ly Christ - child To the hearts of men. A - men.

2 Enters with His blessing
  Into every home,
  Guides and guards our footsteps,
  As we go and come.

3 All unknown, beside me
  He will ever stand,
  And will safely lead me
  With His own right hand.

Georg Friedrich Kayser, 1855.
Tr. Harriett R. Krauth, 1876.

187

89

Sing, Sing for Christmas.

P. M. (*With Chorus.*)

W. W. ROUSSEAU.

1. Sing, sing for Christmas! Welcome happy day! For Christ is born, our Saviour,

To take our sins a - way. Sing, sing a joy-ful song, Loud and clear to - day,

To praise our Lord and Sav - iour, Who in the man - ger lay.

CHORUS.

Sing, sing for Christ-mas! Wel-come hap - py day! For Christ is

born our Sav - iour, To take our sins a - way. A - men.

Sing, Sing for Christmas.—Concluded.

2 Tell, tell the story
  Of the wondrous night
When shepherds who were watching
  Their flocks till morning light,
Saw angel hosts from heaven,
  Heard the angel voice,
And so were told the tidings,
  Which make the world rejoice.
  Sing, sing, etc.

3 Soft, softly shining,
  Stars were in the sky,
And silver fell the moonlight
  On hill and mountain high,
When suddenly the night
  Outshone the bright mid-day,
With angel hosts who herald
  The reign of peace for aye.
  Sing, sing, etc.

4 Hark, hear them singing,
  Singing in the sky,
"Be worship, honor, glory,
  And praise to God on high!
Peace, peace, good-will to men,
  Born the Child from heaven!
The Christ, the Lord, the Saviour,
  The Son to you is given!"
  Sing, sing, etc.

5 Sing, sing for Christmas!
  Echo, earth, the cry
Of worship, honor, glory,
  And praise to God on high!
Sing, sing the joyful song,
  Let it never cease,
Of glory in the highest,
  On earth good-will and peace.
  Sing, sing, etc.

J. H. Egar.

A Great and Mighty Wonder. 90

ICH HAB MIR AUSERWÆHLET. 7, 6, 7, 6.   OLD GERMAN MELODY.

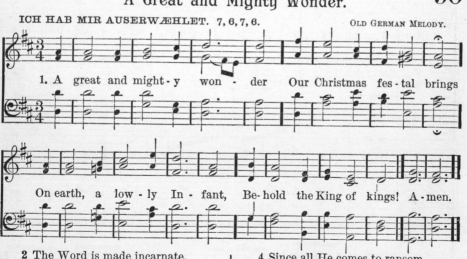

1. A great and might-y won-der Our Christmas fes-tal brings On earth, a low-ly In-fant, Be-hold the King of kings! A-men.

2 The Word is made incarnate,
  Descending from on high;
And cherubim sing anthems
  To shepherds, from the sky.

3 And we with them triumphant,
  Repeat the hymn again:
"To God on high be glory,
  And peace on earth to men!"

4 Since all He comes to ransom,
  By all be He adored,
The Infant born in Bethlehem,
  The Saviour and the Lord!

5 And idol forms shall perish,
  And error shall decay,
And Christ shall wield His sceptre,
  Our Lord and God for aye.

Anatolius, ab., 450.
Tr. John Mason Neale, 1862. a.

189

91

The Darkness has Fallen.

AUF BETHLEHEMS FELDE IM DUNKEL DER NACHT.

A. Spaeth, 1878.

Solo, or Girls.

1. The darkness has fallen, all na - ture is stilled; Lone shepherds are watching on Beth - le-hem's field; Bright stars gleaming o'er them, in num - ber un - told, Their hands, sup-pli - ca - ting they rev - 'rent - ly fold: "O God of our fathers, in -

The Darkness has Fallen.—Concluded.

cline now Thine ear, Look gra-cious-ly down on Thy ser-vants, and hear;

CHORUS.

O send us the Sav-iour, Wake, Arm of the Lord, De-
liv-er Thy peo-ple, Ful-fil now Thy Word. A-men.

2 The woman's Seed crushing the serpent's bold crest;
   And Abraham's Seed, in Whom nations are blest;
   The Prince out of Judah, the Mighty, the Strong,
   Whom Zion receiveth with triumph and song;
   And Jacob's Star, ruling in limitless sway,
   Whose foes fall before Him, all shattered like clay;
      O send us the Saviour, etc.

3 The Son Thou wilt stablish on great David's throne,
   As Priest, and as Prophet, and King all in one;
   The Rod out of Jesse, the Stem from his root,
   Might, counsel and wisdom His heavenly fruit;
   The Wonderful Child that Isaiah portrays;
   The Prince of Peace, Whom years unending shall praise;
      O send us the Saviour, etc.

A. Spaeth, 1878.
Tr. Harriett R. Spaeth, 1894.

92

Thou Didst Leave Thy Throne.

VENI, DOMINE JESU. P. M.

BARNBY.

1. Thou didst leave Thy throne and Thy king-ly crown When Thou cam-est to earth for me; But in Beth-le-hem's home there was found no room For Thy ho-ly na-tiv-i-ty. O come to my heart, Lord Je-sus! There is room in my heart for Thee. A-men.

CHORUS.

2 Heaven's arches rang when the angels sang,
  Proclaiming Thy royal degree;
But in lowly birth didst Thou come to earth,
  And in great humility.
O come to my heart, Lord Jesus!
  There is room in my heart for Thee.

3 The foxes found rest, and the birds had their nest
  In the shade of the forest tree;
But Thy couch was the sod, O Thou Son of God,
  In the desert of Galilee.
O come to my heart, Lord Jesus!
  There is room in my heart for Thee.

Thou Didst Leave Thy Throne.—Concluded.

4 Thou camest, O Lord, with the living
    word,
  That should set Thy people free;
But with mocking scorn, and with crown
    of thorn,
  They bore Thee to Calvary.
O come to my heart, Lord Jesus!
  Thy cross is my only plea.

5 When the heavens shall ring, and the
    angels sing
  At Thy coming to victory,
Let Thy voice call me home, saying,
    "Yet there is room,
There is room at My side for thee."
And my heart shall rejoice, Lord Jesus,
  When Thou comest and callest for me.

Emily E. S. Elliott, 1864.

Sing, oh, Sing, this Blessed Morn.

93

INCARNATION. 7, 7, 7, 7, 7, 7.

HENRY SMART.

1. Sing, oh, sing, this bless-ed morn, Un-to us a Child is born, Un-to us a Son is giv'n, God Him-self comes down from Heav'n. Sing, oh, sing, this bless-ed morn, Je-sus Christ to-day is born. A-men.

2 God of God, and Light of Light,
Comes with mercies infinite,
Joining in a wondrous plan
Heaven to earth, and God to man.
  Sing, oh, sing, etc.

3 God with us, Emmanuel,
Deigns for ever now to dwell;

He on Adam's fallen race
Sheds the fulness of His grace.
  Sing, oh, sing, etc.

4 God comes down that man may rise,
Lifted by Him to the skies;
Christ is Son of man that we
Sons of God in Him may be.
  Sing, oh, sing, etc.

C. Wordsworth, 1862.

THE CHURCH YEAR:
CIRCUMCISION AND THE NAME OF JESUS.

94
There is no Name so Sweet on Earth.

THE BLESSED NAME. 8, 7, 8, 7. D. (*With Chorus.*)

BARNBY.

1. There is no name so sweet on earth, No name so dear in heav-en,

As that be-fore His wondrous birth To Christ the Sav-iour giv-en.

CHORUS.

We love to sing a-round our King, And hail Him bless-ed Je-sus!

For there's no word ear ev-er heard So dear, so sweet as Je-sus! A-men.

There is no Name so Sweet on Earth.—Concluded.

2 His human Name they did proclaim
　　When Abram's Son they sealed Him,—
　The Name that still by God's good will,
　　Deliverer revealed Him.
　　　We love to sing, etc.

3 And when He hung upon the tree,
　　They wrote this Name above Him;
　That all might see the reason we
　For evermore must love Him.
　　　We love to sing, etc.

4 So now, upon His Father's throne,
　　Almighty to release us
　From sin and pains, He gladly reigns,
　　The Prince and Saviour Jesus.
　　　We love to sing, etc.

5 To Jesus every knee shall bow,
　　And every tongue confess Him,
　And we unite with saints in light,
　　Our only Lord to bless Him.
　　　We love to sing, etc.

6 O Jesus, by that matchless Name,
　　Thy grace shall fail us never;
　To-day as yesterday the same,
　　Thou art the same for ever.

CHORUS.—*For last Verse.*
　Then let us sing around our King,
　　The faithful, precious Jesus,
　For there's no word ear ever heard
　　So dear, so sweet as Jesus!

George W. Bethune, 1858.

Jesus! Name of Wondrous Love.　95

WANSTED. 7, 7, 7, 7.　　　　　　　　　　GERMAN.

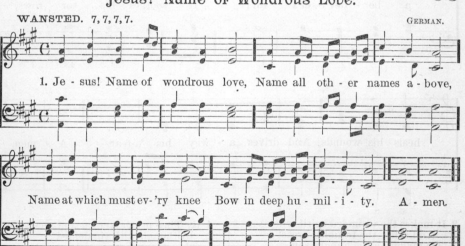

1. Je-sus! Name of wondrous love, Name all oth-er names a-bove,
Name at which must ev-'ry knee Bow in deep hu-mil-i-ty. A-men.

2 Jesus! Name of priceless worth
　To the fallen sons of earth,
　For the promise that it gave—
　"Jesus shall His people save."

3 Jesus! Name of mercy mild,
　Given to the holy Child.
　When the cup of human woe
　First He tasted here below.

4 Jesus! Only Name that's given
　Under all the mighty heaven,
　Whereby man to sin enslaved,
　Bursts his fetters, and is saved.

5 Jesus! Name of wondrous love!
　Human Name of Him above!
　Pleading only this we flee,
　Helpless, O our God, to Thee.

William W. How, 1854.

96

How Sweet the Name of Jesus Sounds.

ST. PETER. C. M.

ALEXANDER R. REINAGLE, 1830.

1. How sweet the Name of Je · sus sounds In a be · liev · er's ear! It soothes his sor · rows, heals his wounds, And drives a · way his fear. A · men.

2 It makes the wounded spirit whole,
   And calms the troubled breast;
'Tis manna to the hungry soul,
   And to the weary rest.

3 Dear Name! the Rock on which I build,
   My Shield and Hiding-place;
My never-failing Treasury, filled
   With boundless stores of grace.

4 By Thee my prayers acceptance gain,
   Although with sin defiled:
Satan accuses me in vain,
   And I am owned a child.

5 Weak is the effort of my heart,
   And cold my warmest thought;
But, when I see Thee as Thou art,
   I'll praise Thee as I ought.

6 Till then, I would Thy love proclaim
   With every fleeting breath;
And may the music of Thy Name
   Refresh my soul in death.

John Newton, 1779.

THE CHURCH YEAR: NEW YEAR.

97

Great God! We Sing that Mighty Hand.

MIGDOL. L. M.

LOWELL MASON.

1. Great God! we sing that might-y Hand, By which sup-port-ed still we stand: The opening year Thy mer-cy shows; Let mer-cy crown it till it close. A-men.

2 By day, by night, at home, abroad,
  Still we are guarded by our God;
  By His incessant bounty fed,
  By His unerring counsel led.

3 With grateful hearts the past we own;
  The future all to us unknown,
  We to Thy guardian care commit,
  And, peaceful, leave before Thy feet.

4 In scenes exalted or deprest,
  Be Thou our joy, and Thou our rest;
  Thy goodness all our hopes shall raise,
  Adored through all our changing days

5 When death shall interrupt our songs,
  And seal in silence mortal tongues;
  Our Helper, God, in Whom we trust,
  In better worlds our souls shall boast.

Doddridge, 1755.

98

Standing at the Portal of the Opening Year.

VALOUR. 6, 5, 6, 5. D. (*With Refrain.*)

A. H. MANN, 1889.

1. Standing at the por-tal of the opening year, Words of comfort meet us, hush-ing ev-'ry fear; Spoken thro' the si-lence by our Father's voice, Tender, strong and faith-ful, making us re-joice, Onward, then, and fear not, children of the day! For His Word shall never, never pass a-way! A-men.

Standing at the Portal of the Opening Year.—Concluded.

2 I, the Lord, am with thee, be not thou afraid,
I will help and strengthen, be thou not dismayed!
Yea, I will uphold thee with My own right hand,
Thou art called and chosen in My sight to stand.
Onward, then, etc.

3 He will never fail us, He will not forsake;
His eternal covenant He will never break;
Resting on His promise, what have we to fear?
God is all-sufficient for the coming year!
Onward, then, etc.   *Frances Ridley Havergal*, 1873.

While with Ceaseless Course the Sun.   99

BENEVENTO. 7, 7, 7, 7. D.   S. WEBBE.

1. While with cease-less course the sun Hast-ed thro' the form-er year,

Ma-ny souls their race have run, Nev-er more to meet us here;

D. S.—We a lit-tle long-er wait, But how lit-tle none can know.

Fixed in an e-ter-nal state, They have done with all be-low; A-men.

2 As the wingéd arrow flies
    Speedily the mark to find;
As the lightning from the skies
    Darts, and leaves no trace behind;
Swiftly thus our fleeting days
    Bear us down life's rapid stream:
Upward, Lord, our spirits raise;
    All below is but a dream.

3 Thanks for mercies past receive,
    Pardon of our sins renew;
Teach us henceforth how to live
    With eternity in view.
Bless Thy Word to young and old,
    Fill us with a Saviour's love;
And when life's short tale is told,
    May we dwell with Thee above.

John Newton, 1779.

100

From Glory Unto Glory!

ST. COLUMB. 13, 13, 13, 14.   W. S. HOYTE, 1889.

1. From glo-ry un-to glo-ry! be this our joy-ful song,

As on the King's own high-way, we brave-ly march a-long!

From glo-ry un-to glo-ry! O word of stir-ring cheer,

As dawns the sol-emn brightness of an-oth-er glad New Year. A-men.

2 From glory unto glory! what great things He hath done,
   What wonders He hath shown us, what triumphs He hath won!
   From glory unto glory! what mighty blessings crown
   As lives for which our Lord hath laid His own so freely down.

3 And closer yet and closer the golden bonds shall be,
   Uniting all who love our Lord in pure sincerity;
   And wider yet and wider shall the circling glory glow,
   As more and more are taught of God that mighty love to know.

4 Now onward, ever onward, from strength to strength we go,
   While grace for grace abundantly shall from His fullness flow,
   To glory's full fruition, from glory's foretaste here,
   Until His very presence crown our happiest New Year.

Frances R. Havergal, 1873

THE CHURCH YEAR: EPIPHANY.

Brightest and Best of the Sons of the Morning. 101

WESLEY. 11, 10, 11, 10.

LOWELL MASON.

1. Bright-est and best of the sons of the morn-ing, Dawn on our
dark-ness and lend us thine aid; Star of the East, the ho-ri-zon a-
dorn-ing, Guide where our In-fant Re-deem-er is laid. A-men.

2 Cold on His cradle the dewdrops are shining,
  Low lies His head with the beasts of the stall;
Angels adore Him in slumber reclining,
  Maker and Monarch and Saviour of all.

3 Say, shall we yield Him, in costly devotion,
  Odors of Edom and offerings divine,
Gems of the mountain and pearls of the ocean,
  Myrrh from the forest, and gold from the mine?

4 Vainly we offer each ample oblation,
  Vainly with gifts would His favor secure;
Richer by far is the heart's adoration,
  Dearer to God are the prayers of the poor.

5 Brightest and best of the sons of the morning,
  Dawn on our darkness and lend us thine aid;
Star of the East, the horizon adorning,
  Guide where our infant Redeemer is laid.

Reginald Heber, 1811.

102

Hail to the Lord's Anointed.

AURELIA. 7, 6, 7, 6. D.   SAMUEL S. WESLEY, 1864.

1. Hail to the Lord's A - noint - ed, Great Da - vid's great - er Son!

Hail, in the time ap - point - ed, His reign on earth be - gun.

He comes to break op - pres - sion, To set the cap - tive free;

To take a - way transgression, And rule in eq - ui - ty. A - men

Hail to the Lord's Anointed.—Concluded.

2 He comes with succor speedy
  To those who suffer wrong;
To help the poor and needy;
  And bid the weak be strong;
To give them songs for sighing;
  Their darkness turn to light,
Whose souls, condemned and dying,
  Were precious in His sight.

3 He shall come down like showers
  Upon the fruitful earth;
And love, joy, hope, like flowers,
  Spring in His path to birth.
Before Him, on the mountains,
  Shall peace, the herald, go;
And righteousness, in fountains,
  From hill to valley flow.

4 For Him shall prayer unceasing
  And daily vows ascend;
His kingdom still increasing,
  A kingdom without end.
The tide of time shall never
  His covenant remove;
His Name shall stand for ever;
  That Name to us is Love.

James Montgomery, 1821.

Bright Was the Guiding Star that Led.

103

MANOAH. C. M.

ROSSINI.

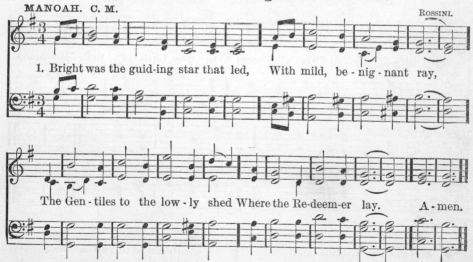

1. Bright was the guid-ing star that led, With mild, be-nig-nant ray,

The Gen-tiles to the low-ly shed Where the Re-deem-er lay. A-men.

2 But, lo! a brighter, clearer light
  Now points to His abode;
It shines through sin and sorrow's night,
  To guide us to our God.

3 O haste to follow where it leads,
  His gracious call obey!
Be rugged wilds, or flowery meads,
  The Christian's destined way.

4 O gladly tread the narrow path,
  While light and grace are given!
For those who follow Christ on earth
  Shall reign with Him in heaven.

Harriet Auber.

104

Songs of Thankfulness and Praise.

ST. EDWARD. 7, 7, 7, 7. D.   CHARLES STEGGALL, 1843.

1. Songs of thank-ful-ness and praise Je-sus, Lord, to Thee we raise,
Man-i-fest-ed by the star To the sa-ges from a-far;
Branch of roy-al Da-vid's stem In Thy birth at Beth-le-hem;
An-thems be to Thee addresst God in Man made man-i-fest. A-men.

2 Manifest at Jordan's stream,
Prophet, Priest, and King supreme;
And at Cana wedding-guest
In Thy Godhead manifest;
Manifest in power Divine,
Changing water into wine;
Anthems be to Thee addrest,
God in Man made manifest.

3 Manifest in making whole
Palsied limbs and fainting soul;
Manifest in valiant fight,
Quelling all the devil's might;

Manifest in gracious will,
Ever bringing good from ill;
Anthems be to Thee addrest,
God in Man made manifest.

4 Grant us grace to see Thee, Lord,
Mirrored in Thy holy Word;
May we imitate Thee now,
And be pure, as pure art Thou;
That we like to Thee may be,
At Thy great Epiphany;
And may praise Thee, ever blest,
God in Man made manifest.

C. Wordsworth, 1862.

As With Gladness Men of Old.

DIX. 7, 7, 7, 7, 7, 7.   ADAPTED 1861, FROM CONRAD KOCHER'S "TREUER HEILAND," &c.

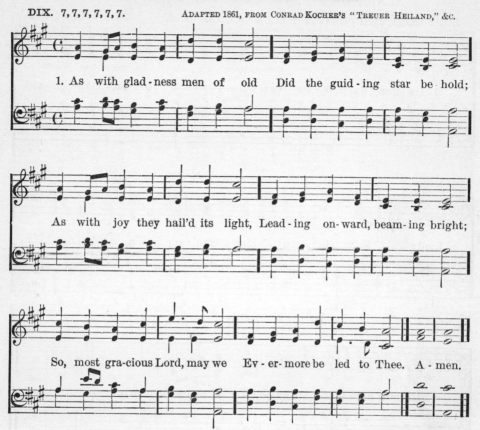

1. As with glad-ness men of old Did the guid-ing star be-hold;

As with joy they hail'd its light, Lead-ing on-ward, beam-ing bright;

So, most gra-cious Lord, may we Ev-er-more be led to Thee. A-men.

2 As with joyful steps they sped
  To that lowly manger-bed,
  There to bend the knee before
  Him whom heaven and earth adore;
  So may we with willing feet
  Ever seek Thy mercy-seat.

3 As they offered gifts most rare
  At that manger rude and bare;
  So may we, with holy joy,
  Pure, and free from sin's alloy,
  All our costliest treasures bring,
  Christ, to Thee, our heavenly King.

4 Holy Jesus! every day
  Keep us in the narrow way;
  And, when earthly things are past,
  Bring our ransomed souls at last
  Where they need no star to guide,
  Where no clouds Thy glory hide.

5 In the heavenly country bright
  Need they no created light:
  Thou its Light, its Joy, its Crown,
  Thou its Sun which goes not down;
  There for ever may we sing
  Hallelujahs to our King.

William C. Dix, 1860.

106

Hosanna! Raise the Pealing Hymn.

LOBT GOTT, IHR CHRISTEN ALLE GLEICH. C. M. NICOLAUS HERMANN, 1560.

1. Ho-san-na! Raise the peal-ing hymn To Da-vid's Son and Lord; With cher-u-bim and ser-a-phim Ex-alt th'incar-nate Word, Ex-alt th'in-car-nate Word. A-men.

2 Hosanna! Lord, our feeble tongue
  No lofty strains can raise:
But Thou wilt not despise the young,
  ‖: Who meekly chant Thy praise. :‖

3 Hosanna! Master, lo! we bring
  Our offerings to Thy throne;
Not gold, nor myrrh, nor mortal thing,
  ‖: But hearts to be Thine own. :‖

4 Hosanna! Once Thy gracious ear
  Approved a lisping throng:
Be gracious still, and deign to hear
  ‖: Our poor but grateful song. :‖

5 O Saviour, if, redeemed by Thee,
  Thy Temple we behold,
Hosannas, through eternity,
  ‖: We'll sing to harps of gold! :‖

W. H. Havergal, 1833.

O Thou, Who By a Star Didst Guide.

ST. LEONARD. C. M. D.

HENRY HILES.

1. O Thou, who by a star didst guide The wise men on their way,

Un-til it came and stood be-side The place where Je-sus lay:

Al-though by stars Thou dost not lead Thy ser-vants now be-low,

Thy Ho-ly Spir-it, when they need, Will show them how to go. A-men.

2 As yet we know Thee but in part,
But still we trust Thy word,
That blessed are the pure in heart,
For they shall see the Lord.
O Saviour, give us then Thy grace
To make us pure in heart,
That we may see Thee face to face,
Hereafter as Thou art.

John Mason Neale (1818—1866), 1842.

108

God of Mercy, God of Grace.

REPASS. 7, 7, 7, 7, 7, 7.   C. A. MARKS.

1. God of mer-cy, God of grace, Show the brightness of Thy Face,
Shine up-on us, Sav-iour, shine, Fill Thy Church with light di-vine;
And Thy sav-ing health ex-tend Un-to earth's re-mot-est end. A-men.

2 Let the people praise Thee, Lord;
Be by all that live adored;
Let the nations shout and sing
Glory to the Saviour King;
At Thy feet their tribute pay,
And Thy holy will obey.

3 Let the people praise Thee, Lord;
Earth shall then her fruits afford;
God to man His blessing give,
Man to God devoted live;
All below and all above,
One in joy, and light, and love.

H. F. Lyte, 1834.

109

Light of the World, we Hail Thee.

DER ABEND SENKT SICH LEISE. 7, 6, 7, 6. D.   J. G. HERZOG.

1. Light of the world, we hail Thee Flush-ing the East-ern skies;

Light of the World, we Hail Thee.—Concluded.

Nev - er shall dark-ness veil Thee A - gain from hu - man eyes;
Too long, a - las, with-hold - en, Now spread from shore to shore, Thy
light so glad and gold - en, Shall set on earth no more. A - men.

2 Light of the world, Thy beauty
   Steals into every heart,
And glorifies with duty
   Life's poorest, humblest part;
Thou robest in Thy splendor
   The simple ways of men,
And helpest them to render
   Light back to Thee again.

3 Light of the world, before Thee
   Our spirits prostrate fall;
We worship, we adore Thee,
   Thou Light, the life of all,

With Thee is no forgetting
   Of all Thine hand hath made;
Thy rising hath no setting,
   Thy sunshine hath no shade.

4 Light of the world, illumine
   This darkened land of Thine,
Till everything that's human
   Be filled with what's divine;
Till every tongue and nation,
   From sin's dominion free,
Rise in the new creation
   Which springs from Love and Thee.

J. S. B. Monsell, 1837.

110

From the Eastern Mountains.

ST. THERESA. 6, 5, (12 lines.)   ARTHUR S. SULLIVAN, (1842——), 1872.

Voices in Unison.

1. From the east - ern mountains, Pressing on, they come, Wise men in their wis - dom To this hum - ble home; Stirr'd by deep de - vo - tion, Starting from a - far, Ev-er journ'ying on-ward, Guided by a star.

From the Eastern Mountains.—Concluded.

CHORUS.

Light of Life, that shin - est Ere the world be - gan,

Draw Thou near and light-en ev - 'ry heart of man. A - men.

2 There their Lord and Saviour
  Meek and lowly lay,
Wondrous light that led them
Onward on their way,
Ever now to lighten
Nations from afar
As they journey homeward
  By that guiding star.
  Light of Life, etc.

3 Thou who in a manger
  Once hast lowly lain,
Who dost now in glory
O'er all kingdoms reign,
Gather in the heathen,
  Who in lands afar
Ne'er have seen the brightness
Of Thy guiding star.
  Light of Life, etc.

4 Onward through the darkness
  Of the lonely night,
Shining still before them
  With Thy kindly light,

Guide them, Jew and Gentile,
  Homeward from afar,
Young and old together,
  By Thy guiding star,
  Light of Life, etc.

5 Gather in the outcasts
  Who have gone astray,
Throw Thy radiance o'er them,
  Guide them on their way.
Those who never knew Thee,
  Or have wandered far,
Guide them by the brightness
  Of Thy guiding star.
  Light of Life, etc.

6 Until every nation
  Whether bond or free,
'Neath Thy starlit banner,
  Jesus, follow Thee
O'er the distant mountains
  To that heavenly home,
Where nor sin nor sorrow
  Evermore shall come.
  Light of Life, etc.

211

G. Thring, (1823 ——).

The Church Year: The Lenten Season.

111

Lord! Who Throughout These Forty Days.

ST. AGNES. C. M.

J. B. DYKES, (1823–1876).

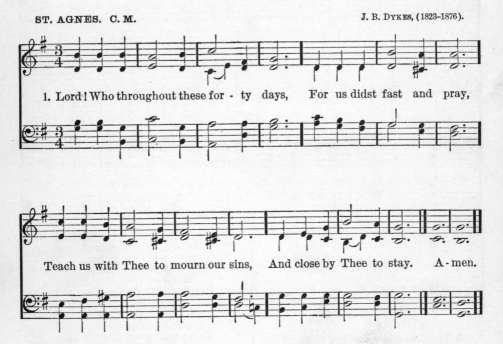

1. Lord! Who throughout these for-ty days, For us didst fast and pray,

Teach us with Thee to mourn our sins, And close by Thee to stay. A-men.

2 As Thou with Satan didst contend,
    And didst the victory win,
Oh, give us strength in Thee to fight,
    In Thee to conquer sin.

3 As Thou didst hunger bear and thirst,
    So teach us, gracious Lord,
To die to self, and chiefly live
    By Thy most holy Word.

4 And through these days of penitence,
    And through Thy Passion tide,
Lord, evermore, in life and death,
    Do Thou with us abide.

5 Abide with us, that so, this life
    Of suffering overpast,
An Easter of unending joy
    We may attain at last.

Mrs. C. F. Hernaman, 1873.

Saviour, When in Dust to Thee.

112

SPANISH HYMN. 7, 7, 7, 7. D.

SPANISH MELODY.

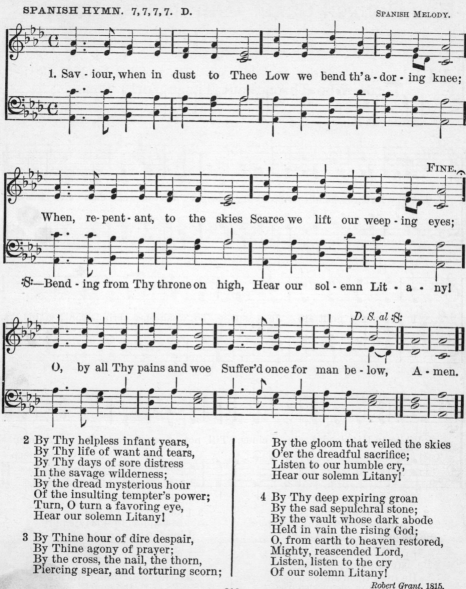

1. Sav - iour, when in dust to Thee Low we bend th'a - dor - ing knee;

When, re - pent - ant, to the skies Scarce we lift our weep - ing eyes;

:S:—Bend - ing from Thy throne on high, Hear our sol - emn Lit - a - ny!

O, by all Thy pains and woe Suffer'd once for man be - low, A - men.

2 By Thy helpless infant years,
By Thy life of want and tears,
By Thy days of sore distress
In the savage wilderness;
By the dread mysterious hour
Of the insulting tempter's power;
Turn, O turn a favoring eye,
Hear our solemn Litany!

3 By Thine hour of dire despair,
By Thine agony of prayer;
By the cross, the nail, the thorn,
Piercing spear, and torturing scorn;

By the gloom that veiled the skies
O'er the dreadful sacrifice;
Listen to our humble cry,
Hear our solemn Litany!

4 By Thy deep expiring groan
By the sad sepulchral stone;
By the vault whose dark abode
Held in vain the rising God;
O, from earth to heaven restored,
Mighty, reascended Lord,
Listen, listen to the cry
Of our solemn Litany!

Robert Grant, 1815.

113

I Lay My Sins on Jesus.

CRUCIFIX. 7, 6, 7, 6. D. (*First tune.*) GREEK MELODY.

1. I lay my sins on Je - sus, The spot - less Lamb of God;

He bears them all, and frees us From the ac - curs - èd load.

I bring my guilt to Je - sus, To wash my crim - son stains

White, in His blood most pre - cious, Till not a spot re - mains. A - men.

2 I lay my wants on Jesus;
 All fulness dwells in Him;
He heals all my diseases,
 He doth my soul redeem.
I lay my griefs on Jesus,
 My burdens and my cares;
He from them all releases,
 He all my sorrows shares.

3 I long to be like Jesus,
 Meek, loving, lowly, mild;
I long to be like Jesus,
 The Father's only child.
I long to be with Jesus
 Amid the heavenly throng,
To sing with saints His praises,
 To learn the angels' song.

Horatius Bonar, 1843.

I Lay My Sins on Jesus.

ELIM. 7, 6, 7, 6. D. (*Second tune.*)   JOHN BAPTISTE CALKIN (1827—), 1867.

1. I lay my sins on Je - sus, The spot - less Lamb of God;

He bears them all, and frees us From the ac - curs - ed load.

I bring my guilt to Je - sus, To wash my crim - son stains

White, in His blood most pre - cious, Till not a spot re - mains. A - men.

114

In the Cross of Christ I Glory.

RATHBUN. 8, 7, 8, 7.

THOMAS CONKEY, 1851.

1. In the Cross of Christ I glo-ry, Tow-'ring o'er the wrecks of time; All the light of sa-cred sto-ry Gath-ers round its head sub-lime. A - men.

2 When the woes of life o'ertake me,
Hopes deceive, and fears annoy,
Never shall the Cross forsake me;
Lo! it glows with peace and joy.

3 When the sun of bliss is beaming
Light and love upon my way,
From the Cross the radiance streaming
Adds new lustre to the day.

4 Bane and blessing, pain and pleasure,
By the Cross are sanctified;
Peace is there that knows no measure,
Joys that through all time abide.

John Bowring, 1825.

115

Jesus, Tender Saviour.

ST. MARY MAGDALENE. 6, 5, 6, 5. D.

J. B. DYKES.

1. Je - sus, ten - der Sav - iour, Hast Thou died for me?
Make me ver - y thank - ful In my heart to Thee.
When the sad, sad sto - ry Of Thy grief I read,
Make me ver - y sor - ry For my sins in - deed. A - men.

2 Now I know Thou livest,
    And dost plead for me;
  Make me very thankful
    In my prayers to Thee.

Soon I hope in glory
    At Thy side to stand;
  Make me fit to meet Thee
    In that happy land.

116

Glory be to Jesus.

CASWALL. 6, 5, 6, 5. (*First tune.*) FR. FILITZ, 1847.

1. Glo - ry be to Je - sus, Who, in bit - ter pains,

Pour'd for me the life - blood From His sa - cred veins! A - men.

2 Grace and life eternal
   In that Blood I find;
   Blest be His compassion,
   Infinitely kind!

3 Blest through endless ages
   Be the precious stream,
   Which from endless torments
   Did the world redeem!

4 Abel's blood for vengeance
   Pleaded to the skies;

But the Blood of Jesus
   For our pardon cries!

5 Oft as earth exulting
   Wafts its praise on high,
   Angel hosts rejoicing
   Make their glad reply.

6 Lift we then our voices,
   Swell the mighty flood;
   Louder still, and louder,
   Praise the precious Blood!

From the Italian by E. Caswall.

Glory be to Jesus.

VIVIA. 6, 5, 6, 5. (*Second tune.*) F. A. MANN.

1. Glo - ry be to Je - sus, Who, in bit - ter pains,

Pour'd for me the life - blood From His sa - cred veins! A - men.

One There is Above All Others.

AMEN RAABE HVER EN TUNGE. 8, 7, 8, 7, 7, 7. FROM DANISH CHORALBOG.

1. One there is a-bove all oth-ers, Well de-serves the name of Friend.

His is love be-yond a broth-er's, Cost-ly, free, and knows no end:

They who once His kindness prove, Find it ev-er-last-ing Love. A-men.

2 Which of all our friends, to save us,
    Could or would have shed his blood?
But this Saviour died to have us
    Reconciled in Him to God:
This was boundless Love indeed:
Jesus is a Friend in need.

3 When He lived on earth abasèd,
    Friend of sinners was His name:
Now, above all glory raisèd,
    He rejoices in the same:
Still He calls them brethren, friends,
And to all their wants attends.

4 O for grace our hearts to soften!
    Teach us, Lord, at length to love.
We, alas! forget too often
    What a Friend we have above:
But when home our souls are brought,
We will love Thee as we ought.

John Newton, 1779.

The Church Year: Palm Sunday.

118

When, His Salvation Bringing.

PALM SUNDAY. 7, 6. 7, 6. D.   J. A. Peter Schultz, d. 1800.   Adap. by H. R. Krauth.

1. When, His sal - va - tion bring - ing, To Zi - on Je - sus came, The chil - dren all stood sing - ing Ho - san - na to His Name. Nor did their zeal of - fend Him, But as He rode a - long, He let them still at - tend Him,

May be sung after each verse.

And smil'd to hear their song.   Ho - san - na, Ho - san - na, To David's roy - al Son,

When, His Salvation Bringing.—Concluded.

Ho-san - na, Ho-san - na, Ho-san - - na. A - men.

2 And since the Lord retaineth
  His love for children still,
Though now as King He reigneth
  On Zion's heavenly hill;
We'll flock around His banner,
  Who sits upon the throne,
And cry aloud, Hosanna
  To David's royal Son.

3 For should we fail proclaiming
  Our great Redeemer's praise,
The stones, our silence shaming,
  Would their Hosannas raise,
But shall we only render
  The tribute of our words?
No; while our hearts are tender,
  They, too, shall be the Lord's.

Joshua King, 1830.

All Glory, Praise, and Honor. 119

ACH SEI MIT DEINER GNADE. 7, 6, 7, 6.   G. E. SALLMANN, 1790.

1. All glo-ry, praise, and hon-or To Thee, Re-deem-er King;

To whom the lips of children Made sweet ho-san-nas ring. A-men.

2 Thou art the King of Israel,
  Thou David's royal Son,
Who in the Lord's name comest,
  The King and Blessed One!

3 The company of angels
  Are praising Thee on high,
And mortal men, and all things
  Created, make reply.

4 The people of the Hebrews
  With palms before Thee went;

Our praise and prayer and anthems
  Before Thee we present.

5 To Thee before Thy Passion
  They sang their hymns of praise;
To Thee, now high exalted,
  Our melody we raise.

6 Thou didst accept their praises;
  Accept the prayers we bring,
Who in all good delightest,
  Thou good and gracious King!

Theodulph of Orleans, d. 821.
Tr. John Mason Neale, 1856. a.

120

Hail, Thou Once Despised Jesus!

PILGRIM. 8, 7, 8, 7. D. (*First tune.*)

1. Hail, Thou once de-spis-éd Je - sus! Hail, Thou Gal-i-le-an King!

Thou didst suf-fer to re-lease us; Thou didst free sal-va-tion bring.

Hail, Thou ag-o-niz-ing Sav-iour, Bear-er of our sin and shame!

By Thy mer-its we find fa-vor; Life is giv-en thro' Thy Name. A-men.

Hail, Thou Once Despised Jesus!—Concluded.

2 Paschal Lamb, by God appointed,
    All our sins on Thee were laid;
By almighty Love anointed,
    Thou hast full Atonement made.
All Thy people are forgiven,
    Through the virtue of Thy Blood:
Opened is the gate of heaven;
    Peace is made 'twixt man and God.

3 Jesus, hail, enthroned in glory,
    There for ever to abide!
All the heavenly hosts adore Thee,
    Seated at Thy Father's side:

There for sinners Thou art pleading,
    There Thou dost our place prepare,
Ever for us interceding,
    Till in glory we appear.

4 Worship, honor, power and blessing,
    Thou art worthy to receive;
Loudest praises, without ceasing,
    Meet it is for us to give.
Help, ye bright angelic spirits,
    Bring your sweetest, noblest lays,
Help to sing our Saviour's merits,
    Help to chant Immanuel's praise.

J. Bakewell.

Hail, Thou Once Despised Jesus!

OTTO. 8, 7, 8, 7. D. (*Second tune.*)   H. K. OLIVER.

1. Hail, Thou once de-spis-éd Je-sus! Hail, Thou Gal-i-le-an King!
Thou didst suf-fer to re-lease us; Thou didst free sal-va-tion bring.

Hail, Thou ag-o-niz-ing Sav-iour, Bear-er of our sin and shame!

By Thy mer-its we find fa-vor; Life is giv-en thro' Thy Name. A-men.

121

The Royal Standard Forward Goes.

ELY. L. M.

TURTON.

1. The Roy-al Stan-dard for-ward goes, The Sa-cred Cross re-ful-gent glows, Where He in flesh, our flesh Who made, Our sen-tence bore, our ran-som paid. A-men.

2 From His pierced hands and riven side
Flows forth the precious crimson tide,
To cleanse us in the mystic flood
Of water mingled with His Blood.

3 Fulfilled is now what David told
In song prophetic, sung of old,
That God should King of nations be,
Ruling and reigning from the Tree.

4 O Tree of glory, Tree most fair,
Ordained those holy Limbs to bear!
Empurpled o'er and o'er it stood—
Empurpled by our Saviour's Blood.

5 How blest upon those branches then
Hung the best gifts of God to men!
A Balance where the price was weighed—
The ransom-price for sinners paid!

6 O wondrous Cross!—Great Victim, hail!
Thy glorious Passion must avail;
The very Life hath Death endured,
And by that Death our life procured.

From the Latin of Fortunatus, 569.

122

Glory and Praise to Thee, Redeemer Blest!

BEECHWOOD. 10, 10, 10, 10.

ARR. FROM NEUKOMM.

1. Glo - ry and praise to Thee, Re - deem - er blest!
By loud Ho - san - nas on Thy road con - fess'd!
Hail! Is - rael's King! Hail! Da - vid's Son a - dor'd, . . .
Who com - est in the Name of Is - rael's Lord! A - men.

2 Thee once with palms the Jews went forth to meet,
Thee now with prayers and holy hymns we greet;
Glory and praise to Thee, Incarnate Word,
Who comest in the Name of Israel's Lord!

3 Thee, on Thy way to die, they crowned with praise!
To Thee, enthroned on high, our song we raise.
Glory and praise, etc.

4 Thy praise in heaven the host angelic sings,
On earth, mankind with all created things.
Glory and praise, etc.

123

Hosanna We Sing.

P. M.

JOHN B. DYKES.

1. Ho - san - na we sing, like the chil - dren dear,

In the old - en days when the Lord lived here;

He blessed lit - tle chil - dren and smiled on them,

While they chant - ed His praise in Je - ru - sa - lem.

Hosanna We Sing.—Concluded.

Al - le - lu - ia we sing, like the chil - dren bright

With their harps of gold and their rai - ment white,

As they fol - low their Shep - herd with lov - ing eyes,

Thro' the beau-ti - ful val-leys of Par - a - dise. A - men.

2 Hosannas we sing, for He bends His ear,
And rejoices the hymns of His own to hear;
We know that His heart will never wax cold
To the lambs that He feeds in His earthly fold.
Alleluia we sing in the Church we love,
Alleluia resounds in the Church above;
To Thy little ones, Lord, may such grace be given,
That we lose not our part in the song of heaven.

G. S. Hodges.

The Church Year: The Passion.

124
O Thou Who Through this Holy Week.

TRIAS. C. M.   GREGORIAN.

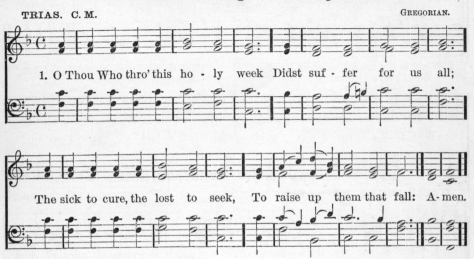

1. O Thou Who thro' this ho - ly week Didst suf - fer for us all;

The sick to cure, the lost to seek, To raise up them that fall: A-men.

2 We cannot understand the woe
Thy Love was pleased to bear:
O Lamb of God, we only know
That all our hopes are there!

3 Thy feet the path of suffering trod;
Thy hand the victory won:

What shall we render to our God
For all that He hath done?

4 To God the Father, God the Son,
And God the Holy Ghost,
By men on earth be honor done,
And by the heavenly host.

J. M. Neale, 1842.

125
There is a Green Hill Far Away.

MED STRAALENKRANS OM SINDE. C. M.   AUG. WINDING.

1. There is a green hill far a - way, With-out a cit - y wall,

There is a Green Hill Far Away.—Concluded.

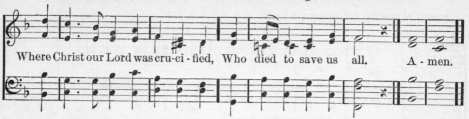

Where Christ our Lord was cru-ci-fied, Who died to save us all. A - men.

2 We may not know, we cannot tell
  What pains He had to bear;
But we believe it was for us
  He hung and suffered there.

3 He died that we might be forgiven,
  He died to make us good,

That we might go at last to heaven,
  Saved by His precious blood.

4 Oh, dearly, dearly has He loved,
  And we must love Him too,
And trust in His redeeming blood,
  And try His works to do.

Cecil F. Alexander, 1848.

When I Survey the Wondrous Cross.

126

O JESU CHRIST, MEINS LEBENS LICHT. L. M.

1630.

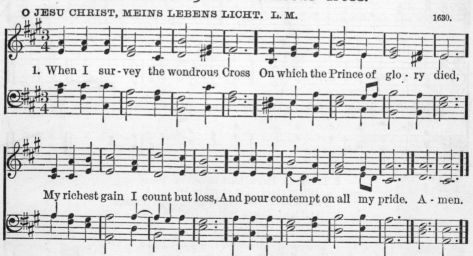

1. When I sur-vey the wondrous Cross On which the Prince of glo-ry died,

My richest gain I count but loss, And pour contempt on all my pride. A - men.

2 Forbid it, Lord, that I should boast,
  Save in the death of Christ, my God;
All the vain things that charm me most,
  I sacrifice them to His Blood.

3 See, from His head, His hands, His feet,
  Sorrow and love flow mingled down!

Did e'er such love and sorrow meet,
  Or thorns compose so rich a crown?

4 Were the whole realm of nature mine,
  That were a tribute far too small;
Love so amazing, so divine,
  Demands my soul, my life, my all.

Watts, 1707.

127

Christ the Life of All the Living.

JESU, MEINES LEBENS LEBEN. 8, 7, 8, 7, 7, 7, 7, 7.

CHRISTOPHER ANTONIUS, 1651.

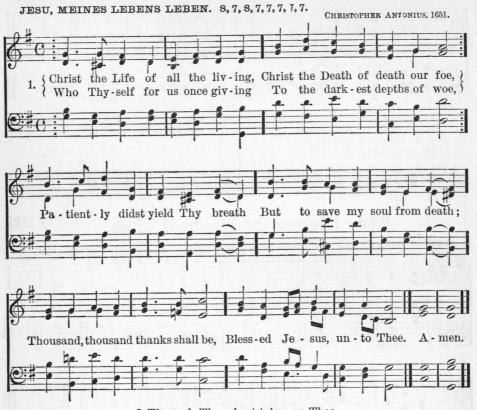

1. Christ the Life of all the liv-ing, Christ the Death of death our foe,
Who Thy-self for us once giv-ing To the dark-est depths of woe,

Pa-tient-ly didst yield Thy breath But to save my soul from death;

Thousand, thousand thanks shall be, Bless-ed Je-sus, un-to Thee. A-men.

2 Thou, ah Thou, hast taken on Thee
   Bitter strokes, a cruel rod;
Pain and scorn were heaped upon Thee,
   O Thou sinless Son of God.
Only thus for me to win
Rescue from the bonds of sin.
Thousand, thousand thanks shall be,
Blessed Jesus, unto Thee.

3 Thou didst bear the smiting only
   That it might not fall on me;
Stoodest falsely charged and lonely,
   That I might be safe and free;
Comfortless that I might know
Comfort from Thy boundless woe.
Thousand, thousand thanks shall be,
Blessed Jesus, unto Thee.

Christ the Life of All the Living.—Concluded.

4 Then for all that wrought our pardon,
  For Thy sorrows deep and sore,
  For Thine anguish in the garden,
  I will thank Thee evermore;
  Thank Thee with my latest breath
  For Thy sad and cruel death,
  For that last and bitter cry:
  Praise Thee evermore on high.

Ernest Christopher Homburg, 1659.
Miss Winkworth, Tr. 1862. *a.*

128

O Perfect Life of Love.

WOOLWICH. S. M.   C. E. KETTLE.

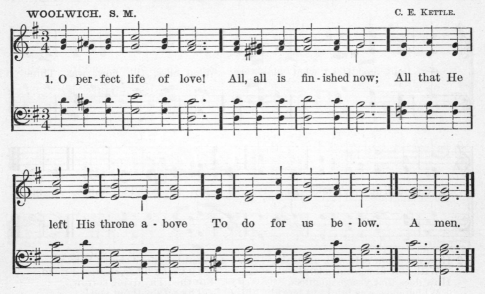

1. O per-fect life of love! All, all is fin-ished now; All that He left His throne a-bove To do for us be-low. A men.

2 No work is left undone
    Of all the Father willed;
  His toil, His sorrows, one by one,
    The Scriptures have fulfilled.

3 No pain that we can share
    But He has felt its smart;
  All forms of human grief and care
    Have pierced that tender heart.

4 And on His thorn-crowned head,
    And on His sinless soul,
  Our sins in all their guilt were laid,
    That He might make us whole.

5 In perfect love He dies—
    For me He dies, for me:
  O all-atoning Sacrifice!
    I cling by faith to Thee!

6 In every time of need,
    Before the judgment-throne,
  Thy work, O Lamb of God! I'll plead—
    Thy merits, not my own.

7 Yet work, O Lord! in me
    As Thou for me hast wrought:
  And let my love the answer be
    To grace Thy love has brought.

Henry W. Baker (1821—1877.)

129

O Sacred Head Now Wounded.

HERZLICH THUT MICH VERLANGEN. 7, 6, 7, 6. D.

SECULAR ORIGIN.

HANS LEO HASSLER, (1564–1612), 1601 AND 1613.

1. { O sa - cred Head now wound - ed, With grief and shame weigh'd down,
   { Now scorn - ful - ly sur - round - ed With thorns, Thy on - ly crown!

O sa - cred Head, what glo - ry, What bliss, till now, was Thine!

Yet, though de - spis'd and go - ry, I joy to call Thee mine. A - men.

2 How art Thou pale with anguish,
   With sore abuse and scorn!
How does that visage languish,
   Which once was bright as morn!
What Thou, my Lord, hast suffered,
   Was all for sinners' gain;
Mine, mine was the transgression,
   But Thine the deadly pain.

3 Lo, here I fall, my Saviour!
   'Tis I deserve Thy place!
Look on me with Thy favor,
   Vouchsafe to me Thy grace.
Receive me, my Redeemer;
   My Shepherd, make me Thine!
Of every good the Fountain,
   Thou art the Spring of mine!

4 What language shall I borrow
   To thank Thee, dearest Friend,
For this, Thy dying sorrow,
   Thy pity without end!
O make me Thine for ever,
   And should I fainting be,
Lord, let me never, never,
   Outlive my love to Thee.

5 Forbid that I should leave Thee;
   O Jesus, leave not me;
In faith may I receive Thee,
   When death shall set me free.
When strength and comfort languish,
   And I must hence depart,
Release me then from anguish
   By Thine own wounded heart.

Bernard of Clairvaux.
P. Gerhardt, by J. W. Alexander.

THE CHURCH YEAR: EASTER.

Day of Wonder, Day of Gladness.

130

ADORATION. 8. 7, 8, 7. D. FROM J. A. SHULTZE, 1780. U. C. BURNAP.

1. { Day of won-der, day of glad-ness, Hail thy ev - er - glo-rious light!
   { Gone is sor-row, gone is sad-ness, End - ed is the

gloom - y night! Lis - ten to the an - gel's sto - ry,

Cast a - way all dark and dread; Give to God the Fa - ther

glo - ry! "Christ is ris - en from the dead!" A - men.

2 In the triumph of this hour,
  Jubilant shall swell the song;
Unto Jesus, honor, power,
  Blessing, victory belong.
Scattered are the clouds of error,
  Sin and hell are captive led:
E'en the grave is free from terror,
  "Christ is risen from the dead!"

3 Every people, every nation,
  Soon shall hear the gladsome sound;
Joyous tidings of salvation,
  Borne to earth's remotest bound.
Then shall rise, in tones excelling,
  Praise for grace so freely shed;
And the Easter hymn be swelling,
  "Christ is risen from the dead!"

R. H. Hall.

131

The Day of Resurrection!

SALVATORI. 7, 6, 7, 6. D. (*First tune.*) S. SALVATORI.

1. The day of Res·ur·rec·tion! Earth! tell it out a·broad!

D. C.—Our Christ hath brought us o·ver, With hymns of vic·to·ry.

The Pass·o·ver of glad·ness, The Pass·o·ver of God!

From death to Life e·ter·nal, From earth un·to the sky, A·men.

2 Our hearts be pure from evil,
  That we may see aright
The Lord in rays eternal
  Of Resurrection light:
And listening to His accents,
  May hear, so calm and plain,
His own All hail!—and hearing,
  May raise the victor strain.

3 Now let the heavens be joyful!
  Let earth her song begin!
Let all the world keep triumph,
  And all that is therein:
In grateful exultation
  Their notes let all things blend
For Christ the Lord hath risen,
  Our Joy that hath no end.

John of Damascus, about 760.
Tr. J. M. Neale. 1862.

The Day of Resurrection!

TOURS. 7, 6, 7, 6. D. (*Second tune.*)

BERTHOLD TOURS.

1. The day of Res - ur - rec - tion! Earth, tell it out a - broad!

The Pass - o - ver of glad - ness, The Pass - o - ver of God!

From death to Life e - ter - nal From earth un - to the sky,

Our Christ hath brought us o - ver, With hymns of vic - to - ry. A - men.

132

Christ the Lord is Risen To-day.

WORGAN. 7, 7, 7, 7. (*With Halleluia.*)　　　　　　　FROM LYRA DAVIDICA.

1. Christ the Lord is ris'n to-day, Hal - - le - lu - ia!
Sons of men and an - gels say. Hal - - le - lu - ia!
Raise your joys and tri - umphs high; Hal - - le - lu - ia!
Sing, ye heav'ns and earth re - ply. Hal - - le - lu - ia! A - men.

2 Love's redeeming work is done,
Fought the fight, the battle won;
Lo! the Sun's eclipse is o'er;
Lo! He sets in blood no more.

3 Vain the stone, the watch, the seal;
Christ has burst the gates of hell!
Death in vain forbids His rise;
Christ hath opened Paradise.

Christ the Lord is Risen To-day.—Concluded.

4 Lives again our glorious King;
　Where, O Death, is now thy sting?
　Dying once, He all doth save;
　Where thy victory, O Grave?

5 Soar we now where Christ has led,
　Following our exalted Head:

Made like Him, like Him we rise;
Ours the cross, the grave, the skies!

6 Hail, the Lord of earth and heaven!
　Praise to Thee by both be given:
　Thee we greet triumphant now;
　Hail, the Resurrection Thou!

Charles Wesley, 1739.

The Strife is O'er, the Battle Done! 133

VICTORY. 8, 8, 8, 4.　　　　　　　　　　　　　PALESTRINA.

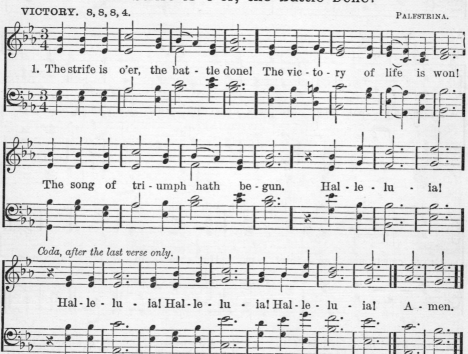

1. The strife is o'er, the bat - tle done! The vic - to - ry of life is won!

The song of tri - umph hath be - gun. Hal - le - lu - ia!

Coda, after the last verse only.

Hal - le - lu - ia! Hal - le - lu - ia! Hal - le - lu - ia! A - men.

2 The powers of death have done their worst,
　But Christ their legion hath dispersed:
　Let shouts of holy joy outburst.
　　Halleluia!

3 The three sad days have quickly sped;
　He rises glorious from the dead:
　All glory to our risen Head!
　　Halleluia!

4 He closed the yawning gates of hell;
　The bars from heaven's high portals fell;
　Let hymns of praise His triumphs tell.
　　Halleluia!

5 Lord, by the stripes which wounded Thee,
　From death's dread sting Thy servants [free,
　That we may live and sing to Thee,
　　Halleluia!

Ancient Latin. Tr. F. Pott, 1859.

134

Jesus Lives! Thy Terrors Now.

ST. ALBINUS. 7, 8, 7, 8. (*With Halleluia.*)

H. J. GAUNTLETT.

1. Je - sus lives! thy ter - rors now Can no long - er, Death, ap - pal us; Je - sus lives! by this we know Thou, O Grave, canst not en - thral us. Hal - le - lu - ia! A - men.

2 Jesus lives! henceforth is death
  But the gate of life immortal;
This shall calm our trembling breath,
  When we pass its gloomy portal.
    Halleluia!

3 Jesus lives! for us He died;
  Then, alone to Jesus living,
Pure in heart may we abide,
  Glory to our Saviour giving.
    Halleluia!

4 Jesus lives! our hearts know well
  Naught from us His love shall sever,
Life, nor death, nor powers of hell
  Tear us from His keeping ever.
    Halleluia!

5 Jesus lives! to Him the throne
  Over all the world is given:
May we go where He has gone,
  Rest and reign with Him in heaven.
    Halleluia!

C. F. Gellert. Tr. F. E. Cox.

135

Let the Song be Begun.

P. M.

G. W. WARREN.

1. Let the song be be-gun, For the bat-tle is done, And the vic-to-ry won, And the foe is scat-ter'd, And the pris-on shat-ter'd: Sing of joy, joy, joy, And to-day Raise the lay, Glo-ry in the high-est. A-men. A-men.

2 They that followed in pain
Shall now follow to reign,
And the crown shall obtain:
  They were sore assaulted,
  They shall be exalted:
Sing of rest, rest, rest;
  And again, Pour the strain,
Glory in the highest. Amen.

3 For the foe never more
Can approach to the shore
Where the conflict is o'er:
  There is joy supernal,

There is life eternal:
Sing of peace, peace, peace;
  Earth and skies Bid it rise,
Glory in the highest. Amen.

4 Then be brave, then be true,
Ye despised and ye few,
For the crown is for you;
  Christ, that went before you,
  Spreads His buckler o'er you;
Sing of hope, hope, hope;
  And to-day Raise the lay,
Glory in the highest. Amen.

J. C. Middleton.

136

Come, Ye Faithful, Raise the Strain.

ST. KEVIN. 7, 6, 7, 6. D. (*First tune.*)　　　　　　　　　　A. S. SULLIVAN.

1. Come, ye faith-ful, raise the strain Of tri-umph-ant glad-ness!
God hath brought His Is-ra-el In-to joy from sad-ness!
'Tis the spring of souls to-day: Christ hath burst His pris-on;
And from three days' sleep in death, As a sun, hath ris-en. A-men.

2 All the winter of our sins,
　Long and dark, is flying
From His light, to whom we give
　Thanks and praise undying.
Neither might the gates of death,
　Nor the tomb's dark portal,
Nor the watchers, nor the seal,
　Hold Thee as a mortal:

3 But to-day amidst the twelve
　Thou didst stand, bestowing
That Thy peace, which evermore
　Passeth human knowing.
Come, ye faithful, raise the strain
　Of triumphant gladness!
God hath brought His Israel
　Into joy from sadness!

John of Damascus, about 760.
John Mason Neale, Tr. 1862.

Come, Ye Faithful, Raise the Strain.

TIL VOR LILLE GJERNING UD. TROCHAIC. 7, 6, 7, 6. D. (*Second tune.*)

C. E. F. WEYSE.

1. Come, ye faith-ful, raise the strain   Of   triumph-ant   glad - ness!

God hath brought His Is - ra - el   In - to   joy from   sad - ness!

'Tis the spring of   souls to - day: Christ hath burst His   pris - on;

And from three days' sleep in death,   As   a   sun, hath ris - en.   A-men.

137

Christ the Lord is Risen Again.

WUERTEMBERG. 7, 7, 7, 7. *(With Halleluia.)* *(First tune.)* JOHANN ROSENMÜLLER, 1694.

1. Christ the Lord is ris'n a-gain; Christ hath bro-ken ev-'ry chain; Hark, an-gel-ic voi-ces cry, Sing-ing ev-er-more on high, Hal - - le - lu - ia! A - men.

2 He, who gave for us His life,
Who for us endured the strife,
Is our Paschal Lamb to-day;
We too sing for joy, and say,
Halleluia!

3 He, who bore all pain and loss
Comfortless upon the Cross,
Lives in glory now on high,
Pleads for us and hears our cry;
Halleluia!

242

Christ the Lord is Risen Again.—Concluded.

4 He, who slumbered in the grave,
Is exalted now to save;
Now through Christendom it rings
That the Lamb is King of kings.
Halleluia!

5 Thou, our Paschal Lamb indeed,
Christ, Thy ransomed people feed;
Take our sins and guilt away,
Let us sing by night and day
Halleluia!

Bohemian, 15th cent. Tr. Miss Winkworth, 1858.

Christ the Lord is Risen Again.

BARNBY'S HYMNARY, No. 289. 7, 7, 7, 7. *(With Halleluia.)* *(Second tune.)* **GERMAN.**

1. Christ the Lord is ris'n a-gain; Christ hath bro-ken ev-'ry
chain; Hark, an-gel-ic voi-ces cry, Sing-ing
ev-er-more on high, Hal-le-lu-ia! A-men.

138

Christ is Risen! Hallelujah!

F. C. MAKER.

1. Christ is ris - en! Hal - le - lu - jah! Ris - en our vic - to - rious Head!

Sing His prais - es! Hal - le - lu - jah! Christ is ris - en from the dead!

Grate - ful - ly our hearts a - dore Him, As His light once more ap - pears,

Bow - ing down in joy be - fore Him, Ris - ing up from grief and tears.

Christ is Risen! Hallelujah!—Concluded.

CHORUS.

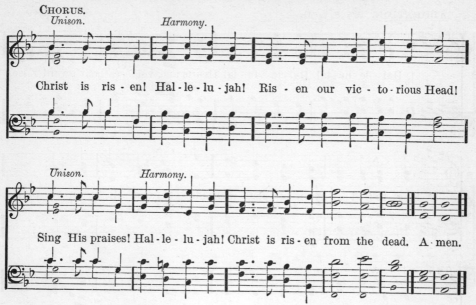

Christ is ris - en! Hal - le - lu - jah! Ris - en our vic - to - rious Head!

Sing His praises! Hal - le - lu - jah! Christ is ris - en from the dead. A - men.

2 Christ is risen! all the sadness
    Of our Lenten fast is o'er,
Through the open gates of gladness
    He returns to life once more:
Death and hell before Him bending,
    He doth rise, the Victor now,
Angels on His steps attending,
    Glory round His wounded brow:

CHO.—Christ is risen! Hallelujah!
    Risen our victorious Head!
    Sing His praises! Hallelujah!
    Christ is risen from the dead.

3 Christ is risen! all the sorrow
    That last evening round Him lay,
Now hath found a glorious morrow
    In the rising of to-day;
And the grave its first fruits giveth,
    Springing up from holy ground,

He was dead, but now He liveth,
    He was lost, but He is found:

CHO.—Christ is risen! Hallelujah!
    Risen our victorious Head!
    Sing His praises! Hallelujah!
    Christ is risen from the dead.

4 Christ is risen! henceforth never
    Death or hell shall us enthrall,
Be we Christ's, in Him for ever
    We have triumphed over all;
All the doubting and dejection
    Of our trembling hearts have ceased,
'Tis His day of Resurrection!
    Let us rise and keep the Feast:

CHO.—Christ is risen! Hallelujah!
    Risen our victorious Head!
    Sing His praises! Hallelujah!
    Christ is risen from the dead.

John S. B. Monsell, (1811–1875), **1863.**

139

Halleluia! Halleluia!

ADORATION. 8, 7, 8, 7. D.

G. J. ELVEY.

1. Hal - le - lu - ia! Hal - le - lu - ia! Hearts and voi - ces heav'nward raise,

Sing to God a hymn of glad - ness, Sing to God a hymn of praise.

He Who on the Cross a Vic - tim For the world's sal - va - tion bled,

Je - sus Christ, the King of Glo - ry, Now is ris - en from the dead. A - men.

2 Now the iron bars are broken;
  Christ from death to life is born,—
Glorious life, and life immortal,
  On this holy Easter morn.
Christ hath triumphed, and we conquer
  By His mighty enterprise:
We with Christ to life eternal
  By His Resurrection rise.

3 Christ is risen, we are risen:
  Shed on us Thy heavenly grace,
Rain, and dew, and gleams of glory,
  From the brightness of Thy face;
That we, Lord, with hearts in heaven,
  Here on earth may fruitful be,
And by angel-hands be gathered,
  And be ever safe with Thee.

Wordsworth, 1865.

Ye Happy Bells of Easter Day.

8, 4, 4, 6, 8, 6.

Organ.

1. Ye hap-py bells of Eas-ter-Day!

Ring, ring your joy   Thro' earth and sky,   Ye ring a   glorious word.

The notes that swell in glad-ness tell   The ris-ing of the   Lord!

Organ.

A - men.

2 Ye glory-bells of Easter-Day!
　　The hills that rise
　　Against the skies,
　　Re-echo with the word—
The victor-breath that conquers death—
　　The rising of the Lord!

3 Ye mercy-bells of Easter-Day!
　　His tender side
　　Was riven wide,

　　Where floods of mercy poured:
Redeemèd clay doth sing to-day
　　The rising of the Lord!

4 Ye victor-bells of Easter-Day!
　　The thorny crown
　　He layeth down:
　　Ring! ring! with strong accord—
The mighty strain of love and pain
　　The rising of the Lord!

141

We Will Carol Joyfully.

FERDINAND. 7, 7, 7, 7, 8, 7.

C. A. MARKS, 1895.

1. We will car - ol joy - ful - ly On this ho - ly fes - tal day; To our ris - en Lord and King Grate - ful hom - age we will bring. Car - ol, car - ol, car - ol, car - ol, To our ris - en Lord and King. A - men.

2 We will carol joyfully,
As with sweet accord we bring
Praise from every heart and voice
To our risen Lord and King.
Carol, carol, etc.

3 We will carol joyfully,
While our love and thanks we give
To our risen Lord and King,
Him who died that we might live.
Carol, carol, etc.

4 We will carol joyfully,
And to Him our offerings bring—
Grateful hearts, with love and praise,
To our risen Lord and King.
Carol, carol, etc.

Christ the Lord is Risen To-day.

ST. GEORGE'S, WINDSOR. 7, 7, 7, 7. D.   GEORGE J. ELVEY, (1816—).

142

1. Christ the Lord is ris'n to-day; Chris-tians, haste your vows to pay;
Of-fer ye your prais-es meet At the Pas-chal vic-tim's feet.
For the sheep the Lamb hath bled, Sin-less in the sin-ner's stead;
"Christ is ris'n," to-day we cry; Now He lives no more to die. A-men.

2 Christ, the victim undefiled,
Man to God hath reconciled;
While in strange and awful strife
Met together Death and Life:
Christians, on this happy day
Haste with joy your vows to pay;
"Christ is risen," to-day we cry;
Now He lives no more to die.

3 Christ, who once for sinners bled,
Now the first-born from the dead,
Throned in endless might and power
Lives and reigns for evermore.
Hail, Eternal Hope on high!
Hail, Thou King of victory!
Hail, Thou Prince of life adored!
Help and save us, gracious Lord.

Latin Sequence, Tr. by Jane E. Leeson, 1851

143

O Sons and Daughters, let us Sing!

GELOBT SEI GOTT IM HŒCHSTEN THRON. 8, 8, 8. (*With Halleluia.*)

MELCHIOR VULPIUS, 1609.

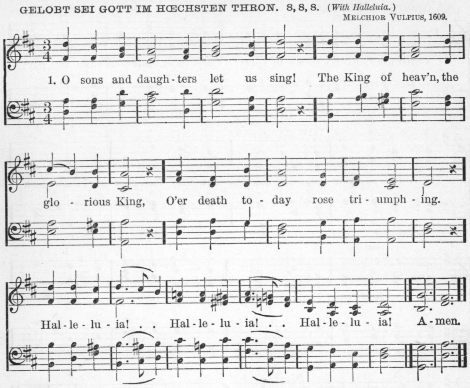

1. O sons and daugh-ters let us sing! The King of heav'n, the glo - rious King, O'er death to - day rose tri - umph - ing.

Hal - le - lu - ia! . . Hal - le - lu - ia! . . Hal - le - lu - ia! A - men.

2 That Sunday morn, at break of day,
The faithful women went their way
To seek the tomb where Jesus lay.
    Halleluia! Halleluia! Halleluia!

3 An angel clad in white they see,
Who sat and spake unto the three,
"Your Lord doth go to Galilee."
    Halleluia! Halleluia! Halleluia!

4 That night the Apostles met in fear;
Amidst them came their Lord most dear,
And said, "My peace be on all here."
    Halleluia! Halleluia! Halleluia!

5 When Didymus the tidings heard,
He doubted if it were the Lord,
Until He came and spake this word:
    Halleluia! Halleluia! Halleluia!

6 "My piercèd Side, O Thomas, see;
My Hands, My Feet, I show to thee;
Nor faithless, but believing be."
    Halleluia! Halleluia! Halleluia!

7 No longer Thomas then denied;
He saw the Feet, the Hands, the Side:
"Thou art my Lord and God," he cried.
    Halleluia! Halleluia! Halleluia!

8 How blest are they who have not seen,
And yet whose faith hath constant been;
For they eternal life shall win.
    Halleluia! Halleluia! Halleluia!

9 On this most holy day of days,
To God your hearts and voices raise
In laud, and jubilee, and praise.
    Halleluia! Halleluia! Halleluia!

J. M. Neale, and compilers: from the Latin.

Welcome, Thou Victor in the Strife.

144

GERONTIUS. C. M.

J. B. DYKES.

1. Wel-come, Thou Vic-tor in the strife, Wel-come from out the cave! To-day we tri-umph in Thy life A-round Thine emp-ty grave. A-men.

2 Our enemy is put to shame,
  His short-lived triumph o'er;
Our God is with us, we exclaim,
  We fear our foe no more.

3 The dwellings of the just resound
  With songs of victory;
For in their midst Thou, Lord, art found,
  And bringest peace with Thee.

4 O let Thy conquering banner wave
  O'er hearts Thou makest free;
And point the path that from the grave
  Leads heavenward up to Thee.

5 We bury all our sin and crime
  Deep in our Saviour's tomb,
And seek the treasure there, that time
  Nor change can e'er consume.

Benjamin Schmolk, 1712.
Tr. Cath. Winkworth, 1855.

259

THE CHURCH YEAR: ASCENSION.

145

The Head That Once Was Crowned With Thorns.

WIE IST ES HEUT SO STILL UND KLAR. C. M.　　　　　H. W. STORK, 1868.

1. The Head that once was crowned with thorns Is crowned with glo - ry now;

A roy - al dia - a - dem a - dorns The mighty Vic-tor's brow. A - men.

2 The highest place that heaven affords
  Is His by sovereign right:
The King of kings and Lord of lords,
  And heaven's eternal Light.

3 The joy of all who dwell above,
  The joy of all below,
To whom He manifests His love,
  And grants His Name to know.

4 To them the Cross, with all its shame,
  With all its grace, is given;
Their name an everlasting name,
  Their joy the joy of heaven.

5 The Cross He bore is life and health,
  Though shame and death to Him:
His people's hope, His people's wealth,
  Their everlasting theme.

Thomas Kelly, 1820.

146

See the Conqueror Mounts in Triumph.

REX GLORIAE. 8, 7, 8, 7. D.

H. SMART.

1. See the Conqu'ror mounts in triumph; See the King in roy-al state,
Rid-ing on the clouds, His char-iot, To His heav'nly pal-ace gate!
Hark! the choirs of an-gel voi-ces Joy-ful Al-le-lu-ias sing,
And the por-tals high are lift-ed To receive their heav'nly King. A-men.

2 Who is this that comes in glory,
   With the trump of Jubilee?
Lord of battles, God of armies,
   He has gained the victory!
Jesus reigns, adored by angels;
   Man with God is on the throne:
Mighty Lord in Thine ascension
   We by faith behold our own.

C. Wordsworth, 1862

147

Draw us to Thee, Lord Jesus.

EDEN. 7, 6, 7, 6. (*First tune.*)   St. Alban's Tune Book.

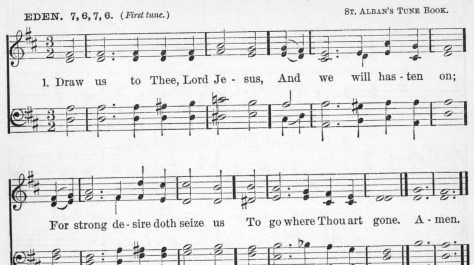

1. Draw us to Thee, Lord Je - sus, And we will has - ten on;

For strong de - sire doth seize us To go where Thou art gone. A - men.

2 Draw us to Thee; enlighten
  These hearts to find Thy way,
That else the tempests frighten,
  Or pleasures lure astray.

3 Draw us to Thee; and teach us
  Even now that rest to find,

Where turmoils cannot reach us,
  Nor cares weigh down the mind.

4 Draw us to Thee; nor leave us
  Till all our path is trod,
Then in Thine arms receive us,
  And bear us home to God.

*Ludaemilia Elizabeth, Countess of Schwarzberg Rudolstadt. d. 1672.
Tr. Miss Winkworth, 1862.*

Draw us to Thee, Lord Jesus.

KOCHER. 7, 6, 7, 6. (*Second tune.*)   J. H. Knecht.

1. Draw us to Thee, Lord Je - sus, And we will has - ten on;

Draw us to Thee, Lord Jesus.—Concluded.

For strong de - sire doth seize us   To go where Thou art gone.   A-men.

A Hymn of Glory let us Sing.

148

PARK ST. L. M.

F. M. A. VENUA.

1. A hymn of glo - ry let   us sing; New hymns throughout the

world shall ring; By a new way none ev - er trod, Christ mounteth

to the throne of God, Christ mounteth to the throne of God.   A - men.

2 May our affections thither tend,
  And thither constantly ascend,
  Where, seated on the Father's throne,
‖: Thee reigning in the heavens we own! :‖

3 Be Thou our present Joy, O Lord,
  Who wilt be ever our Reward :
  And as the countless ages flee,
‖: May all our glory be in Thee! :‖

From Bede, 8th Century, by E. R. Charles, **1858,**

149

Hark, Ten Thousand Harps and Voices.

NAAR SKAL DA MIN TID FAA ENDE. 8, 7, 8, 7, 7, 7.   P. C. Krossing, 1824.

1. Hark, ten thous-and harps and voi-ces Sound the note of praise a-bove!

Je-sus reigns, and heav'n re-joi-ces; Je-sus reigns, the God of love.

See, He sits on yon-der throne; Je-sus rules the world a-lone.   A-men.

2 Jesus, hail! whose glory brightens
  All above, and makes it fair:
Lord of life, Thy smile enlightens,
  Cheers and charms Thy people here.
When we think of Love like Thine,
Lord, we own it Love divine.

3 King of glory, reign for ever;
  Thine an everlasting crown:
Nothing from Thy Love shall sever
  Those whom Thou hast made Thine
Happy objects of Thy grace,   [own
Destined to behold Thy face.

4 Saviour, hasten Thine appearing;
  Bring, O bring the glorious day,
When, the awful summons hearing,
  Heaven and earth shall pass away.
Then, with golden harps we'll sing,
"Glory, glory to our King."
        Thomas Kelly, 1804.

Look, ye Saints! the Sight is Glorious.

CORONAE. 8, 7, 8, 7, 4, 7.

WILLIAM H. MONK, (1823–1889.)

1. Look, ye saints! the sight is glo-rious! See the Man of sor-rows now!

From the fight re-turn'd vic-to-rious, Ev-'ry knee to Him shall bow:

Crown Him! crown Him! Crowns be come the Vic - tor's brow. A - men.

2 Crown the Saviour! angels, crown Him!
  Rich the trophies Jesus brings;
On the seat of power enthrone Him,
  While the vault of heaven rings:
    Crown Him! crown Him!
  Crown the Saviour King of kings.

3 Sinners in derision crowned Him,
  Mocking thus the Saviour's claim;
Saints and angels crowd around Him,
  Own His title, praise His Name:
    Crown Him! crown Him!
  Spread abroad the Victor's fame!

4 Hark! those bursts of acclamation!
  Hark! those loud triumphant chords!
Jesus takes the highest station:
  O what joy the sight affords!
    Crown Him! crown Him!
  King of kings, and Lord of lords.

Thomas Kelly, (1769–1855), 1806.

THE CHURCH YEAR: PRAISE TO CHRIST.

151

All Hail the Power of Jesus' Name!

CORONATION. C. M. (*First tune.*)   O. HOLDEN.

1. All hail the power of Je-sus' Name! Let an-gels pros-trate fall; Bring forth the roy-al di-a-dem, And crown Him Lord of all; Bring forth the roy-al di-a-dem, And crown Him Lord of all. A-men.

All Hail the Power of Jesus' Name!—Concluded.

2 Hail Him, ye heirs of David's line,
 Whom David Lord did call;
 The God incarnate, Man divine :
 And crown Him Lord of all.

3 Let every kindred, every tribe,
 On this terrestrial ball,
 To Him all majesty ascribe,
 And crown Him Lord of all.

4 O that with yonder sacred throng
 We at His feet may fall;
 We'll join the everlasting song,
 And crown Him Lord of all.

Edward Perronet, 1785.

All Hail the Power of Jesus' Name!

LAUD. C. M. (*Second tune.*)   J. B. DYKES, (1823–1876).

1. All hail the power of Je sus' Name! Let an - gels pros - trate fall; Bring forth the roy - al di - a - dem, And crown Him Lord of all. A - men.

152

Beautiful Saviour.

CRUSADERS' HYMN. 5, 5, 7, 5, 5, 8.   SILESIAN MELODY, 1842.

1. Beau-ti-ful Sav-iour! King of Cre-a-tion! Son of God and Son of Man! Tru-ly I'd love Thee, Tru-ly I'd serve Thee, Light of my soul, my Joy, my Crown. A-men.

2 Fair are the meadows,
    Fair are the woodlands,
Robed in flowers of blooming spring;
    Jesus is fairer,
    Jesus is purer;
He makes our sorrowing spirit sing.

3 Fair is the sunshine,
    Fair is the moonlight
And the sparkling stars on high;

Jesus shines brighter,
Jesus shines purer,
Than all the angels in the sky.

4 Beautiful Saviour!
    Lord of the nations!
Son of God and Son of Man!
    Glory and honor,
    Praise, adoration,
Now and for evermore be Thine!

From the German in the Fulda Hymn Book, 1695.
Tr. Joseph A. Seiss, 1873.

Humble Praises, Holy Jesus.

VESPER HYMN. 8, 7, 8, 7. *(With Chorus.)*   DEMETRIUS BORTNIANSKY.

1. Hum - ble prais - es, ho - ly Je - sus, In - fant voi - ces raise to Thee:

In Thy mer - cy, O re - ceive us! Suf - fer us Thy lambs to be.

CHORUS.

Hal - le - lu - ia, sweet - ly sing - ing, Joy - ful trib - ute now we bring.

Hal - le - lu - ia, Hal - le - lu - ia! Hal - le - lu - ia, to our King. A - men.

2 Gracious Saviour, be Thou with us;
   Let Thy mercy richly flow:
Give Thy Spirit, Blessed Jesus!
   Light and life on us bestow.
     Halleluia, sweetly singing, etc.

Composite.

154

Come, Let Us Sing of Jesus.

ROMAINE. 7, 6, 7, 6. D.

J. BANNISTER.

1. Come, let us sing of Je-sus, While hearts and ac-cents blend;
Come, let us sing of Je-sus, The sin-ner's on-ly friend;
His ho-ly soul re-joic-es A-mid the choirs a-bove,
To hear our youthful voi-ces Ex-ult-ing in His love. A men.

2 We love to sing of Jesus,
    Who wept our path along;
We love to sing of Jesus,
    The tempted and the strong;
None who besought His healing,
    He passed unheeded by;
He still retains His feeling
    For us above the sky.

3 We love to sing of Jesus,
    Who died our souls to save;
We love to sing of Jesus,
    Triumphant o'er the grave;

And in our hour of danger,
    We'll trust His love alone,
Who once slept in a manger,
    And now sits on a throne.

4 Then let us sing of Jesus,
    While yet on earth we stay,
And hope to sing of Jesus
    Throughout eternal day.
For those who here confess Him,
    He will in heaven confess,
And faithful hearts that bless Him,
    He will for ever bless.

G. W. Bethune, 1850.

We Gather, We Gather.

IHR KINDERLEIN, KOMMET. 11, 11, 11, 11.

J. A. P. Schultz, 1800.

1. We gath-er, we gath-er, dear Je-sus, to bring
The breath-ings of love 'mid the blos-soms of Spring;

Our Mak-er, Re-deem-er, we grate-ful-ly raise

Our hearts and our voi-ces in hymn-ing Thy praise. A-men.

2 When stooping to earth from the brightness of Heaven,
Thy blood for our ransom so freely was given,
Thou deignedst to listen while children adored,
With joyful Hosannas, the bless'd of the Lord.

3 Those arms, which embraced little children of old,
Still love to encircle the lambs of the fold;
That grace which inviteth the wandering home,
Hath never forbidden the youngest to come.

4 Hosanna! Hosanna! Great Teacher! we raise
Our hearts and our voices in hymning Thy praise
For precept and promise so graciously given,—
For blessings of earth, and glories of Heaven.

J. N. Van Harlingen.

156

Jesus Christ, our Saviour.

PRINCETHORPE. 6, 5, 6, 5. D.

WM. PITTS.

1. Je-sus Christ, our Sav - iour, Once for us a child, In Thy whole be- hav - ior Meek, o - be-dient, mild; In Thy footsteps tread-ing We Thy lambs will be, Foe nor dan - ger dread - ing While we fol - low Thee. A - men.

2 For all Thou bestowest,
    All Thou dost withhold;
Whatsoe'er Thou knowest,
    Best for us, Thy fold;
For all gifts and graces
    While we live below,
Till in heavenly places
    We Thy face shall know.

3 We, Thy children, raising
    Unto Thee our hearts,
In Thy constant praising
    Bear our duteous parts.

As Thy love hath won us
    From the world away,
Still Thy hands put on us;
    Bless us day by day.

4 Let Thine angels guide us;
    Let Thine arms enfold;
In Thy bosom hide us,
    Sheltered from the cold;
To Thyself us gather,
    'Mid the ransomed host,
Praising Thee, the Father,
    And the Holy Ghost.

William Whiting, (1825–1878), 1860. *Abridged.*

O Saviour, Precious Saviour.

NORWICH. 7, 6, 7, 6. D.

ARTHUR H. MANN, (1850——).

1. O Sav - iour, pre - cious Sav - iour, Whom yet un - seen we love,

O Name of might and fa - vor, All oth - er names a - bove;

We wor - ship Thee, we bless Thee, To Thee a - lone we sing;

We praise Thee, and con - fess Thee, Our ho - ly Lord and King. A - men.

2 O Bringer of salvation,
    Who wondrously hast wrought,
Thyself the revelation
    Of love beyond our thought;
We worship Thee, we bless Thee,
    To Thee alone we sing;
We praise Thee, and confess Thee,
    Our gracious Lord and King.

3 In Thee all fullness dwelleth,
    All grace and power divine;
The glory that excelleth,
    O Son of God, is Thine;

We worship Thee, we bless Thee,
    To Thee alone we sing;
We praise Thee, and confess Thee,
    Our glorious Lord and King.

4 O grant the consummation
    Of this our song above,
In endless adoration,
    And everlasting love;
Then shall we praise and bless Thee,
    Where perfect praises ring,
And evermore confess Thee,
    Our Saviour and our King.

Frances Ridley Havergal, (1836–1879)

158

Saviour, Teach Me Day by Day.

FERRIER. 7, 7, 7, 7.

J. B. DYKES, (1823–1876).

1. Sav - iour, teach me day by day, Love's sweet les - son to o - bey; Sweet - er les - son can - not be, Lov - ing Him who first loved me. A - men.

2 With a childlike heart of love,
At Thy bidding may I move;
Prompt to serve and follow Thee,
Loving Him who first loved me.

3 Teach me all Thy steps to trace,
Strong to follow in Thy grace;
Learning how to love from Thee,
Loving Him who first loved me.

4 Love in loving finds employ,
In obedience all her joy;
Ever new that joy will be,
Loving Him who first loved me.

5 Thus may I rejoice to show
That I feel the love I owe;
Singing, till Thy face I see,
Of His love who first loved me.

Jane Elizabeth Leeson, 1842. Alt. and abridged

159

Singing for Jesus.

BROMHAM. 10, 10, 10, 10.

T. R. MATTHEWS, 1886.

1. Sing-ing for Je-sus, our Saviour and King, Sing-ing for Je-sus, the Lord whom we love; All ad-o-ra-tion we joy-ous-ly bring, Long-ing to praise as they praise Him a-bove. A-men.

2 Singing for Jesus, and trying to win
　Many to love Him, and join in the song;
Calling the weary and wandering in,
　Rolling the chorus of gladness along.

3 Singing for Jesus, our Shepherd and Guide,
　Singing for gladness of heart that He gives;
Singing for wonder and praise that He died,
　Singing for blessing and joy that He lives.

4 Singing for Jesus—yes, singing for joy;
　Thus will we praise Him and tell out His love,
Till He shall call us to brighter employ,
　Singing for Jesus, for ever above.

Frances R. Havergal.

160

Thou that art the Father's Word.

AL DEN GANSKE KRISTENHED. 7, 7, 7, 7, 7, 7, 5.   G. MATTHISON—HANSEN.

1. Thou that art the Fa-ther's Word, Thou that art the Lamb of God,

Thou that art the Vir-gin's Son, Thou that sav-est souls un-done,

Sa-cred Sac-ri-fice for sin, Fount of pi-e-ty with-in;

Hail, hail, Lord Je - sus! A - men.

2 Thou to whom the angels raise
   Choiring songs of sweetest praise,
   Thou that art the Flower and Fruit,
   Virgin born from Jesse's root,
     Shedding holy peace abroad,
     Perfect Man and perfect God;
       Hail, hail, Lord Jesus!

3 Thou that art the God of heaven,
   Living Bread in mercy given,
   Brightness of the Father's face,
   Everlasting Prince of Peace,

   Precious Pearl beyond all price,
   Brightest Star in all the skies;
     Hail, hail, Lord Jesus!

4 King and Spouse of holy hearts,
   Fount of love that ne'er departs,
   Sweetest Life and brightest Day,
   Truest Truth and surest Way,
     That leads onward to the blest
     Sabbath of eternal rest:
       Hail, hail, Lord Jesus!

Dean H. Alford, 1867.

161

I Know that my Redeemer Lives!

REDEEMER. L. M.

ADAPTED FROM K. WONNBERGER.

1. I know that my Re-deem-er lives! What com-fort this sweet sen-tence gives! He lives, He lives, who once was dead, He lives, my ev-er-liv-ing Head. A-men.

2 He lives to bless me with His Love,
He lives to plead for me above,
He lives my hungry soul to feed,
He lives to help in time of need.

3 He lives to grant me rich supply,
He lives to guide me with His eye,
He lives to comfort me when faint,
He lives to hear my soul's complaint.

4 He lives to silence all my fears,
He lives to wipe away my tears,

He lives to calm my troubled heart,
He lives all blessings to impart.

5 He lives, and grants me daily breath;
He lives, and I shall conquer death;
He lives, my mansion to prepare;
He lives, to bring me safely there.

6 He lives, all glory to His Name!
He lives, my Jesus, still the same;
O the sweet joy this sentence gives,
I know that my Redeemer lives!

From Samuel Medley, 1800.

269

162

We Sing a Loving Jesus.

THANET. 7, 6, 7, 6. D.

Voices in unison.

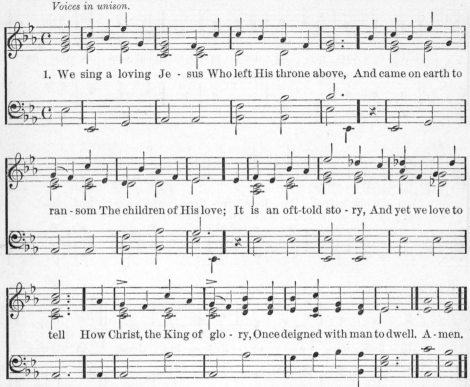

1. We sing a loving Je - sus Who left His throne above, And came on earth to ran - som The children of His love; It is an oft-told sto - ry, And yet we love to tell How Christ, the King of glo - ry, Once deigned with man to dwell. A - men.

2 We sing a holy Jesus;
　No taint of sin defiled
The Babe of David's City.
　The pure and stainless child:
O teach us, blessed Saviour,
　Thy heavenly grace to seek,
And let our whole behaviour,
　Like Thine, be mild and meek.

3 We sing a lowly Jesus,
　No kingly crown He had;
His heart was bowed with anguish,
　His face was marred and sad;
In deep humiliation
　He came, His work to do;
O Lord of our salvation,
　Let us be humble too.

4 We sing a mighty Jesus,
　Whose voice could raise the dead;
The sightless eyes He opened,
　The famished souls He fed.
Thou camest to deliver
　Mankind from sin and shame;
Redeemer and life giver,
　We praise Thy holy Name!

5 We sing a coming Jesus;
　The time is drawing near,
When Christ with all His Angels
　In glory shall appear;
Lord, save us, we entreat Thee,
　In this Thy day of grace,
That we may gladly meet Thee,
　And see Thee face to face.

Sarah Daneney, 1871.

In Thee is Gladness.

IN DIR IST FREUDE.

GIOVANNI GIACOMO GASTOLDO, 1591.

1. In Thee is glad-ness A-mid all sad-ness, Je-sus, sunshine of the heart.
By Thee are giv-en The gifts of heav-en, Thou the true Re-deem-er art.

Our souls Thou wak-est, Our bonds Thou break-est, Who trusts Thee sure-ly,

D.S.—Our hearts are pin-ing To see Thy shin-ing, Dy-ing or liv-ing.

Hath built se-cure-ly, He stands for-ev-er: Hal-le-lu-jah! A-men.

To Thee are cleaving, Naught can us sev-er: Hal-le-lu-jah!

2 If He is ours
We fear no powers,
Nor of earth, nor sin, nor death,
He sees and blesses
In worst distresses,
He can change them with a breath.
Wherefore the story
Tell of His glory
With heart and voices;

All heaven rejoices
In Him forever:
Hallelujah!
We shout for gladness,
Triumph o'er sadness,
Love Him and praise Him,
And still shall raise Him,
Glad hymns forever:
Hallelujah!

Dresden Gsgb., 1611. *Lindeman.*
Tr. Miss Catharine Winkworth, 1858.

164

Jesus, King of Glory.

ST. ALBAN. 6, 5, 6, 5. D. (*With Chorus.*)　　　　　　　HAYDN, 1775.

1. Je - sus, King of glo - ry, Throned a - bove the sky,

Je - sus, ten - der Sav - iour, Hear Thy chil - dren cry.

Par - don our trans - gres - sions, Cleanse us from our sin;

By Thy Spir - it help us Heav'n - ly life to win.

Jesus, King of Glory.—Concluded.

Je-sus, King of glo-ry, Throned a-bove the sky,

Je-sus, ten-der Sav-iour, Hear Thy chil-dren cry. A-men.

2 On this day of gladness,
    Bending low the knee
In Thine earthly temple,
    Lord, we worship Thee,—
Celebrate Thy goodness,
    Mercy, grace, and truth,
All the loving guidance
    Of our heedless youth.
        Jesus, King of glory, etc.

3 For the little children
    Who have come to Thee;
For the glad, bright spirits
    Who Thy glory see;
For the loved ones resting
    In Thy dear embrace;
For the pure and holy
    Who behold Thy face;
        Jesus, King of glory, etc.

4 For Thy faithful servants
    Who have entered in;
For Thy fearless soldiers
    Who have conquered sin;
For the countless legions
    Who have followed Thee,
Heedless of the danger,
    On to victory;
        Jesus, King of glory, etc.

5 Help us ever steadfast
    In the faith to be:
In Thy Church's conflicts
    Fighting valiantly.
Loving Saviour! strengthen
    These weak hearts of ours,
Through Thy cross to conquer
    Crafty evil powers.
        Jesus, King of glory, etc.

6 When the shadows lengthen,
    Show us, Lord, Thy way;
Through the darkness lead us
    To the heavenly day:
When our course is finished,
    Ended all the strife,
Grant us, with the faithful,
    Palms and crowns of life.
        Jesus, King of glory, etc.

E. Husband, 1863.

273

The Church Year: Whitsuntide.

165

Let Songs of Praises Fill the Sky.

PENTECOST. C. H. M.

Ad. Goss, 1854.

1. Let songs of prais-es fill the sky: Christ our as-cend-ed Lord, Sends down His

Spir-it from on high, Ac-cord-ing to His word: All hail the day of

Pen-te-cost, The com-ing of the Ho-ly Ghost! All hail the day of

Pen-te-cost, The com-ing of the Ho-ly Ghost! A-men.

Let Songs of Praises Fill the Sky.—Concluded.

2 The Spirit, by His heavenly breath,
Creates new life within;
He quickens sinners from the death
Of trespasses and sin:
‖: All hail the day of Pentecost,
The coming of the Holy Ghost! :‖

3 The things of Christ the Spirit takes,
And shows them unto men:
The fallen soul His temple makes;

God's image stamps again:
‖: All hail the day of Pentecost,
The coming of the Holy Ghost! :‖

4 Come, Holy Spirit, from above,
With Thy celestial fire;
Come, and with flames of zeal and love
Our hearts and tongues inspire!
‖: Be this our day of Pentecost,
The coming of the Holy Ghost! :‖

Thomas Cotterill, 1819.

166

Holy Ghost, With Light Divine.

MORGENSTERN, AUF FINSTRE NACHT. 7, 7, 7, 7.   MEININGEN GESANGBUCH, 1693.

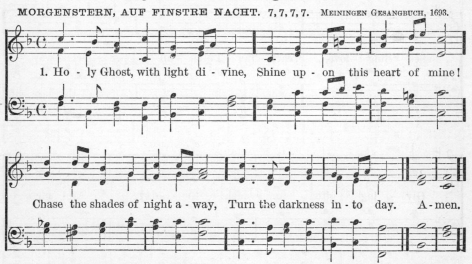

1. Ho - ly Ghost, with light di - vine, Shine up - on this heart of mine!

Chase the shades of night a - way, Turn the darkness in - to day.   A - men.

2 Let me see my Saviour's face,
Let me all His beauties trace;
Show those glorious truths to me,
Which are only known to Thee.

3 Holy Ghost, with power divine,
Cleanse this guilty heart of mine:
In Thy mercy pity me,
From sin's bondage set me free.

4 Holy Ghost, with joy divine,
Cheer this saddened heart of mine;

Yield a sacred, settled peace,
Let it grow and still increase.

5 Holy Spirit, all divine,
Dwell within this heart of mine;
Cast down every idle throne,
Reign supreme, and reign alone.

6 See, to Thee, I yield my heart;
Shed Thy life through every part.
A pure temple I would be,
Wholly dedicate to Thee.

Andrew Reed, 1842.

167

Thou, Who Camest From Above.

VIENNA. 7, 7, 7, 7.

JUSTIN HEINRICH KNECHT (1752–1817.)

1. Thou, Who cam-est from a-bove, Bring-ing light, and shed-ding love, Teach-ing Thine all-per-fect way, Giv-ing gifts to men to-day: A-men.

2 Thou Who changest our lost state,
Making us regenerate,
Help us evermore to be
Faithful subjects unto Thee.

3 Where Thou art not, none can do
What is holy, just and true;
Those whose hearts Thy wisdom leads
Think good thoughts and do good deeds.

4 We have often grieved Thee sore;
Never let us grieve Thee more.
Thou the feeble canst protect,
Thou the wandering canst direct.

5 We are dark—be Thou our Light
We are blind—be Thou our Sight.
Be our Comfort in distress,
Guide us through the wilderness.

6 To the blessed Three in One,
To the Father, and the Son,
And the Holy Ghost, arise
Praise from all below the skies.

John Mason Neale, 1844.

Spirit of Mercy, Truth, and Love.

MELCOMBE. L. M.

SAMUEL WEBBE, 1792.

1. Spir - it of mer - cy, truth, and love, O shed Thine in - fluence from a - bove; And still from age to age con - vey The won - ders of this sa - cred day. A - men.

2 In every clime, by every tongue,
Be God's surpassing glory sung:
Let all the listening earth be taught
The wonders by our Saviour wrought.

3 Unfailing Comfort, heavenly Guide,
Still o'er Thy holy Church preside;
Still let mankind Thy blessing prove;
Spirit of mercy, truth, and love.

Found. Hosp. Coll. **1774.**

169

Come, Holy Spirit, Come.

FRANCONIA. S. M. (*First tune.*)

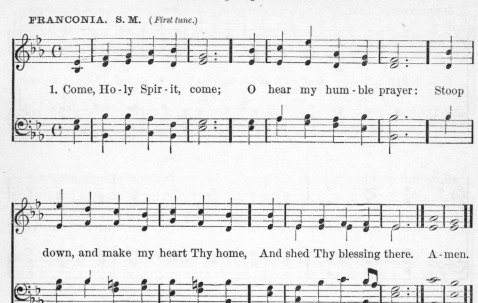

1. Come, Ho-ly Spir-it, come; O hear my hum-ble prayer: Stoop

down, and make my heart Thy home, And shed Thy blessing there. A-men.

2 Thy light, Thy love impart,
  And let it ever be
A holy, humble, happy heart,
  A dwelling-place for Thee.

3 Let Thy rich grace increase,
  Through all my early days,
The fruits of righteousness and peace,
  To Thine eternal praise.

Dorothy A. Thrupp (1779—1847), 1835.

Come, Holy Spirit, Come.

NEWLAND. S. M. (*Second tune.*)   HENRY J. GAUNTLETT, (1806–1876).

1. Come, Ho-ly Spir-it, come; O hear my hum-ble prayer: Stoop

Come, Holy Spirit, Come.—Concluded.

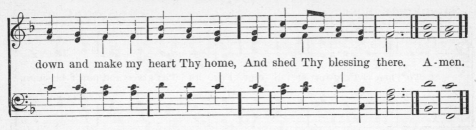

down and make my heart Thy home, And shed Thy blessing there. A-men.

170

Holy Spirit! Hear Us.

ST. LUCIAN. 6, 5, 6, 5.　　　　　　JOH. CHRIST. HEINR. RINK (1770—1846).

1. Ho - ly Spir - it! hear us On this sa - cred day;

Come to us with bless - ing, Come with us to stay. A - men.

2 Come, as once Thou camest
　To the faithful few,
　Patiently awaiting
　Jesus' promise true.

3 Up to heaven ascending
　Our dear Lord has gone;
　Yet His little children
　Leaves He not alone.

4 To His blessèd promise
　Now in faith we cling:—
　Comforter, most holy!
　Spread o'er us Thy wing.

5 Lighten Thou our darkness,
　Be Thyself our light;
　Strengthen Thou our weakness,
　Spirit of all might!

6 Spirit of adoption!
　Make us overflow
　With Thy sevenfold blessing,
　And in grace to grow.

7 Into Christ baptizèd
　Grant that we may be,
　Day and night, dear Spirit,
　Perfected by Thee!

171

To Thee, O Comforter Divine.

SUNDRIDGE. 8, 8, 6, 8, 8, 6.   WILLIAM C. FILBY, (1836 ——).

1. To Thee, O Com-fort-er di-vine, For all Thy grace and pow'r be-nign,

Sing we Al-le-lu-ia! To Thee, whose faith-ful love had place

In God's great cov-e-nant of grace, Sing we Al-le-lu-ia! A-men.

2 To Thee, whose faithful voice doth win
The wandering from the ways of sin,
   Sing we Alleluia!
To Thee, whose faithful power doth heal,
Enlighten, sanctify, and seal,
   Sing we Alleluia!

3 To Thee, whose faithful truth is shown
By every promise made our own,
   Sing we Alleluia!
To Thee, our Teacher and our Friend,
Our faithful Leader to the end,
   Sing we Alleluia!

4 To Thee, by Jesus Christ sent down,
Of all His gifts the sum and crown,
   Sing we Alleluia!
To Thee, who art with God the Son
And God the Father ever One,
   Sing we Alleluia!

Frances Ridley Havergal, (1836–1879), 1872.

Jesus is Glorified.

CROFT'S 148 PSALM. H. M.

WM. CROFT, 1703.

1. Je-sus is glo-ri-fied, And gives the Com-fort-er, His Spir-it, to re-side In all His mem-bers here: Re-joice, the Ho-ly Ghost is giv'n, Sent down by Je-sus Christ from heav'n. A-men.

2 He brings His kingdom in
    Peace, righteousness, and **joy,**
To make an end of sin,
    And Satan's works destroy:
Rejoice, the Holy Ghost is given,
Sent down by Jesus Christ from heaven.

3 Sent down to make us meet
    To see His glorious face,
And raise us to a seat
    In that thrice happy place:
Rejoice, the Holy Ghost is given,
Sent down by Jesus Christ from heaven.

4 Jesus from heaven once more
    In triumph shall descend,
And all His saints restore
    To joys that never end;
Then, then, when all our joys are **given,**
Shall we rejoice in God, in heaven.

J. Wesley. a.

281

THE CHURCH YEAR: TRINITY.

173 Holy, Holy, Holy, Lord God Almighty!

NICÆA. 11, 12, 11, 10.

J. B. DYKES, 1861.

1. Ho - ly, Ho - ly, Ho - ly, Lord God Al-might - y! Ear - ly in the morn - ing our song shall rise to Thee: Ho - ly, Ho - ly, Ho - ly, mer - ci - ful and might-y; God in Three Persons, Blessed Trini - ty! Amen.

2 Holy, Holy, Holy! all the saints adore Thee,
Casting down their golden crowns around the glassy sea;
Cherubim and Seraphim falling down before Thee,
Which wert, and art, and evermore shalt be.

3 Holy, Holy, Holy! though the darkness hide Thee,
Though the eye of sinful man Thy glory may not see,
Only Thou art holy : there is none beside Thee
Perfect in power, in love, and purity.

4 Holy, Holy, Holy, Lord God Almighty!
All Thy works shall praise Thy Name, in earth, and sky, and sea:
Holy, Holy, Holy! merciful and mighty;
God in Three Persons, Blessed Trinity!

Reginald Heber, 1827.

Blessed Father! Great Creator!

REGENT SQUARE. 8, 7, 8, 7, 4, 7.

HENRY SMART, 1867.

1. Bless-ed Fa-ther! Great Cre-a-tor! Hum-bly at Thy feet we bend;

To Thy throne for all Thy fa-vors, Youth-ful prais-es now we send.

Bless-ed Father! Bless-ed Father! To our youthful songs at-tend. A-men.

2 Blessed Jesus! Great Redeemer!
   Sadly by Thy Cross we stand;
On that Cross Thou diedst to bring us
To the joys of Thy right hand.
   Blessed Jesus!
Bring us to Thy heavenly land.

3 Blessed Spirit! Great Consoler!
   Make our hearts Thy dwelling place;
Teach us, guide us, sanctify us,
And console us all our days.
   Blessed Spirit!
Ever cheer us with Thy grace.

4 Blessed Father, Son, and Spirit,
   Glorious Godhead, Three in One!
Guide us to the heaven of heavens,
Through the merits of the Son.
   Guide and guard us,
Till we see Him on the throne.

John Cawood, 1837.

175

Come, Thou Almighty King.

ITALIAN HYMN. (MOSCOW.) 6, 6, 4, 6, 6, 6, 4.   FELICE DE GIARDINI, 1769.

1. Come, Thou al - might - y King, Help us Thy Name to sing,
Help us to praise! Fa - ther all glo - ri - ous, O'er all vic -
to - ri - ous, Come and reign o - ver us, An - cient of days. A - men.

2 Jesus, our Lord, descend;
  From all our foes defend,
    Nor let us fall;
  Let Thine almighty aid
  Our sure defence be made;
  Our souls on Thee be stayed;
    Lord, hear our call!

3 Come, Thou incarnate Word,
  Gird on Thy mighty sword,
    Our prayer attend:
  Come, and Thy people bless,
  And give Thy word success;
  Spirit of holiness,
    On us descend.

4 Come, holy Comforter,
  Thy sacred witness bear
    In this glad hour:
  Thou who almighty art,
  Now rule in every heart,
  And ne'er from us depart,
    Spirit of power!

5 To the great One in Three
  Eternal praises be,
    Hence, evermore!
  His sovereign Majesty
  May we in glory see
  And to eternity
    Love and adore

Glory be to God the Father!

ST. PETER'S WESTMINSTER. 8, 7, 8, 7, 8, 7.   J. TURLE.

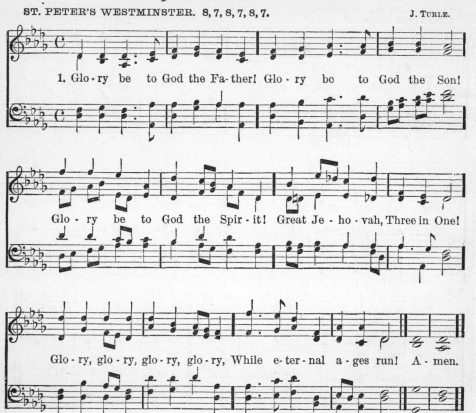

1. Glo-ry be to God the Fa-ther! Glo-ry be to God the Son!

Glo-ry be to God the Spir-it! Great Je-ho-vah, Three in One!

Glo-ry, glo-ry, glo-ry, glo-ry, While e-ter-nal a-ges run! A-men.

2 Glory be to Him who loved us,
    Washed us from each spot and stain!
Glory be to Him who bought us,
    Made us kings with Him to reign!
    Glory, glory, glory, glory,
    To the Lamb that once was slain!

3 Glory to the King of angels!
    Glory to the Church's King.
Glory to the King of nations!
    Heaven and earth your praises bring;
    Glory, glory, glory, glory,
    To the King of glory bring!

4 Glory, blessing, praise eternal!
    Thus the choir of angels sings;
Honor, riches, power, dominion!
    Thus its praise creation brings;
    Glory, glory, glory, glory,
    Glory to the King of kings!

Horatius Bonar, (1808–1889), 1867.

177

The God Who Reigns on High.

LEONI. 6, 6, 8, 4. D.

JEWISH MELODY.

1. The God who reigns on high, The great arch-an-gels sing, And "Ho-ly, ho-ly, ho-ly," cry, "Al-might-y King! Who was and is the same, And ev-er-more shall be; Je-ho-vah, Fa-ther, great I Am, We wor-ship Thee." A-men.

The God Who Reigns on High.—Concluded.

2 Before the Saviour's face
  The ransomed nations bow,
O'erwhelmed at His almighty grace,
    For ever new:
  He shows His prints of love;
  They kindle to a flame,
And sound, through all the worlds above,
  The slaughtered Lamb.

3 The whole triumphant host
  Give thanks to God on high;
"Hail, Father, Son, and Holy Ghost!"
    They ever cry:
  Hail, Abraham's God, and mine!
  I join the heavenly lays;
All might and majesty are Thine,
  And endless praise.

Thomas Olivers, 1772.

178

Glory to the Father Give.

DAY BY DAY. 7, 7, 7, 7.   E. S. CARTER.

1. Glo-ry to the Fa-ther give, God in whom we move and live;

Children's pray'rs He deigns to hear, Children's songs delight His ear. A men.

2 Glory to the Son we bring,
Christ our Prophet, Priest and King;
Children, raise your sweetest strain
To the Lamb, for He was slain.

3 Glory to the Holy Ghost,
Who reclaims the sinner lost;
Children's minds may He inspire,
Touch their tongues with holy fire.

4 Glory in the highest be
To the blessèd Trinity,
For the gospel from above,
For the word that God is love.

James Montgomery, (1771—1854).

179

Holy, Holy, Holy, Lord.

ST. ATHANASIUS. 7, 7, 7, 7, 7, 7.

E. J. HOPKINS.

1. Ho - ly, ho - ly, ho - ly, Lord God of hosts, e - ter - nal King, By the heav'ns and earth a - dored; An - gels and arch - an - gels sing, Chant - ing ev - er - last - ing - ly To the bless-ed Trin - i - ty. A - men.

2 Since by Thee were all things made,
  And in Thee do all things live,
Be to Thee all honor paid,
  Praise to Thee let all things give,
Singing everlastingly
To the blessed Trinity.

3 Thousands, tens of thousands stand,
  Spirits blest before Thy throne,
Speeding thence at Thy command;
  And when Thy command is done,
Singing everlastingly
To the blessed Trinity.

4 Cherubim and seraphim
  Veil their faces with their wings;
Eyes of angels are too dim

To behold the King of kings,
While they sing eternally
To the blessed Trinity.

5 Thee, apostles, prophets Thee,
  Thee, the noble martyr band,
Praise with solemn jubilee,
  Thee, the Church in every land;
Singing everlastingly
To the blessed Trinity.

6 Alleluia! Lord to Thee
  Father, Son, and Holy Ghost,
Three in One, and One in Three,
  Join we with the heavenly host,
Singing everlastingly
To the blessed Trinity.

C. Wordsworth, 1862.

THE CHURCH: FOUNDATION AND NATURE.

The Church's One Foundation.

WEBB. 7, 6, 7, 6. D.

G. J. WEBB.

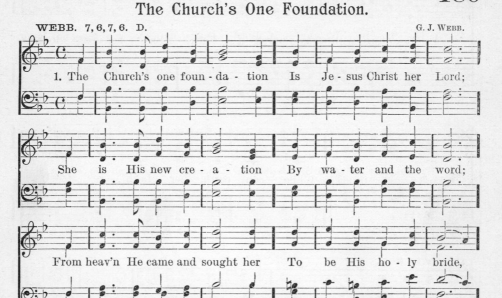

1. The Church's one foun-da-tion Is Je-sus Christ her Lord;
She is His new cre-a-tion By wa-ter and the word;
From heav'n He came and sought her To be His ho-ly bride,
With His own blood He bought her, And for her life He died. A-men.

2 Elect from every nation,
  Yet one o'er all the earth,
Her charter of salvation
  One Lord, one Faith, one Birth:
One holy Name she blesses,
  Partakes one holy food,
And to one hope she presses,
  With every grace endued.

3 Though with a scornful wonder
  Men see her sore opprest,
By schisms rent asunder,
  By heresies distrest,

Yet saints their watch are keeping,
  Their cry goes up, "How long?"
And soon the night of weeping
  Shall be the morn of song.

4 'Mid toil, and tribulation,
  And tumult of her war,
She waits the consummation
  Of peace for evermore;
Till with the vision glorious
  Her longing eyes are blest,
And the great Church victorious
  Shall be the Church at rest.

S. J. Stone, 1868.

181

Jesus, With Thy Church Abide.

LITANY. 7, 7, 7, 6.   W. H. MONK.

1. Jesus, with Thy Church abide, Be her Saviour, Lord and Guide While on earth her faith is tried: We beseech Thee, hear us. Amen.

2 Arms of love around her throw,
Shield her safe from every foe,
Comfort her in time of woe:
    We beseech Thee, hear us.

3 Keep her life and doctrine pure,
Grant her patience to endure,
Trusting in Thy promise sure:
    We beseech Thee, hear us.

4 May she one in doctrine be,
One in truth and charity,
Winning all to faith in Thee:
    We beseech Thee, hear us.

5 May she guide the poor and blind,
Seek the lost until she find,
And the broken-hearted bind:
    We beseech Thee, hear us.

6 May she soon all glorious be,
Spotless and from wrinkle free,
Pure, and bright, and worthy Thee:
    We beseech Thee, hear us.

7 Fit her all Thy joy to share
In the home Thou dost prepare,
And be ever blessèd there:
    We beseech Thee, hear us.

Thomas Benson Pollock, (1836 ——).
Abridged.

I Love Thy Zion, Lord.

ST. THOMAS. S. M.

A. WILLIAMS.

1. I love Thy Zi - on, Lord; The house of Thine a - bode; The Church our blest Re - deem - er sav'd With His own pre - cious Blood. A - men.

2 I love Thy Church, O God!
  Her walls before Thee stand,
Dear as the apple of Thine eye,
  And graven on Thy hand.

3 For her my tears shall fall;
  For her my prayers ascend:
To her my cares and toils be given,
  Till toils and cares shall end.

4 Beyond my highest joy
  I prize her heavenly ways,
Her sweet communion, solemn vows,
  Her hymns of love and praise.

5 Jesus, Thou Friend divine,
  Our Saviour and our King,
Thy hand from every snare and foe,
  Shall great deliverance bring.

6 Sure as Thy truth shall last,
  To Zion shall be given
The brightest glories earth can yield,
  And brighter bliss of heaven.

Timothy Dwight, 1800. *a.*

THE CHURCH: REFORMATION.

183

Glorious Things of Thee are Spoken.

AUSTRIA. 8, 7, 8, 7. D. (*First tune.*)   HAYDN, 1797.

1. Glo - rious things of thee are spo - ken, Zi - on, cit - y of our God;

He, whose word can - not be bro - ken, Form'd thee for His own a - bode;

On the Rock of A - ges found-ed, What can shake thy sure re - pose?

With sal - va-tion's walls surrounded, Thou may'st smile at all thy foes. A - men

Glorious Things of Thee are Spoken.—Concluded.

2 See the streams of living waters
　Springing from eternal love,
Well supply thy sons and daughters,
　And all fear of want remove.
Who can faint while such a river
　Ever flows their thirst to assuage?
Grace, which, like the Lord, the Giver,
　Never fails from age to age.

3 Saviour, if of Zion's city
　I, through grace, a member am,
Let the world deride or pity,
　I will glory in Thy Name.
Fading is the worldling's pleasure,
　All his boasted pomp and show;
Solid joys and lasting treasure
　None but Zion's children know.

John Newton, 1779.

Glorious Things of Thee are Spoken.

HARWELL. 8, 7, 8, 7. D. (*Second tune.*)　　　　L. MASON.

1. { Glo-rious things of thee are spo-ken, Zi-on, cit-y of our God; }
{ He, whose word can-not be bro-ken, Form'd thee for His own a-bode. }

On the Rock of A-ges founded, What can shake thy sure re-pose?

With sal-va-tion's walls surrounded, Thou may'st smile at all thy foes. A-men.

184

A Mighty Fortress is Our God.

EIN FESTE BURG IST UNSER GOTT.   MARTIN LUTHER (1483—1546), 1529.

1. A mighty For-tress is   our God,   A trust-y Shield and Weap - on;
2. With might of ours can naught be done, Soon were our loss ef - fect - ed;

He helps us free from ev - 'ry need That hath us now o'er - tak - en.
But for us fights the Val - iant One Whom God Himself e - lect - ed.

The old   bit - ter foe Means us dead - ly woe: Deep guile and great might
Ask ye,   Who is this? Je - sus Christ it is,   Of Sab - a - oth   Lord,

Are his dread arms in fight,   On earth is   not his e - qual.
And there's none oth - er God; He holds the field for ev - er.

A Mighty Fortress is Our God.—Concluded.

3 Though devils all the world should fill,
   All watching to devour us,
We tremble not, we fear no ill,
   They cannot overpower us.
      This world's prince may still
      Scowl fierce as he will,
      He can harm us none,
      He's judged, the deed is done,
   One little word o'erthrows him.

4 The Word they still shall let **remain**,
   And not a thank have for it,
He's by our side upon the plain,
   With His good gifts and Spirit,
      Take they then our life,
      Goods, fame, child and wife;
      When their worst is done,
      They yet have nothing won,
   The Kingdom ours remaineth.

Martin Luther, 1528.

Zion Stands With Hills Surrounded. 185

O JERUSALEM, DU SCHŒNE. 8, 7, 8, 7, 4, 7. J. G. C. STOERL, 1711.

1. Zi - on stands with hills sur-rounded; Zi - on kept by pow'r di - vine;

All her foes shall be con-founded, Tho' the world in arms com - bine.

Hap - py Zi - on, What a fa - vored lot is thine! A - men.

2 Every human tie may perish;
   Friend to friend unfaithful prove;
Mothers cease their own to cherish;
   Heaven and earth at last remove:
      But no changes
   Can attend Jehovah's love.

3 In the furnace God may prove thee,
   Thence to bring thee forth more bright,
But can never cease to love thee;
   Thou art precious in His sight:
      God is with thee,
   God, thine everlasting Light.

T. Kelly, 1806.

186

My Church! My Church!

ATHENS. C. M. D. (*First tune.*)

F. GIARDINI.

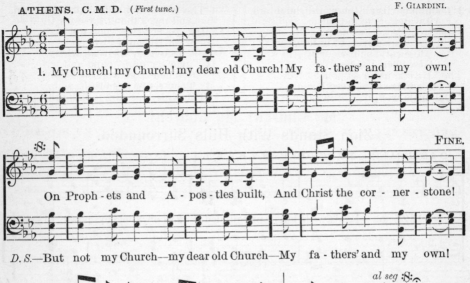

1. My Church! my Church! my dear old Church! My fa - thers' and my own!

On Proph - ets and A - pos - tles built, And Christ the cor - ner - stone!

FINE.

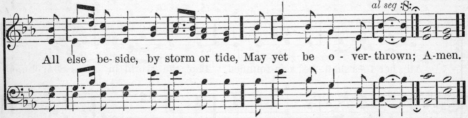

D. S.—But not my Church—my dear old Church—My fa - thers' and my own!

All else be - side, by storm or tide, May yet be o - ver - thrown; A - men.

2 My Church! my Church! my dear old Church!
My glory and my pride!
Firm in the Faith Immanuel taught,
She holds no faith beside.
Upon this Rock, 'gainst every shock,
Though gates of hell assail,
She stands secure, with promise sure,
"They never shall prevail."

3 My Church! my Church! my dear old Church!
I love her ancient name;
And God forbid, a child of hers
Should ever do her shame!
Her mother-care, I'll ever share;
Her child I am alone,
Till He who gave me to her arms
Shall call me to His own.

4 My Church! my Church! my dear old Church!
I've heard the tale of blood,
Of hearts that loved her to the death—
The great, the wise, the good.
Our martyred sires defied the fires
For Christ the crucified;
The once delivered Faith to keep,
They burned, they bled, they died.

5 My Church! my Church! I love my Church!
For she exalts my Lord!
She speaks, she breathes, she teaches not,
But from His written Word.
And if her voice bids me rejoice,
From all my sins released;
'Tis through the atoning sacrifice,
And Jesus is the Priest.

My Church! My Church!—Concluded.

6 My Church! my Church! I love my
  For she doth lead me on   [Church!
To Zion's Palace Beautiful,
  Where Christ the Lord hath gone.
From all below, she bids me go,
  To Him, the Life, the Way,
The Truth to guide my erring feet
  From darkness into day.

7 Then here, my Church! my dear old
  Thy child would add a vow, [Church!
To that whose token once was signed
  Upon his infant brow:—
Assault who may, kiss and betray,
  Dishonor and disown,
My Church shall yet be dear to me,
  My fathers' and my own!

My Church! My Church!

EPIPHANY. C. M. D. (*Second tune.*)   E. J. HOPKINS.

1. My Church! my Church! my dear old Church! My fa-thers' and my own!

On Proph-ets and A-pos-tles built, And Christ the cor-ner-stone!

All else be-side, by storm or tide, May yet be o-ver-thrown;

But not my Church—my dear old Church—My fa-thers' and my own! A-men.

187

Jehovah, Thee to Praise.

AMERICA. 6, 6, 4, 6, 6, 6, 4.

HANDEL.
ADAPTED BY HENRY CAREY, 1739.

1. Je - ho - vah, Thee to praise In all Thy wondrous ways, Teach us this hour.

Thy voice the Church a - woke Thy hand her fet - ters broke,

Through Thee her Cham - pion spoke, Thy Word His power. A - men.

2 Shepherd of souls abide
   Thy faithful people's guide,
      Fresh pasture give.
   Faith in Thy saving grace,
   Faith in Thy will to bless,
   Be this our righteousness,
      In Thee we live.

3 O Spirit, Comforter,
   On us Thy gift confer
      All truth to see;
   And, where the ways divide,
   Do Thou our paths decide,
   Thus shall we, sanctified,
      Still walk in Thee.

Harriett R. Spaeth, 1883.

THE CHURCH: MISSIONS.

Thou, Whose Almighty Word.

188

DORT. 6, 6, 4, 6, 6, 6, 4.

L. MASON.

Thou, whose al-might-y word Cha-os and darkness heard, And took their flight;
Hear us, we hum-bly pray; And where the Gos-pel day
Sheds not its glo-rious ray, Let there be light! A-men.

2 Thou, who didst come to bring,
On Thy redeeming wing,
    Healing and sight,
Health to the sick in mind,
Sight to the inly-blind,
O, now to all mankind
    Let there be light!

3 Spirit of truth and love,
Life-giving, holy Dove,
    Speed forth Thy flight;

Move on the waters' face,
Bearing the lamp of grace,
And in earth's darkest place
    Let there be light!

4 Holy and blessed Three,
Glorious Trinity,
    Wisdom, Love, Might!
Boundless as ocean's tide
Rolling in fullest pride,
Through the earth, far and wide,
    Let there be light!

J. Marriott, 1813.

189

From Greenland's Icy Mountains.

MISSIONARY HYMN. 7, 6, 7, 6. D.

L. MASON.

1. From Greenland's i - cy moun - tains, From In - dia's cor - al strand,

Where Af - ric's sun - ny foun - tains, Roll down their gold - en sand;

From many an an - cient riv - er, From many a palm - y plain,

They call us to de - liv - er Their land from er - ror's chain. A - men.

From Greenland's Icy Mountains.—Concluded.

2 What though the spicy breezes
  Blow soft o'er Ceylon's isle;
Though every prospect pleases,
  And only man is vile;
In vain with lavish kindness
  The gifts of God are strown:
The heathen in his blindness,
  Bows down to wood and stone.

3 Shall we, whose souls are lighted
  With wisdom from on high,
Shall we to men benighted
  The lamp of life deny?

Salvation, O salvation!
  The joyful sound proclaim,
Till each remotest nation
  Has learned Messiah's Name.

4 Waft, waft, ye winds, His story,
  And you, ye waters, roll,
Till, like a sea of glory,
  It spreads from pole to pole;
Till o'er our ransomed nature
  The Lamb for sinners slain,
Redeemer, King, Creator,
  In bliss returns to reign.

Reginald Heber, 1819.

190

Hasten, Lord, the Glorious Time.

BETHLEHEM. 7, 7, 7, 7.   C. KOCHER, 1837.

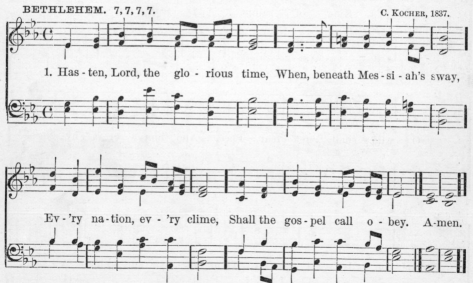

1. Has - ten, Lord, the glo - rious time, When, beneath Mes - si - ah's sway,

Ev - 'ry na - tion, ev - 'ry clime, Shall the gos - pel call o - bey. A - men.

2 Mightiest kings His power shall own,
  Heathen tribes His Name adore;
Satan and his host, o'erthrown,
  Bound in chains shall hurt no more.

3 Then shall war and tumult cease,
  Then be banished grief and pain;
Righteousness and joy and peace
  Undisturbed shall ever reign.

4 Bless we, then, our gracious Lord,
  Ever praise His glorious Name;
All His mighty acts record,
  All His wondrous Love proclaim.

Harriet Auber.

191

How Wondrous and Great.

LYONS. 5, 5, 5, 5, 5, 5, 6, 5.

HAYDN, 1770.

1. How won-drous and great Thy works, God of praise!
How just, King of saints, And true are Thy ways!
O who shall not fear Thee, And hon-or Thy Name?
Thou on-ly art ho-ly, Thou on-ly su-preme. A men.

2 To nations long dark
  Thy light shall be shown;
Their worship and vows
  Shall come to Thy throne:

Thy truth and Thy judgments
  Shall spread all abroad,
Till earth's every people
  Confess Thee their God.

H. U. Onderdonk, 1826.

302

Jesus Shall Reign Where'er the Sun.

DUKE STREET. L. M.

JOHN HATTON, 1800.

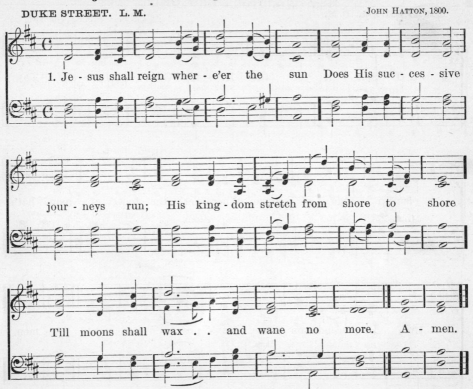

1. Je - sus shall reign wher - e'er the sun Does His suc - ces - sive jour - neys run; His king - dom stretch from shore to shore Till moons shall wax . . and wane no more. A - men.

2 For Him shall endless prayer be made,
And endless praises crown His head;
His Name, like sweet perfume, shall rise
With every morning sacrifice.

3 People and realms of every tongue
Dwell on His love with sweetest song:
And infant voices shall proclaim
Their early blessings on His Name.

4 Blessings abound where'er He reigns;
The prisoner leaps to lose his chains;
The weary find eternal rest,
And all the sons of want are blest.

5 Where He displays His healing power,
Death and the curse are known no more;
In Him the tribes of Adam boast
More blessings than their father lost.

6 Let every creature rise and bring
Peculiar honors to our King;
Angels descend with songs again,
And earth repeat the loud Amen.

Watts, 1719.

193

O Spirit of the Living God!

ROCKINGHAM. L. M.

E. MILLER.

1. O Spir-it of the liv-ing God! In all Thy plen-i-tude of grace, Wher-e'er the foot of man hath trod, De-scend on our a-pos-tate race! A-men.

2 Give tongues of fire and hearts of love,
  To preach the reconciling Word;
Give power and unction from above,
  Where'er the joyful sound is heard.

3 Be darkness, at Thy coming, light;
  Confusion, order, in Thy path;
Souls without strength inspire with might;
  Bid mercy triumph over wrath.

4 Baptize the nations; far and nigh
  The triumphs of the Cross record;
The Name of Jesus glorify,
  Till every kindred call Him Lord.

5 God from eternity hath willed,
  All flesh shall His salvation see;
So be the Father's Love fulfilled,
  The Saviour's sufferings crowned through Thee.

James Montgomery, 1825.

Happy Are We, God's Own Little Flock.

ST. ASAPH. 10, 10, 10, 7.

A. H. MANN.

1. Hap - py are we, God's own lit - tle flock, Shel - tered so close in the cleft of the Rock, Far a-bove tem-pest, or dan - ger or shock, Hap - py are we in Je - sus. A - men.

2 What shall we do for the Master so dear?
Oh, there are many in need of our cheer,
Souls that know nothing but darkness and **fear,**
Souls in the dark without Jesus.

3 Many He has who are not of this fold,
Out in the storm and the pitiless cold;
These we will win by our pray'rs and our **gold,**
Win them to love our Jesus.

4 Over the mountains and over the seas,
Lovingly, joyfully, speed we to these,
Seeking to save them by tenderest **pleas,**
Save by the blood of Jesus.

5 Joyfully, then, let us spread the glad **news,**
Never this service for Jesus refuse,
Never a moment to work for Him lose;
Joyfully work for Jesus.

Mrs. Herrick Johnson.

195

Lord of the Living Harvest.

SAINTS' DAYS. 7, 6, 7, 6. D.   SAMUEL SMITH.

1. Lord of the liv-ing har-vest That whit-en's o'er the plain,

Where an gels soon shall gath - er Their sheaves of gold - en grain;

Ac - cept these hands to la - bor, These hearts to trust and love,

And deign with them to hast - en Thy king-dom from a - bove. A - men.

2 As laborers in Thy vineyard
　Still faithful may we be,
Content to bear the burden
　Of weary days for Thee;
We ask no other wages,
　When Thou shalt call us home,
But to have shared the travail
　Which makes Thy kingdom come.

3 Come down, Thou Holy Spirit,
　And fill our hearts with light,
Clothe us in spotless raiment,
　In vestures clean and white;

Within Thy sacred temple
　Be with us where we stand,
And sanctify Thy people
　Throughout this happy land.

4 Be with us, God the Father!
　Be with us, God the Son!
And God the Holy Spirit!
　O blessèd Three in One!
Make us a royal priesthood,
　Thee rightly to adore,
And fill us with Thy fulness
　Both now and evermore.

J. S. B. Monsell, 1866.

Christ for the World we Sing.

DYB AF KJÆRLIGHED. 6, 6, 4, 6, 6, 6, 4.

J. P. E. HARTMAN.

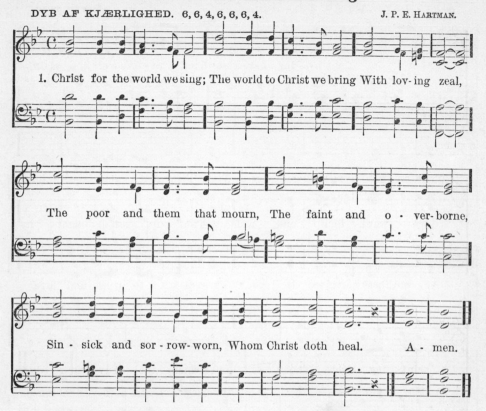

1. Christ for the world we sing; The world to Christ we bring With lov-ing zeal,

The poor and them that mourn, The faint and o-ver-borne,

Sin-sick and sor-row-worn, Whom Christ doth heal. A-men.

2 Christ for the world we sing;
The world to Christ we bring,
 With fervent prayer;
The wayward and the lost,
By restless passions tossed,
Redeemed at countless cost,
 From dark despair.

3 Christ for the world we sing;
The world to Christ we bring,
 With one accord;
With us the work to share,
With us reproach to dare,
With us the cross to bear,
 For Christ our Lord.

4 Christ for the world we sing;
The world to Christ we bring,
 With joyful song;
The new-born souls, whose days,
Reclaimed from error's ways,
Inspired with hope and praise,
 To Christ belong.

S. Wolcott, 1869.

197

Uplift the Banner! Let it Float.

1. Up - lift the ban - ner! Let it float Sky - ward and sea - ward, high and wide; The sun shall light its shin - ing folds, The Cross on which the Sav - iour died. Up - lift the ban - ner! An - gels bend, In

Uplift the Banner! Let it Float.—Concluded.

anx - ious si - lence, o'er the Sign; And vain - ly seek to

com - pre - hend The won - der of the love di - vine. A - men.

2 Uplift the banner! Let it float
   Skyward and seaward, high and wide;
Our glory only in the Cross,
   Our only hope the Crucified.
Uplift the banner! Heathen lands
   Shall see from far the glorious sight,
And nations, gathering at the call,
   Their spirits kindle in its light.

3 Uplift the banner! Wide and high,
   Skyward and seaward, let it shine:
Nor skill, nor might, nor merit ours,
   We conquer only in that Sign.
Uplift the banner! Sin-sick souls,
   That sink and perish in the strife,
Shall touch in faith its radiant hem,
   And spring immortal into life!

4 Uplift the banner! Manfully
   Conquer the foe by Jesus' might;
The faith which stirs the soldier's breast,
   Upholds the soldier in the fight.
Uplift the banner! All the foes
   Of earth or hell can ne'er prevail;
In vain shall they contend with us,
   For Jesus' promise cannot fail!

George W. Doane, (1799–1859), 1824.

198

Who Is On the Lord's Side?

SUMUS TIBI. 6, 5, 12 lines.

H. ELLIOT BUTTON.

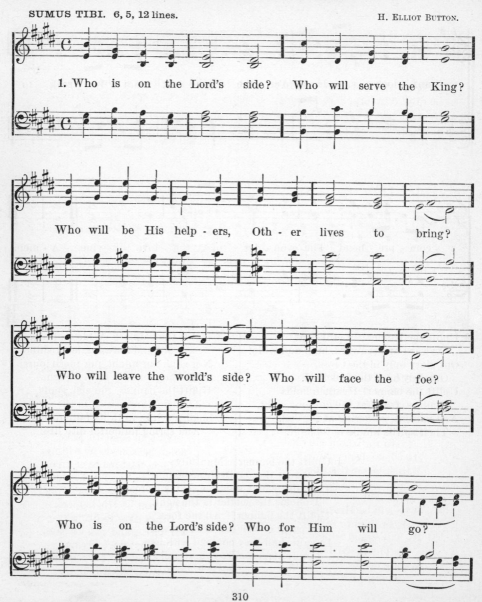

1. Who is on the Lord's side? Who will serve the King?

Who will be His help - ers, Oth - er lives to bring?

Who will leave the world's side? Who will face the foe?

Who is on the Lord's side? Who for Him will go?

Who Is On the Lord's Side?—Concluded.

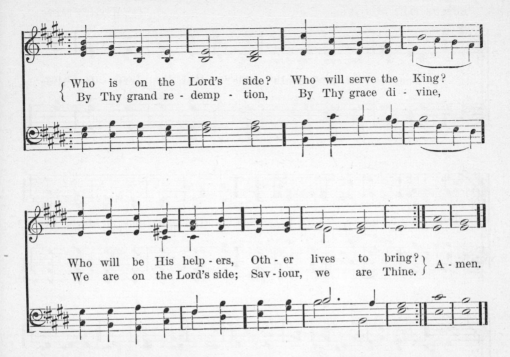

Who is on the Lord's side? Who will serve the King?
By Thy grand re - demp - tion, By Thy grace di - vine,

Who will be His help - ers, Oth - er lives to bring?
We are on the Lord's side; Sav - iour, we are Thine. } A - men.

2 Not for weight of glory,
   Not for crown and palm,
Enter we the army,
   Raise the warrior-psalm;
But for love that claimeth
   Lives for whom He died,
He whom Jesus nameth
   Must be on His side.
Who is on the Lord's side?
   Who will serve the King?
Who will be His helpers,
   Other lives to bring?
By Thy grand redemption,
   By Thy grace divine,
We are on the Lord's side;
   Saviour, we are Thine.

3 Jesus, Thou hast bought us,
   Not with gold or gem,
But with Thine own life-blood,
   For Thy diadem;
With Thy blessing filling
   All who come to Thee,
Thou hast made us willing,
   Thou hast made us free.
Who is on the Lord's side?
   Who will serve the King?
Who will be His helpers,
   Other lives to bring?
By Thy grand redemption,
   By Thy grace divine,
We are on the Lord's side;
   Saviour, we are Thine.

Frances Ridley Havergal.

199

Tell it Out Among the Heathen.

P. M.

FREDERICK STEVENSON.

1. Tell it out a-mong the heathen that the Lord is King!

Tell it out! Tell it out! Tell it out a-mong the

nations; bid them shout and sing! Tell it out! Tell it out! Tell it

out with ad - o - ra-tion that He shall in-crease, That the might-y King of

Tell it Out Among the Heathen.—Concluded.

Glo-ry is the King of Peace; Tell it out with ju-bi-la-tion, tho' the waves may roar, That He sit-teth on the wa-ter-floods, our King for ev-er-more! Tell it out! Tell it out! A-men.

2 Tell it out among the heathen that the
    Saviour reigns;
  Tell it out! Tell it out!
Tell it out among the nations, bid them
    burst their chains;
  Tell it out! Tell it out!
'Tell it out among the weeping ones that
    Jesus lives;
Tell it out among the weary what sweet
    rest He gives;
Tell it out among the sinners that He
    came to save;
Tell it out among the dying that He tri-
    umphed o'er the grave.
  Tell it out! Tell it out!

3 Tell it out among the heathen, Jesus
    reigns above;
  Tell it out! Tell it out!
Tell it out among the nations that His
    reign is love;
  Tell it out! Tell it out!
Tell it out among the highways and the
    lanes at home;
Let it ring across the mountains and the
    ocean foam;
Like the sound of many waters let the
    glad shout be,
Till it echo and re-echo from the islands
    of the sea.
  Tell it out! Tell it out!

Frances Ridley Havergal, (1836–1879). 1872.

200

O Zion Haste.

O ZION HASTE. 11, 10, 11, 10. D. (*With Chorus.*)   Geo. C. F. Haas.

1. O Zi - on haste, thy mis - sion high ful - fill - ing, To tell to

all the world that God is Light; That He who made all na-tions is not will-ing,

One soul should per-ish, lost in shades of night. Be - hold how ma - ny

thousands still are ly - ing Bound in the dark - some prison-house of sin,

O Zion Haste.—Concluded.

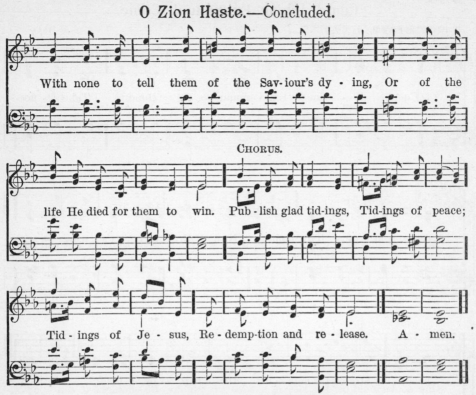

With none to tell them of the Sav-iour's dy - ing, Or of the

CHORUS.

life He died for them to win. Pub - lish glad tid-ings, Tid-ings of peace;

Tid - ings of Je - sus, Re - demp-tion and re - lease. A - men.

2 'Tis thine to save from peril of perdition
   The souls for whom the Lord His life laid down;
Beware lest, slothful to fulfill thy mission,
   Thou lose one jewel that should deck His crown.
Proclaim to every people, tongue and nation,
   That God, in whom they live and move, is love;
Tell, how He stooped to save His lost creation,
   And died on earth that man might live above.
      Publish glad tidings, etc.

3 Give of thy sons to bear the message glorious;
   Give of thy wealth to speed them on their way;
Pour out thy soul for them in prayer victorious;
   And all thou spendest Jesus will repay,
He comes again—O Zion, ere thou meet Him,
   Make known to every heart His saving grace;
Let none whom He hath ransomed fail to greet Him,
   Through thy neglect, unfit to see His face.
      Publish glad tidings, etc.
                                    M. A. Thomas. a.

201

Come, Divine Emmanuel, Come.

LOWESTOFT. 7, 7, 7, 7.

1. Come, di - vine Em - manu - el, come, Take pos -
ses - sion of Thy home; Now thy mer - cy's wings ex -
pand, Stretch through - out the hap - py land. A - men.

2 Carry on Thy victory,
  Spread Thy rule from sea to sea;
  Rescue all Thy ransomed race,
  Save us, save us, Lord, by grace.

3 Take the purchase of Thy Blood,
  Bring us to a pardoning God:
  Give us eyes to see our day,
  Hearts the Gospel truth to obey:

4 Ears to hear the Gospel sound,—
  Grace doth more than sin abound;
  God appeased, and man forgiven,
  Peace on earth, and joy in heaven.

5 O that every soul might be
  Perfectly subdued to Thee!
  O that all in Thee might know
  Everlasting life below!

6 Now Thy mercy's wings expand,
  Stretch throughout the happy land:
  Take possession of Thy home;
  Come, divine Emmanuel, come!

C. Wesley, 1749. *a.*

316

THE WORD OF GOD.

Lord of All Power and Might.

202

FIAT LUX. 6, 6, 4, 6, 6, 6, 4.

J. B. DYKES.

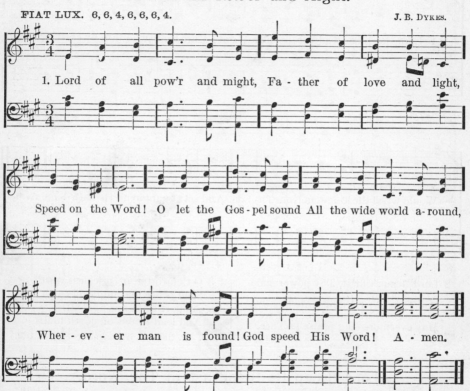

1. Lord of all pow'r and might, Fa-ther of love and light,
Speed on the Word! O let the Gos-pel sound All the wide world a-round,
Wher-ev-er man is found! God speed His Word! A-men.

2 On this high Jubilee
  Thine let the glory be:
    Hallelujah!
  Thine was the mighty plan,
  From Thee the work began:
  Away with praise to man.
    Glory to God!

3 Lo! what embattled foes,
  Stern in their hate, oppose
    God's holy Word;
  One for His truth we stand,
Strong in His own right hand,
Firm as a martyr band.
  God shield His Word!

4 Onward shall be our course,
  Despite of fraud and force;
    God is before:
  His Word ere long shall run
  Free as the noon-day sun;
  His purpose must be done:
    God bless His Word!

Hugh Stowell, 1858.

203

Lord, Keep Us Steadfast in Thy Word.

ERHALT UNS, HERR, BEI DEINEM WORT. L. M. (*First tune.*)

"GEISTLICHE LIEDER," WITTENBERG, 1543.

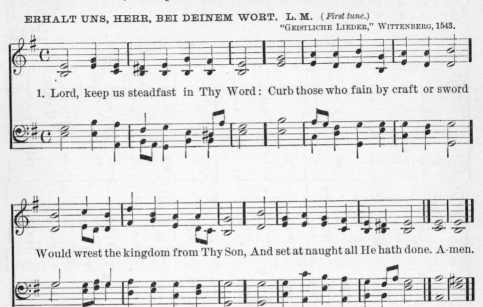

1. Lord, keep us steadfast in Thy Word: Curb those who fain by craft or sword

Would wrest the kingdom from Thy Son, And set at naught all He hath done. A-men.

2 Lord Jesus Christ, Thy power make
    known;
For Thou art Lord of lords alone:
Defend Thy Christendom, that we
May evermore sing praise to Thee.

3 O Comforter, of priceless worth,
Send peace and unity on earth,
Support us in our final strife,
And lead us out of death to life.

Martin Luther (1483—1546), 1541.   *Tr. Catharine Winkworth* (1827—1878), 1862.

Lord, Keep Us Steadfast in Thy Word.

MENDON. L. M. (*Second tune.*)

Arr. by LOWELL MASON.

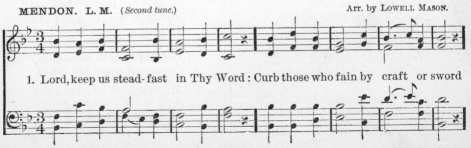

1. Lord, keep us stead-fast in Thy Word: Curb those who fain by craft or sword

Lord, Keep Us Steadfast in Thy Word.—Concluded.

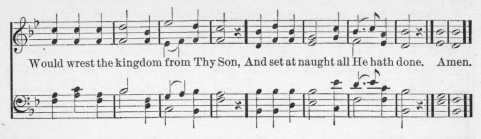

Would wrest the kingdom from Thy Son, And set at naught all He hath done. Amen.

204

Lord, Thy Word Abideth.

LEOMINSTER. 6, 6, 6, 6.

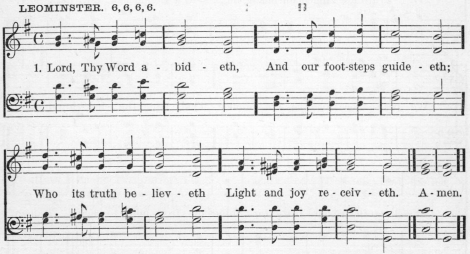

1. Lord, Thy Word a - bid - eth, And our foot-steps guide - eth;

Who its truth be - liev - eth Light and joy re - ceiv - eth. A - men.

2 When our foes are near us,
Then Thy Word doth cheer us,
Word of consolation,
Message of salvation.

3 When the storms are o'er us,
And dark clouds before us,
Then its light directeth,
And our way protecteth.

4 Who can tell the pleasure,
Who recount the treasure,
By Thy Word imparted
To the simple-hearted?

5 Word of mercy, giving
Succor to the living;
Word of life, supplying
Comfort to the dying;

6 O that we, discerning
Its most holy learning,
Lord, may love and fear Thee,
Evermore be near Thee!

Henry William Baker, 1861.

319

205

O Word of God Incarnate.

EVARTS. 7, 6, 7, 6. D.

1. O Word of God In-car-nate, O Wis-dom from on high,
O Truth unchanged, un-chang-ing, O Light of our dark sky;
We praise Thee for the ra-diance That from the hal-low'd page,
A lan-tern to our foot-steps, Shines on from age to age. A-men.

2 The Church from her dear Master
   Received the gift divine,
And still that light she lifteth
   O'er all the earth to shine.
It is the golden casket
   Where gems of truth are stored;
It is the heaven-drawn picture
   Of Christ, the living Word.

3 It floateth like a banner
   Before God's host unfurled;
It shineth like a beacon
   Above the darkling world:

It is the chart and compass,
   That o'er life's surging sea,
'Mid mists, and rocks, and quicksands,
   Still guides, O Christ, to Thee.

4 O make Thy Church, dear Saviour,
   A lamp of burnished gold,
To bear before the nations
   Thy true light as of old:
O teach Thy wandering pilgrims
   By this their path to trace,
Till, clouds and darkness ended,
   They see Thee face to face.

Wm. W. How, 1867.

BAPTISM.

Father, Son, and Holy Spirit.

206

VERONA. 8, 7, 8, 7, 8, 7.

J. H. DEANE.

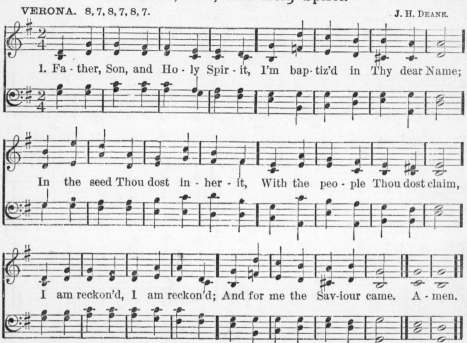

1. Fa-ther, Son, and Ho-ly Spir-it, I'm bap-tiz'd in Thy dear Name;

In the seed Thou dost in-her-it, With the peo-ple Thou dost claim,

I am reckon'd, I am reckon'd; And for me the Sav-iour came. A-men.

2 Thou receivest me, O Father,
  As a child and heir of Thine;
Jesus, Thou who diedst, yea, rather
  Ever livest, Thou art mine.
‖: Thou, O Spirit, :‖
  Art my Guide, my Light divine.

3 I have pledged, and would not falter,
  Truth, obedience, love to Thee;
I have vows upon Thine altar,
  Ever Thine alone to be;
‖: And for ever :‖
  Sin and all its lusts to flee.

4 Gracious God, all Thou hast spoken
  In this covenant shall take place;
But if I, alas! have broken

These my vows, hide not Thy face;
‖: And from falling :‖
  O restore me by Thy grace!

5 Lord, to Thee I now surrender
  All I have, and all I am;
Make my heart more true and tender,
  Glorify in me Thy Name.
‖: Let obedience: ‖
  To Thy will be all my aim.

6 Help me in this high endeavor,
  Father, Son, and Holy Ghost!
Bind my heart to Thee for ever,
  Till I join the heavenly host.
‖: Living, dying :‖
  Let me make in Thee my boast.

From J. J. Rambach, by C. W. Schaeffer.

207

I Was Made a Christian.

WARUM SIND DER THRÆNEN. 6, 5, 6, 5. D.

J. A. P. Schulz, 1785.

1. I was made a Chris - tian When my name was giv'n,
One of God's dear chil - dren, And an heir of heav'n.
In the name of Chris - tian I will glo - ry now,
Ev - er - more re - mem - ber My bap - tis - mal vow. A - men.

2 I must, like a Christian,
  Shun all evil ways,
Keep the faith of Jesus,
  Serve Him all my days.
Called to be a Christian,
  I will praise the Lord,
Seek for His assistance
  So to keep my word.

3 All a Christian's blessings,
  I will claim for mine,
Holy work and worship,
  Fellowship Divine,
Father, Son and Spirit,
  Give me grace, that I
Still may live a Christian,
  And a Christian die.

O Lord, our Strength in Weakness.

LANCASHIRE. 7, 6, 7, 6. D.   H. SMART.

1. O Lord, our strength in weak - ness, We pray to Thee for grace;
For pow'r to fight the bat - tle, For speed to run the race;
When Thy bap - tis - mal wa - ters Were pour'd up - on our brow,
We then were made Thy chil - dren, And pledg'd our ear - liest vow. A - men.

2 We then were sealed and hallowed
  By Thy life-giving word;
Were made the Spirit's temples,
  And members of the Lord;
With His own blood He bought us,
  And made the purchase sure;
His are we: may He keep us
  Sober, and chaste, and pure.

3 Conformed to His own likeness
  May we so live and die,
That in the grave our bodies
  In holy peace may lie;

And at the resurrection
  Forth from those graves may spring,
Like to the glorious body
  Of Christ, our Lord and King.

4 The pure in heart are blessèd,
  For they shall see the Lord
For ever and for ever
  By seraphim adored;
And they shall drink the pleasures,
  Such as no tongue can tell,
From the clear crystal river,
  And life's eternal well.

C. Wordsworth.

CONFIRMATION.

Thine Forever! God of Love.

INNOCENTS. 7, 7, 7, 7.

1. Thine for ev - er! God of love, Hear us from Thy throne a - bove;

Thine for ev - er may we be, Here and in e - ter - ni - ty. A - men.

2 Thine for ever! Lord of Life,
   Shield us through our earthly strife;
   Thou, the Life, the Truth, the Way,
   Guide us to the realms of day.

3 Thine for ever! O how blest
   They who find in Thee their rest;
   Saviour, Guardian, heavenly Friend,
   O defend us to the end.

4 Thine for ever! Thou our Guide,
   All our wants by Thee supplied,
   All our sins by Thee forgiven,
   Lead us, Lord, from earth to heaven.

Mary F. Maude.

Holy Spirit, Lord of Love.

HOLY JESUS. 7, 7, 7, 7, 7, 7.

G. B. Lissant.

1. Ho-ly Spir-it, Lord of love, Thou who cam-est from a-bove,

Gifts of bless-ing to be-stow On Thy wait-ing Church be-low;

Once a-gain in love draw near To Thy children gathered here. A-men.

2 From their bright baptismal day,
Through their childhood's onward way,
Thou hast been their constant guide,
Watching ever by their side;
May they now till life shall end,
Choose and know Thee as their friend.

3 Give them light Thy truth to see,
Give them life to live for Thee,
Daily power to conquer sin,
Patient faith the crown to win;
Shield them from temptation's breath,
Keep them faithful unto death.

4 When the holy vow is made,
When the hands are on them laid,
Come in this most solemn hour,
With Thy sevenfold gifts of power;
Come, Thou blessed Spirit, come,
Make each heart Thy happy home.

W. D. Maclagan, 1873.

211

O Jesus, I Have Promised.

DAY OF REST. 7, 6, 7, 6, D.

J. W. ELLIOTT.

1. O Jesus, I have prom-is'd To serve Thee to the end;
Be Thou for-ev-er near me, My Mas-ter and my Friend!
I shall not fear the bat-tle If Thou art by my side,
Nor wan-der from the path-way If Thou wilt be my Guide. A-men.

2 Oh, let me feel Thee near me!
The world is ever near;
I see the sights that dazzle;
The tempting sounds I hear;
My foes are ever near me,
Around me and within;
But, Jesus, draw Thou nearer,
And shield my soul from sin.

3 Oh, let me hear Thee speaking
In accents dear and still,
Above the storms of passion,
The murmurs of self-will!
Oh, speak to reassure me,
To hasten or control!
Oh, speak, and make me listen,
Thou Guardian of my soul!

O Jesus, I Have Promised.—Concluded.

4 O Jesus, Thou hast promised
   To all who follow Thee,
That where Thou art in glory
   There shall Thy servant be;
And, Jesus, I have promised
   To serve Thee to the end;
Ah, give me grace to follow,
   My Master and my Friend!

5 Oh, let me see Thy foot-marks,
   And in them plant my own!
My hope to follow duly
   Is in Thy strength alone.
Oh, guide me, call me, draw me,
   Uphold me to the end!
At last in heaven receive me,
   My Saviour and my Friend!

J. E. Bode, 1869.

O Thou Best Gift of Heaven!

212

NU LUKKER SIG MIT OEGE. 6, 6, 4, 6, 6, 4.   PETER CASPER KROSSING.

1. O Thou best Gift of Heav'n! Thou who Thy-self hast giv'n,—
For Thou hast died! This hast Thou done for me:
What have I done for Thee, Thou Cru-ci-fied, Thou Cru-ci-fied? A-men.

2 I long to serve Thee more:
   Reveal an open door,
      Saviour to me;
   Then, counting all but loss,
   I'll glory in Thy Cross,
   ‖: And follow Thee. :‖

3 Do Thou but point the way,
   And give me strength to obey;
      Thy will be mine:
   Then can I think it joy
   To suffer or to die,
   ‖ Since I am Thine. :‖

Nicholls, 1837.

CALLING.

213

Life Everlasting He Offers to Thee.

KLYNKE OG KLAGE. 10, 10, 10, 10, 8.

JOHANNE FENGER.
REFRAIN BY F. F. BUERMEYER.

1. "Life ev-er-last-ing" He of-fers to Thee— Par-don-ing grace set-ting sin's cap-tive free; Love that is in-fi-nite, per-fect, Di-vine—

REFRAIN.

Such is the portion which now may be Thine. Why not! O, why not trust Je-sus?

Why not! O, why not trust Je-sus? Why not! O, why not trust Je-sus? A-men.

2 "Peace, passing knowledge," He giveth His own;
Joy that thou otherwise never hadst known,
Wilt thou not come? and, in coming, be blest,
Proving the sweetness of perfect heart-rest.
‖: Why not! O, why not trust Jesus? :‖

Life Everlasting He Offers to Thee.—Concluded.

3 Treasures unfathomed are hid in His store,
　Drawing from which thou but findest still more;
　Fear not to bathe in love's ocean so wide,
　'Neath the deep waves of that ne'er ebbing tide.
　‖: Why not! O, why not trust Jesus? :‖

4 "Fullness of blessing" there dwelleth in Him—
　Fullness o'erflowing that fills to the brim:
　"His is the bounty"—but thine is the need;
　Grace, only grace, can the poor sinner plead,
　‖: Why not! O, why not trust Jesus? :‖

5 "Marvellous love," passing all human thought,
　Love which alone could these wonders have wrought—
　Such is the love that is waiting for thee,
　Tenderly whispering, "Come unto Me."
　‖: Why not! O, why not trust Jesus? :‖

6 Perfect in loveliness, matchlessly fair,
　Peerless in beauty, beyond all compare;
　Christ the unchanging, who loves to the end—
　This thy Belovèd, and this is thy Friend.
　‖: Why not! O, why not trust Jesus? :‖

Art Thou Weary, Art Thou Languid? 214

STEPHANOS. 8, 5, 8, 3.　　　　　　　　HENRY WILLIAMS BAKER, 1868.

1. Art thou wea-ry, art thou lan-guid? Art thou sore dis-tress'd?

"Come to Me, saith One, and com-ing, Be at rest." A-men.

2 Hath He marks to lead me to Him,
　　If He be my Guide?
"In His feet and hands are wound-prints,
　　And His side."

3 Is there diadem, as Monarch,
　　That His brow adorns?
"Yea, a crown in very surety,
　　But of thorns."

4 If I find Him, if I follow,
　　What His guerdon here?
"Many a sorrow, many a labor,
　　Many a tear."

5 If I still hold closely to Him,
　　What hath He at last?
"Sorrow vanquished, labor ended,
　　Jordan passed."

6 If I ask Him to receive me,
　　Will He say me nay?
"Not till earth, and not till heaven
　　Pass away."

7 Finding, following, keeping, struggling,
　　Is He sure to bless?
Saints, apostles, prophets, martyrs,
　　Answer, "Yes."

St. Stephen the Sabaite, 775.
John Mason Neale. Tr.

215

I Heard the Voice of Jesus Say.

VOX DILECTI. C. M. D. (*First tune.*)　　　　　　　　J. B. DYKES.

1. I heard the voice of Je - sus say, "Come un - to me and rest; Lay down, thou wea - ry one, lay down Thy head up - on my breast." I came to Je - sus as I was, Wea - ry, and worn and sad; I found in Him a rest - ing place, And He has made me glad. A - men.

I Heard the Voice of Jesus Say.—Concluded.

2 I heard the voice of Jesus say,
  "Behold, I freely give
The living water; thirsty one,
  Stoop down, and drink, and live."
I came to Jesus and I drank
  Of that life-giving stream :
My thirst was quenched, my soul revived,
  And now I live in Him.

3 I heard the voice of Jesus say,
  "I am this dark world's Light;
Look unto Me, thy morn shall rise,
  And all thy day be bright."
I looked to Jesus, and I found
  In Him, my Star, my Sun;
And in that Light of life I'll walk,
  Till travelling days are done.

Horatius Bonar, 1856.

I Heard the Voice of Jesus Say.

SWEDISH MELODY. C. M. D. (*Second tune.*)　　　I. H. BOETHIUS.

1. I heard the voice of Je - sus say, "Come un - to me and rest;
Lay down, thou weary one, lay down Thy head up - on my breast."

I came to Je - sus as I was, Weary, and worn, and sad; I found in Him a

rest-ing-place, And He has made me glad, And He has made me glad. A-men.

216

O Come to the Merciful Saviour.

NU TITTE TIL HINANDEN DE FAVRE BLOMSTER SMAA. 12, 11, 12, 11.

C. E. F. WEYSE.

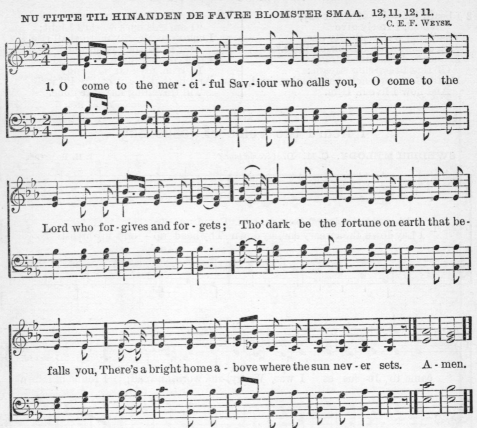

1. O come to the mer-ci-ful Sav-iour who calls you, O come to the Lord who for-gives and for-gets; Tho' dark be the fortune on earth that be-falls you, There's a bright home a-bove where the sun nev-er sets. A-men.

2 O come then to Jesus, whose arms are extended,
To fold His dear children in closest embrace;
O come! for your exile will shortly be ended,
And Jesus will show you His beautiful face.

3 Yes! come to the Saviour, whose mercy grows brighter,
The longer you look at the depths of His love;
And fear not, 'tis Jesus! and life's cares grow lighter
As you think of the home and the glory above.

4 Come, come to His feet, and lay open your story
Of suffering and sorrow, of guilt and of shame;
For the pardon of sin is the crown of His glory,
And the joy of our Lord to be true to His name.

F. W. Faber, 1854.

PRAYER.

Come, My Soul, Thy Suit Prepare.

217

NEW CALABAR. 7, 7, 7, 7.

J. D. FARRER.

1. Come, my soul, thy suit pre-pare, Je - sus loves to an - swer pray'r: He Him-self has bid thee pray, There - fore will not say thee nay. A - men.

2 Thou art coming to a King;
  Large petitions with thee bring;
  For His grace and power are such,
  None can ever ask too much.

3 With my burden I begin;
  Lord, remove this load of sin!
  Let Thy Blood, for sinners spilt,
  Set my conscience free from guilt.

4 Lord, I come to Thee for rest!
  Take possession of my breast;
  There Thy blood-bought right maintain,
  And without a rival reign.

5 While I am a pilgrim here,
  Let Thy love my spirit cheer;
  As my Guide, my Guard, my Friend,
  Lead me to my journey's end.

6 Show me what I have to do,
  Every hour my strength renew;
  Let me live a life of faith,
  Let me die Thy people's death.

John Newton, 1779.

218

Heavenly Father, from Thy Throne.

MISERERE DOMINE. 7, 7, 7, 7.

R. BROWN-BORTHWICK.

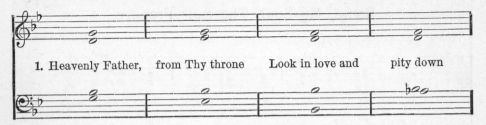

1. Heavenly Father, from Thy throne Look in love and pity down

On each lowly little one; Fa - ther, Lord, de - liv - er us. A - men.

2 Jesus, Saviour | undefiled,
Once on earth a | little Child,
Thou on little | ones hast smiled;
Jesus Lord, deliver us.

3 Blessed Spirit, | gentle Dove,
From Thy home in | heaven above,
Come, and fill our | hearts with love;
Spirit, Lord, deliver us.

4 Heavenly Father, | Spirit, Son,
Glorious Godhead, | Three in One,
Thou canst hear, and | Thou alone;
Three in One, deliver us.

5 By the great and | tender love
Thou didst once for | sinners prove.
Love which brought Thee | from
above,
Jesus, Lord, deliver us.

6 When the evil | spirits throng,
Whispering words and | thoughts of
wrong,
Let our prayer be | all along.
Jesus, Lord, deliver us.

7 When they tempt our | feet to stray
From Thy pure and | perfect way,
Teach us from our | hearts to say,
Jesus, Lord, deliver us.

8 When we yield our | feeble breath
When the awful | hour of death
Calls us to the | tomb beneath,
Jesus, Lord, deliver us.

9 When Thy voice shall | bid us rise,
When we meet Thee | in the skies,
By Thy perfect | Sacrifice,
Jesus, Lord, deliver us.

Jesus, from Thy Throne on High.

LITANY. 7, 7, 7, 6.

W. S. HOYTE.

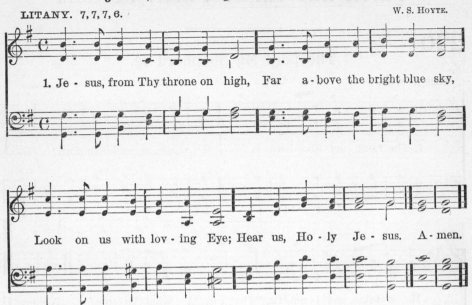

1. Je - sus, from Thy throne on high, Far a - bove the bright blue sky,

Look on us with lov - ing Eye; Hear us, Ho - ly Je - sus. A - men.

2 Little hearts may love Thee well,
Little lips Thy love may tell,
Little hymns Thy praises swell;
    Hear us, Holy Jesus.

3 Little lives may be divine,
Little deeds of love may shine,
Little ones be wholly Thine;
    Hear us, Holy Jesus.

4 Be Thou with us every day,
In our work and in our play,
When we learn and when we pray;
    Hear us, Holy Jesus.

5 When we lie asleep at night,
Ever may Thy Angels bright;
Keep us safe till morning light;
    Hear us, Holy Jesus.

6 Make us brave, without a fear;
Make us happy, full of cheer,
Sure that Thou art always near;
    Hear us, Holy Jesus.

7 May we grow from day to day,
Glad to learn each holy way,
Ever ready to obey;
    Hear us, Holy Jesus.

8 May we ever try to be
From our sinful tempers free,
Pure and gentle, Lord, like Thee;
    Hear us, Holy Jesus.

9 May our thoughts be undefiled;
May our words be true and mild;
Make us each a holy child;
    Hear us, Holy Jesus.

10 Jesus, Son of God most high,
Who didst in the manger lie,
Who upon the Cross didst die;
    Hear us, Holy Jesus.

11 Jesus, from Thy heavenly Throne
Watching o'er each little one,
Till our life on earth is done;
    Hear us, Holy Jesus.

T. B. Pollock.

Faith and Life: Faith in God.

220

The Lord My Shepherd Is.

REST. S. M.

GOODRICH'S SERVICE AND TUNE BOOK.

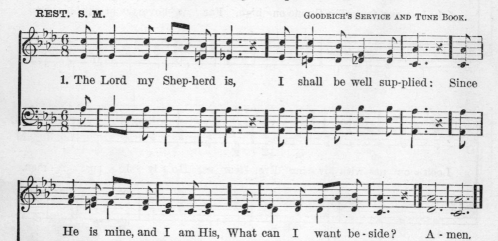

1. The Lord my Shep-herd is, I shall be well sup-plied: Since

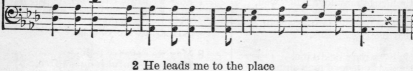

He is mine, and I am His, What can I want be - side? A - men.

2 He leads me to the place
　　Where heavenly pasture grows,
　Where living waters gently pass,
　　And full salvation flows.

3 If e'er I go astray,
　　He doth my soul reclaim,
　And guides me in His own **right way**,
　　For His most holy Name.

4 While He affords His aid,
　　I cannot yield to fear:
　Though I should walk through death's **dark shade**,
　　My Shepherd's with me there.

5 The bounties of Thy love
　　Shall crown my following days;
　Nor from Thy house will I remove,
　　Nor cease to speak Thy praise.

Watts.

Nearer, My God, to Thee.

BETHANY. 6, 4, 6, 4, 6, 6, 6, 4.

L. MASON.

1. Near - er, my God to Thee, Near - er to Thee! E'en tho' it be a cross

That rais - eth me; Still all my song shall be, Near - er, my God, to Thee,

Near - er my God to Thee, Near - er to Thee! A - men.

2 Though, like the wanderer,
  The sun gone down,
Darkness be over me,
  My rest a stone,
Yet in my dreams I'd be
‖: Nearer, my God, to Thee, :‖
  Nearer to Thee!

3 There let my way appear
  Steps unto heaven;
All that Thou sendest me
  In mercy given;
Angels to beckon me
‖: Nearer, my God, to Thee, :‖
  Nearer to Thee!

4 Then with my waking thoughts
  Bright with Thy praise,
Out of my stony griefs
  Bethel I'll raise;
So by my woes to be
‖: Nearer, my God, to Thee, :‖
  Nearer to Thee!

6 Or if on joyful wing
  Cleaving the sky,
Sun, moon, and stars forgot,
  Upwards I fly;
Still all my song shall be,
‖: Nearer, my God, to Thee, :‖
  Nearer to Thee.

Mrs. Sarah Adams, 1841.

222

The Lord My Pasture Shall Prepare.

S. FINBAR. L. M. 6 lines.

1. The Lord my pas - ture shall pre - pare, And feed me with a
shep - herd's care; His pres - ence shall my wants sup - ply,
And guard me with a watch - ful eye: My noon - day walks He
shall at - tend, And all my mid - night hours de - fend. A - men.

2 When in the sultry glebe I faint,
Or in the thirsty mountains pant,
To fertile vales and dewy meads
My weary, wandering steps He leads,
Where peaceful rivers, soft and slow,
Amid the verdant landscape flow.

3 Though in a bare and rugged way,
Through devious, lonely wilds I stray,
His bounty shall my pains beguile;

The barren wilderness shall smile,
With lively green and herbage crowned,
And streams shall murmur all around.

4 Though in the paths of death I tread,
With gloomy horrors overspread,
My steadfast heart shall fear no ill,
For Thou, O Lord! art with me still;
Thy friendly crook shall give me aid,
And guide me through the dismal shade.

Joseph Addison, 1712.

What Cheering Words are These!

HOLBORN. S. M.

1. What cheer - ing words are these! Their sweet - ness who can tell?

In time and to e - ter - nal days, "'T is with the right - eous well."

A - men.

2 In every state secure,
   Kept by Jehovah's eye,
'T is well with them while life endure,
   And well when called to die.

3 'T is well when joys arise;
   'T is well when sorrows flow;
'T is well when darkness veils the skies,
   And strong temptations blow.

4 'T is well when on the mount
   They feast on dying Love:
And 't is as well in God's account,
   When they the furnace prove.

5 'T is well when Jesus calls,
   "From earth and sin arise,
Join with the hosts of ransomed souls,
   Made to salvation wise."

John Kent, 1803.

224

Father! I Know That All My Life.

DEIN GUTER VATER IST DIR NAH. 8, 6, 6 lines.

W. PETERSON.

1. Father! I know that all my life Is por-tion'd out for me; The changes that will sure-ly come, I do not fear to see: I ask Thee for a pres-ent mind, In-tent on pleasing Thee. A-men.

2 I ask Thee for a thoughtful love,
  Through constant watchings wise,
To meet the glad with joyful smiles,
  To wipe the weeping eyes,—
A heart at leisure with itself,
  To soothe and sympathize.

3 I ask Thee for the daily strength
  To none that ask denied,
A mind to blend with outward life,
  While keeping at Thy side,—
Content to fill a little space,
  If Thou be glorified.

4 And if some things I do not ask
  Among my blessings be,
I'd have my spirit filled the more
  With grateful love to Thee,
And careful less to serve Thee much
  Than please Thee perfectly.

A. L. Waring, (1820 ——

Faith and Life: Faith in Christ.

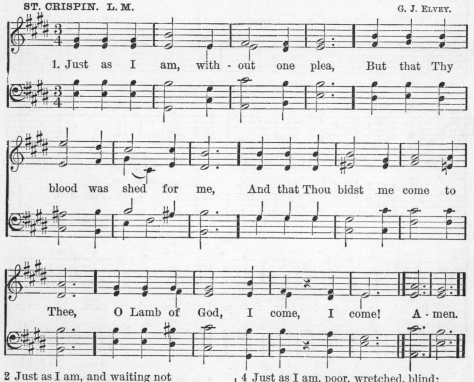

Just As I Am, Without One Plea.

ST. CRISPIN. L. M.

G. J. ELVEY.

225

1. Just as I am, with-out one plea, But that Thy
blood was shed for me, And that Thou bidst me come to
Thee, O Lamb of God, I come, I come! A-men.

2 Just as I am, and waiting not
  To rid my soul of one dark blot, [spot,
  To Thee, whose Blood can cleanse each
  O Lamb of God, I come, I come!

3 Just as I am, though tossed about
  With many a conflict, many a doubt,
  Fightings and fears within, without,
  O Lamb of God, I come, I come!

4 Just as I am, poor, wretched, blind;
  Sight, riches, healing of the mind,
  Yea, all I need, in Thee to find,
  O Lamb of God, I come, I come!

5 Just as I am; Thou wilt receive,
  Wilt welcome, pardon, cleanse, relieve,
  Because Thy promise I believe;
  O Lamb of God, I come, I come!

6 Just as I am; Thy Love unknown
  Has broken every barrier down;
  Now to be Thine, yea, Thine alone,
  O Lamb of God, I come, I come!

Charlotte Elliott, 1836. a.

226

Rock of Ages, Cleft for Me.

TOPLADY. 7, 7, 7, 7, 7, 7.

T. HASTINGS.

1. Rock of A-ges, cleft for me, Let me hide my-self in Thee;

Let the wa-ter and the blood, From Thy riv-en side which flowed,

Be of sin the per-fect cure, Save me, Lord, and make me pure. A-men.

2 Not the labors of my hands,
Can fulfil Thy law's demands:
Could my zeal no respite know,
Could my tears for ever flow,
All for sin could not atone:
Thou must save, and Thou alone!

3 Nothing in my hand I bring,
Simply to Thy Cross I cling;
Naked, come to Thee for dress;
Helpless, look to Thee for grace;
Foul, I to the Fountain fly;
Wash me, Saviour, or I die!

4 While I draw this fleeting breath,
When my eyelids close in death,
When I soar to worlds unknown,
See Thee on Thy judgment throne,
Rock of Ages, cleft for me,
Let me hide myself in Thee!

Augustus M. Toplady, (1740—1778), 1776. *Altered.*

My Faith Looks Up to Thee.

FAITH. 6, 6, 4, 6, 6, 6, 4.

J. R. FAIRLAMB.

1. My faith looks up to Thee, Thou Lamb of Cal - va - ry,
Sav - iour di - vine! Now hear me while I pray; Take all my
guilt a - way; O let me from this day Be whol-ly Thine. A - men.

2 May Thy rich grace impart
  Strength to my fainting heart,
    My zeal inspire;
  As Thou hast died for me,
  O may my love to Thee
  Pure, warm, and changeless be,
    A living fire.

3 While life's dark maze I tread,
  And griefs around me spread,
    Be Thou my Guide;
  Bid darkness turn to day,
  Wipe sorrow's tears away,
  Nor let me ever stray
    From Thee aside.

4 When ends life's transient dream,
  When death's cold sullen stream
    Shall o'er me roll;
  Blest Saviour, then, in love,
  Fear and distrust remove;
  O bear me safe above.
    A ransomed soul.

Ray Palmer, 1830.

228

Jesus, Lover of My Soul.

MARTYN. 7, 7, 7, 7. D.

SIMEON MARSH.

1. Je - sus, Lov - er of my soul, Let me to Thy bos - om fly,

While the near - er wa - ters roll, While the tem - pest still is high!

Hide me, O my Sav - iour, hide, Till the storm of life is past;

Safe in - to the ha - ven guide; O receive my soul at last! A - men.

2 Other refuge have I none;
   Hangs my helpless soul on Thee:
Leave, ah, leave me not alone,
   Still support and comfort me!
All my trust on Thee is stayed,
   All my help from Thee I bring:
Cover my defenceless head
   With the shadow of Thy wing.

3 Thou, O Christ, art all I want;
   More than all in Thee I find:
Raise the fallen, cheer the faint,
   Heal the sick, and lead the blind.

Just and holy is Thy Name;
   I am all unrighteousness:
False and full of sin I am;
   Thou art full of truth and grace.

4 Plenteous grace with Thee is found,
   Grace to cover all my sin;
Let the healing streams abound;
   Make and keep me pure within.
Thou of life the Fountain art,
   Freely let me take of Thee:
Spring Thou up within my heart,
   Rise to all eternity.

C. Wesley, 1740.

Ask Ye What Great Thing I Know.

WOLLT IHR WISSEN, WAS MEIN PREIS. 7, 7, 7, 7, 7, 7.

JOHANN BALTHASAR REIMANN, 1747.

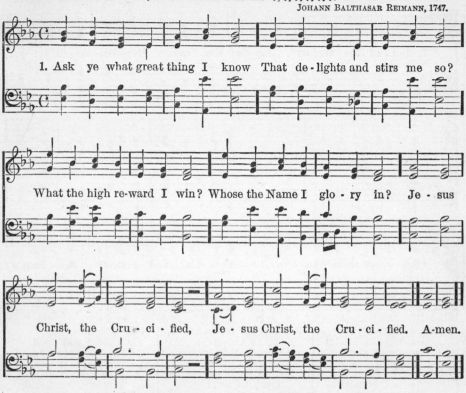

1. Ask ye what great thing I know That de-lights and stirs me so? What the high re-ward I win? Whose the Name I glo-ry in? Je-sus Christ, the Cru-ci-fied, Je-sus Christ, the Cru-ci-fied. A-men.

2 What is faith's foundation strong?
What awakes my lips to song?
He who bore my sinful load,
Purchased for me peace with God.
‖: Jesus Christ, the Crucified. :‖

3 Who is He that makes me wise,
To discern where duty lies?
Who is He that makes me true,
Duty, when discerned, to do?
‖: Jesus Christ, the crucified. :‖

4 Who defeats my fiercest foes?
Who consoles my saddest woes?
Who revives my fainting heart?

Healing all its hidden smart?
‖: Jesus Christ, the Crucified. :‖

5 Who is life in life to me?
Who the death of death will be?
Who will place me on His right
With the countless hosts of light?
‖: Jesus Christ, the Crucified. :‖

6 This is the great thing I know;
This delights and stirs me so;
Faith in Him who died to save,
Him who triumphed o'er the grave
‖: Jesus Christ, the Crucified. :‖

Johann Christoph Schwedler, 1721.
Tr. Benjamin Holl Kennedy, 1804.

230

Rest of the Weary.

PALMER. 5, 4, 5, 4. D. (*First tune.*)

1. Rest of the wea-ry, Joy of the sad; Hope of the drear-y,
Light of the glad; Home of the stran-ger, Strength to the end;
Ref - uge from dan - ger, Sav - iour and Friend. A - men.

2 Pillow, where, lying,
  Love rests its head;
Peace of the dying,
  Life of the dead;
Path of the lowly,
  Prize at the end;
Breath of the holy,
  Saviour and Friend.

3 When my feet stumble,
  I'll to Thee cry;
Crown of the humble,
  Cross of the high:
When my steps wander,
  Over me bend,
Truer and fonder,
  Saviour and Friend.

4 Ever confessing
  Thee, I will raise
Unto Thee blessing,
  Glory, and praise:—
All my endeavor,
  World without end,
Thine to be ever,
  Saviour and Friend.

Ray Palmer.

Rest of the Weary.

THEODORA. 5, 4, 5, 4. D. (*Second tune.*)   A. LEGGE, 1845.

1. Rest of the wea - ry, Joy of the sad; Hope of the drear - y,

Rest of the Weary.—Concluded.

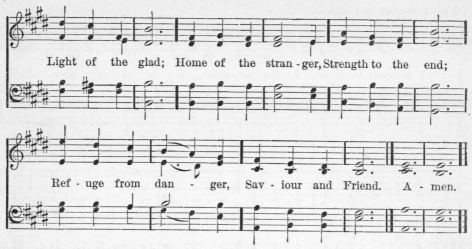

Light of the glad; Home of the stran-ger, Strength to the end;

Ref-uge from dan-ger, Sav-iour and Friend. A-men.

I Am Trusting Thee, Lord Jesus.

231

ST. HELEN'S. 8, 5, 8, 3.

R. P. STEWART (1825—1894).

1. I am trust-ing Thee, Lord Je-sus, Trust-ing on-ly Thee,

Trust-ing Thee for full sal-va-tion, Great and free. A-men.

2 I am trusting Thee for pardon;
   At Thy feet I bow;
For Thy grace and tender mercy,
   Trusting now.

3 I am trusting Thee, Lord Jesus,
   Never let me fall;
I am trusting Thee for ever,
   And for all.

F. R. Havergal, 1874.

232

Jesus Loves Me, Jesus Loves Me.

LUX VITÆ. 8, 7, 8, 7.

SACRED MUSICAL CABINET.

1. Je - sus loves me, Je - sus loves me, He is al - ways, al - ways near:

If I try to please Him tru - ly, There is nought that I can fear. A - men.

2 Jesus loves me,—well, I know it,
   For to save my soul He died;
   He for me bore pain and sorrow;
   Nailèd hands and piercèd side.

3 Jesus loves me,—night and morning
   Jesus hears the prayers I pray;
   And He never, never leaves me,
   When I work or when I play.

4 Jesus loves me,—and He watches
   Over me with loving eye,
   And He sends His holy angels,
   Safe to keep me till I die.

5 Jesus loves me,—O Lord Jesus,
   Now I pray Thee by Thy love,
   Keep me ever pure and holy,
   Till I come to Thee above!

233

Jesus, When He Left the Sky.

ST. RAPHAEL. 7, 7, 7, 5.

MRS. FRANCIS.

1. Je - sus, when He left the sky, And for sin - ners came to die,

Jesus, When He Left the Sky.—Concluded.

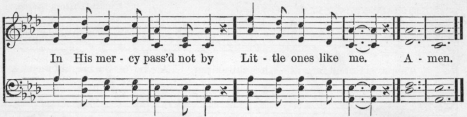

In His mer - cy pass'd not by Lit - tle ones like me. A - men.

2 Mothers then the Saviour sought
In the places where He taught,
And to Him their children brought—
Little ones like me.

3 Did the Saviour say them nay?
No, He kindly bade them stay;
Suffered none to turn away
Little ones like me.

4 'Twas for them His life He gave,
To redeem them from the grave;
Jesus able is to save
Little ones like me.

5 Children, then, should love Him too,
Strive His holy will to do,
Pray to Him, and praise Him too—
Little ones like me.

Mrs. M. Ramsey.

Jesus, I Live to Thee. 234

EMMAUS. S. M.   ADAPTED BY H. R. KRAUTH, 1871.

1. Je - sus, I live to Thee, The lov - li - est and best; My life in
Thee, Thy life in me, In Thy blest love I rest. A - men.

2 Jesus, I die to Thee,
    Whenever death shall come;
To die in Thee is life to me,
    In my eternal home.

3 Whether to live or die,
    I know not which is best;

To live in Thee is bliss to me,
    To die is endless rest.

4 Living or dying, Lord,
    I ask but to be Thine;
My life in Thee, Thy life in me,
    Makes heaven forever mine.

Henry Harbaugh, 1850.

235

There's a Friend for Little Children.

EDENGROVE. 7, 6, 7, 6. D. (*First tune.*) SAMUEL SMITH.

1. There's a Friend for lit-tle chil-dren A - bove the bright blue sky,

A Friend who nev - er chan - ges, Whose love will nev - er die.

Un - like our friends by na - ture Who change with changing years,

This Friend is al - ways wor - thy The precious Name He bears. A-men

2 There's a rest for little children,
　Above the bright blue sky,
Who love the blessèd Saviour,
　And to the Father cry.—
A rest from every trouble,
　From sin and danger free;
There every little pilgrim
　Shall rest eternally.

3 There's a home for little children,
　Above the bright blue sky,
Where Jesus reigns in glory,
　A home of peace and joy;
No home on earth is like it,
　Nor can with it compare,
For every one is happy,
　Nor can be happier there.

There's a Friend for Little Children.—Concluded.

4 There are crowns for little children
  Above the bright blue sky,
And all who look to Jesus
  Shall wear them by-and-by;
Yea, crowns of brightest glory
  Which He shall sure bestow,
On all who loved the Saviour
  And walked with Him below.

5 There are songs for little children,
  Above the bright blue sky,
And harps of sweetest music
  For their hymns of victory:
And all above is pleasure,
  And found in Christ alone;
Lord, grant Thy little children,
  To know Thee as their own.

A. Midlane, 1859.

There's a Friend for Little Children.

FRIEND. 7, 6, 7, 6. D. (*Second tune.*) FELIX MENDELSSOHN–BARTHOLDY, 1847.

1 There's a Friend for lit-tle chil-dren, A-bove the bright blue sky, A Friend who nev-er chan-ges, Whose love will nev-er die. Unlike our friends by na-ture, Who change with changing years, This Friend is always wor-thy The precious Name He bears, This Friend is always worthy The precious Name He bears. A-men.

236

Jesus, Thou Joy of Loving Hearts.

MT. AIRY. L. M.

J. B. DYKES.

1. Jesus, Thou Joy of loving hearts, Thou Fount of life! Thou light of men! From the best bliss that earth imparts, We turn unfilled to Thee again. A-men.

2 Thy truth unchanged hath ever stood;
   Thou savest those that on Thee call;
   To them that seek Thee, Thou art good,
   To them that find Thee, All in all.

3 We taste Thee, O Thou Living Bread,
   And long to feast upon Thee still;
   We drink of Thee, the Fountain Head,
   And thirst our souls from Thee to fill.

4 Our restless spirits yearn for Thee,
   Where'er our changeful lot is cast;
   Glad, that Thy gracious smile we see,
   Blest, that our faith can hold Thee fast.

5 O Jesus, ever with us stay!
   Make all our moments calm and bright;
   Chase the dark night of sin away,
   Shed o'er the world Thy holy light.

Bernard of Clairvaux, 1153.
Ray Palmer, 1858. a.

Seeing I am Jesus' Lamb.

WEIL ICH JESU SCHÆFLEIN BIN. 7, 7, 8, 8, 7, 7.   GERMAN.

1. See-ing I am Je - sus' lamb, Ev - er glad at heart I am

O'er my Shepherd kind and good, Who provides me dai - ly food,

And His lamb by name doth call, For He knows and loves us all. A-men.

2 Guided by His gentle staff
Where the sunny pastures laugh,
I go in and out and feed,
Lacking nothing that I need.
When I thirst, my feet He brings
To the fresh and living springs.

3 Shall I not rejoice for this?
He is mine, and I am His:
And when these bright days are past,
Safely in His arms at last
He will bear me home to heaven;
Ah, what joy hath Jesus given!

Henrietta Louisa von Hayn, 1778.
Miss Winkworth, Tr. 1858. a.

238

Come, Jesus, Redeemer, Abide Thou With Me.

SO NIMM DENN MEINE HÆNDE. 11s.

F. SILCHER, † 1860.

1. Come, Je - sus, Re - deem - er, a - bide Thou with me;
Come, glad - den my spir - it that wait - eth for Thee;

Thy smile ev - 'ry shad - ow shall chase from my heart,

And soothe ev - 'ry sor - row, though keen be the smart. A - men.

2 Without Thee but weakness, with Thee I am strong;
By day Thou shalt lead me, by night be my song;
Though dangers surround me, I still every fear,
Since Thou, the most Mighty, my Helper, art near.

3 Thy love, O how faithful! so tender, so pure!
Thy promise, faith's anchor, how steadfast and sure!
That love, like sweet sunshine, my cold heart can warm,
That promise make steady my soul in the storm.

4 Breathe, breathe on my spirit, oft ruffled, Thy peace;
From restlesss, vain wishes, bid Thou my heart cease;
In Thee all its longings henceforward shall end,
Till, glad, to Thy presence my soul shall ascend.

5 O then, blessed Jesus, who once for me died,
Made clean in the fountain that gushed from Thy side,
I shall see Thy full glory, Thy face shall behold,
And praise Thee with raptures for ever untold!

Ray Palmer, 1867.

Saviour, Like a Shepherd Lead Us.

O DU LIEBE MEINER LIEBE. 8, 7, 8, 7. D.

BASEL, 1745.

1. Sav-iour, like a shepherd lead us, Much we need Thy tend'rest care;
In Thy pleas-ant pastures feed us, For our use Thy folds pre - pare.
Bless - ed Je - sus, Blessed Je - sus, Thou hast bought us, Thine we are,
Blessed Je - sus, Blessed Je - sus, Thou hast bought us, Thine we are. A-men.

2 Thou hast promised to receive us,
  Poor and sinful though we be;
Thou hast mercy to relieve us,
  Grace to cleanse, and power to free.
  ‖: Blessed Jesus,
Let us early turn to Thee. :‖

3 Early let us seek Thy favor,
  Early let us do Thy will;
Blessed Lord and only Saviour,
  With Thy love our bosoms fill.
  ‖: Blessed Jesus,
Thou hast loved us, love us still. :‖

H. F. Lyte, 1836.

240

I Think, When I Read That Sweet Story.

11, 8, 12, 9.

GREEK MELODY.

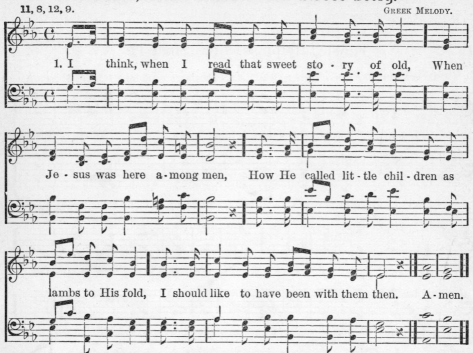

1. I think, when I read that sweet sto-ry of old, When Je-sus was here a-mong men, How He called lit-tle chil-dren as lambs to His fold, I should like to have been with them then. A-men.

2 I wish that His hands had been placed on my head,
  That His arm had been thrown around me,
And that I might have seen His kind look when He said,
  "Let the little ones come unto Me."

3 Yet still to His footstool in prayer I may go,
  And ask for a share in His love;
And if I thus earnestly seek Him below,
  I shall see Him and hear Him above;

4 In that beautiful place He has gone to prepare
  For all who are washed and forgiven;
Full many dear children are gathering there,
  "For of such is the kingdom of heaven."

5 But thousands and thousands who wander and fall,
  Never heard of that heavenly home
I wish they could know there is room for them all,
  And that Jesus has bid them to come.

6 And O, how I long for that glorious time,
  The sweetest and brightest and best,
When the dear little children of every clime,
  Shall crowd to His arms and be blest.

Jemima Luke, 1841.

Faith and Life: Following Christ.

Feeble, Helpless, How Shall I?

241

ELLASUR. 7, 7, 7, 7.

1. Fee - ble, help - less, how shall I Learn to live, and learn to die? Who, O God, my guide shall be? Who shall lead Thy child to Thee? A - men.

2 Blessed Father, gracious One,
Thou hast sent Thy holy Son;
He will give the light I need,
He my trembling steps will lead.

3 Through this world, uncertain, dim,
Let me ever lean on Him;
From His precepts wisdom draw,
Make His life my solemn law.

4 Thus in deed, and thought, and word,
Led by Jesus Christ the Lord,
In my weakness, thus shall I
Learn to live and learn to die.

Wm. H. Furness, 1844.

242

My Jesus, as Thou Wilt!

SUBMISSION. 6, 6, 6, 6. D. (*First tune.*) ARR.

1. My Je-sus, as Thou wilt! O may Thy will be mine!

In-to Thy hand of love I would my all re-sign.

Through sor-row or through joy Con-duct me as Thine own,

And help me still to say, My Lord Thy will be done. A-men.

2 My Jesus, as Thou wilt!
　If needy here and poor,
Give me Thy people's bread,
　Their portion rich and sure.
The manna of Thy word
　Let my soul feed upon;
And if all else should fail,
　My Lord, Thy will be done!

3 My Jesus, as Thou wilt!
　Though seen through many a tear,
Let not my star of hope
　Grow dim or disappear:
Since Thou on earth hast wept
　And sorrowed oft alone,
If I must weep with Thee,
　My Lord, Thy will be done!

My Jesus, as Thou Wilt!—Concluded.

4 My Jesus, as Thou wilt!
    When death itself draws nigh,
To Thy dear wounded side
    I would for refuge fly.
Leaning on Thee, to go
    Where Thou before hast gone:
The rest as Thou shalt please:
    My Lord, Thy will be done!

5 My Jesus, as Thou wilt!
    All shall be well for me:
Each changing future scene
    I gladly trust with Thee.
Thus to my home above
    I travel calmly on,
And sing, in life or death,
    My Lord, Thy will be done!

Benjamin Schmolk, d. 1737.
Tr. Jane Borthwick, 1853.

My Jesus, as Thou Wilt!

LADD. 6, 6, 6, 6. D. (*Second tune.*)

F. F. BUERMEYER.

1. My Je-sus, as Thou wilt! O may Thy will be mine!
In-to Thy hand of love I would my all re-sign.
Through sor-row or through joy Con-duct me as Thine own,
And help me still to say, My Lord, Thy will be done. A-men.

243

Saviour, Blessed Saviour.

EGBERT. 6, 5, 6, 5. D.

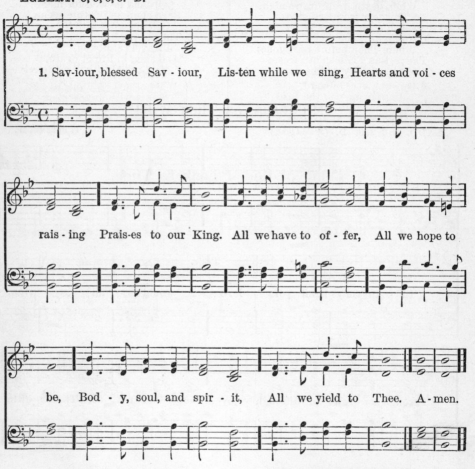

1. Sav-iour, blessed Sav - iour, Lis-ten while we sing, Hearts and voi - ces rais - ing Prais-es to our King. All we have to of - fer, All we hope to be, Bod - y, soul, and spir - it, All we yield to Thee. A - men.

2 Nearer, ever nearer,
  Christ, we draw to Thee,
 Deep in adoration,
  Bending low the knee;
 Thou for our redemption
  Cam'st on earth to die;
 Thou, that we might follow,
  Hast gone up on high.

3 Great and ever greater
  Are Thy mercies here,
 True and everlasting
  Are the glories there,
 Where no pain or sorrow,
  Toil or care is known,
 Where the angel legions
  Circle round the throne.

Saviour, Blessed Saviour.—Concluded.

4 Brighter still and brighter
  Glows the western sun,
Shedding all its gladness
  O'er our work that's done;
Time will soon be over,
  Toil and sorrows past,
May we, blessed Saviour,
  Find a rest at last.

5 Onward, ever onward,
  Journeying o'er the road
Worn by saints before us,
  Journeying on to God;

Leaving all behind us,
  May we hasten on,
Backward never looking
  Till the prize is won.

6 Bliss, all bliss excelling,
  When the ransomed soul
Earthly toils forgetting
  Finds its promised goal;
Where the joys unheard of
  Saints with angels sing,
Never weary raising
  Praises to their King.

Godfrey Thring.

244

Lamb of God, I Look to Thee.

EDYFIELD. 7, 7, 7, 7.

C. J. LATROBE.

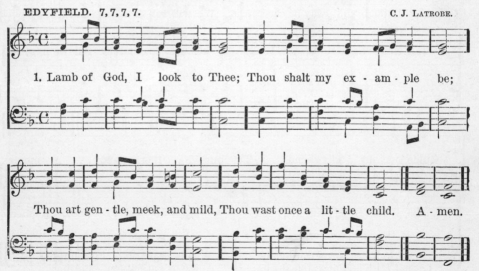

1. Lamb of God, I look to Thee; Thou shalt my ex - am - ple be;

Thou art gen - tle, meek, and mild, Thou wast once a lit - tle child. A - men.

2 Fain I would be as Thou art,
  Give me Thy obedient heart.
Thou art pitiful and kind:
  Let me have Thy loving mind.

3 Loving Jesus, gentle Lamb,
  In Thy gracious hands I am.
Make me, Saviour, what Thou art,
  Live Thyself within my heart.

4 I shall then show forth Thy praise,
  Serve Thee all my happy days:
Then the world shall always see
  Christ, the holy Child, in me.

C. Wesley, 1742.

Jesus, Still Lead On.

SEELENBRÄUTIGAM. 5, 5, 8, 8, 5, 5.

A. DRESE, 1698.

1. Je - sus, still lead on, Till our rest be won!
And although the way be cheer - less, We will fol - low, calm and fear - less.
Guide us by Thy hand To our Fa - ther - land! A - men.

2 If the way be drear,
  If the foe be near,
Let not faithless fears o'ertake us,
Let not faith and hope forsake us;
  For through many a foe
  To our home we go!

3 When we seek relief
  From a long-felt grief;
When temptations come alluring,
Make us patient and enduring:
  Show us that bright shore
  Where we weep no more!

4 Jesus, still lead on,
  Till our Rest be won;
Heavenly Leader, still direct us,
Still support, console, protect us,
  Till we safely stand
  In our Fatherland!

Nicholas Louis, Count Zinzendorf, 1721.
Jane Borthwick, Tr. 1853. a.

I Will Leave My Jesus Never!

ACH! WAS SIND WIR OHNE JESUS. 8, 7, 8, 7, 8, 8.   17TH CENTURY.

1. I will leave my Je-sus nev-er! On the Cross for me He died;
Love shall draw me to Him ev-er, At His feet I will a-bide.
Of my life the Light for ev-er, I will leave my Je-sus nev-er! A-men.

2 In His Name I stand acquitted
    While upon the earth I stay:
What I have to Him committed
    He will keep until that day.
Be His service my endeavor;
I will leave my Jesus never!

3 Dwelling in His presence holy,
    I at length shall reach the place
Where with all His saints in glory
    I shall see His lovely face;
Nothing then but bliss for ever:
I will leave my Jesus never!

4 Not the earth with all its treasure
    Could content this soul of mine;
Not alone for heavenly pleasure
    Doth my thirsty spirit pine;
For its Saviour yearning ever:
I will leave my Jesus never!

5 From that living Fountain drinking,
    Walking always at His side,
Christ shall lead me without sinking
    Through the river's rushing tide,
With the blest to sing for ever;
I will leave my Jesus never!

Christian Keymann, 1656.
Tr. Unknown, 1864.

247

Take My Life and Let it Be.

AVE MARIS STELLA. 7, 7, 7, 7. D. (*First tune.*)

1. Take my life and let it be Con-se-cra-ted, Lord, to Thee; Take my mo-ments and my days,— Let them flow in cease-less praise; 2. Take my hands, and let them move At the im-pulse of Thy love; Take my feet and

Take My Life and Let it Be.—Concluded.

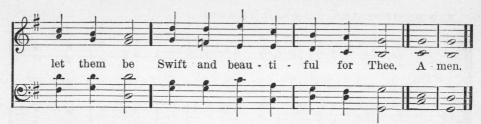

let them be Swift and beau-ti-ful for Thee. A-men.

2 Take my hands, and let them move
At the impulse of Thy love;
Take my feet and let them be
Swift and beautiful for Thee.

3 Take my voice, and let me sing
Always, only for my King;
Take my lips, and let them be
Filled with messages from Thee:

4 Take my silver and my gold,—
Not a mite would I withhold;

Take my intellect, and use
Every power as Thou shalt choose.

5 Take my will and make it Thine;
It shall be no longer mine;
Take my heart it is Thine own;
It shall be Thy royal throne:

6 Take my love; my Lord, I pour
At Thy feet its treasure store;
Take myself, and I will be
Ever, only, all for Thee.

Frances Ridley Havergal, 1874.

Take My Life and Let it Be.

LITANY TUNE. 7, 7, 7, 7. (*Second tune.*)　　　J. WHITAKER.

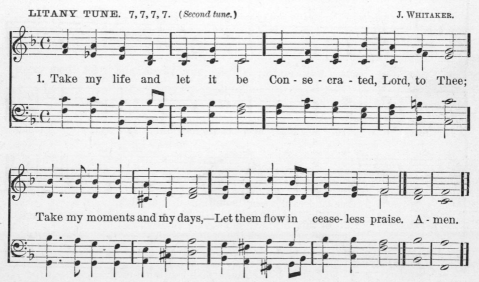

1. Take my life and let it be Con-se-cra-ted, Lord, to Thee;

Take my moments and my days,—Let them flow in cease-less praise. A-men.

248

I'm a Pilgrim and Will Walk With Jesus.

NUR MIT JESU WILL ICH PILGER WANDERN.

P. SCHÜCK.

1. I'm a pil - grim and will walk with Je - sus, In Him al - so are our go - ings blest; All the way from doubts and fears He frees us, He a - lone keeps heart and mind at rest, He a - lone keeps heart and mind at rest. A - men.

2 Seas, lands, vales, and mountains firm abiding,
  Joyful I traverse held by His hand;
 But for this, my Saviour's loving guiding,
  I could never reach the promised land.

3 When I sleep He keepeth guard around me,
  When I wake He is my strength and stay,
 He takes care that nothing shall confound me,
  Leads me right when doubtful is the way.

I'm a Pilgrim and Will Walk With Jesus.—Concluded.

4 In Him ever would I be abiding,
In Him meat and drink and peace I have,
In His gracious arms my place of hiding;
Soul and body both His love will save.

5 Him I follow till my days are ended,
Till Himself shall call me home to rest,
In the Father's house there'll be extended
The glad welcome of a heavenly guest.

P. Schück. Tr. by C. W. Schaeffer.

249

Christ is Kind and Gentle.

CUTHBERT. 6, 5, 6, 5.

G. A. MACFARREN.

1. Christ is kind and gen - tle, Christ is pure and true,

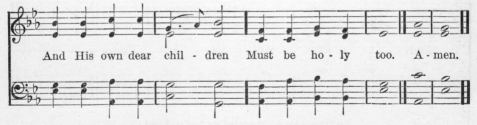

And His own dear chil - dren Must be ho - ly too. A - men.

2 There's a wicked spirit
Watching round us still,
And he tries to tempt us
To all harm and ill.

3 But we must not hear him,
Nor his bidding do,
But resist the evil
And the good pursue.

4 For we promised truly
In our infant days,
To renounce him wholly
And forsake his ways.

5 We are new-born Christians,
We must learn to fight
With the bad within us,
And to do the right.

6 Christ is our own Master,
He is good and true,
And His little children
Must be holy too.

C. F. Alexander. a.

250

Lord Jesus, Point Thou Out the Way.

RANFORD. 8, 8, 8, 4.

ARTHUR SULLIVAN.

1. Lord Je - sus, point Thou out the way, Nor suf - fer Thou our steps to stray; Then in that path that leads to day We fol low Thee. A - men.

2 Through good report and evil, Lord,
Still guided by Thy faithful word,—
Our staff, our buckler, and our sword,—
We follow Thee.

3 Thou hast passed on before our face;
Thy footsteps on the way we trace;
Oh, keep us, aid us by Thy grace:
We follow Thee.

4 Whom have we in the heaven above,
Whom on this earth, save Thee, to love?
Still in Thy light we onward move;
We follow Thee!

Horatius Bonar. a.

Jesus, When a Little Child.

JESUS, DU, DU, BIST MEIN LEBEN. 7, 7, 7, 7, 7, 7.　　WERNER FABRICIUS, 1659.

1. Je - sus, when a lit - tle Child, Taught us what we ought to be;

Ho - ly, harm - less, un - de - fil'd, Was the Sav - iour's in - fan - cy;

All the Fa - ther's glo - ry shone In the per - son of His Son. A - men.

2 As in age and strength He grew,
　Heavenly wisdom filled His breast;
Crowds attentive round Him drew,
　Wondering at their infant Guest;
Gazed upon His lovely face,
Saw Him full of truth and grace.

3 In His heavenly Father's house,
　Jesus spent His early days;
There He paid His solemn vows,
　There proclaimed His Father's praise;
Thus it was His lot to gain
Favor both with God and man.

4 Father, guide our steps aright
　In the way that Jesus trod;
May it be our great delight
　To obey Thy will, O God!
Then to us shall soon be given
Endless bliss with Christ in heaven.

Sunday School Union H. B. 1845

Various Occasions: Charity.

252

O Lord of Heaven, and Earth, and Sea.

ALMSGIVING. (GRATITUDE.). 8, 8, 8, 4.

J. B. DYKES.

1. O Lord of heav'n, and earth, and sea, To Thee all praise and glo - ry be; How shall we show our love to Thee, Giv - er of all? A - men.

2 The golden sunshine, vernal air,
Sweet flowers and fruits, Thy love declare;
Where harvests ripen, Thou art there,
   Giver of all!

3 For peaceful homes and healthful days,
For all the blessings earth displays,
We owe Thee thankfulness and praise,
   Giver of all!

4 Thou didst not spare Thine only Son,
But gav'st Him for a world undone,
And freely with that blessèd One
   Thou givest all!

5 Thou giv'st the Holy Spirit's dower
Spirit of life, and love, and power,
And dost His sevenfold graces shower,
   Upon us all.

O Lord of Heaven, and Earth, and Sea.—Concluded.

3 For souls redeemed, for sins forgiven,
  For means of grace, and hopes of heaven,
  Father, what can to Thee be given;
    Who givest all?

  We lose what on ourselves we spend:
  We have as treasure without end
  Whatever, Lord, to Thee we lend,
    Who givest all!

8 Whatever, Lord, we lend to Thee,
  Repaid a thousandfold will be;
  Then gladly will we give to Thee,
    Giver of all!

9 To Thee, from whom we all derive
  Our life, our gifts, our power to give.
  Oh, may we ever with Thee live,
    Giver of all!

C. Wordsworth, 1863.

We Give Thee But Thine Own. 253

ST. GEORGE. S. M.   GAUNTLETT.

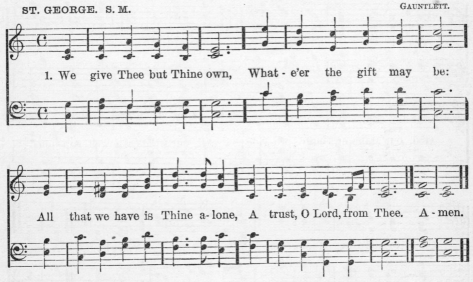

1. We give Thee but Thine own, What-e'er the gift may be:

All that we have is Thine a-lone, A trust, O Lord, from Thee. A-men.

2 May we Thy bounties thus
    As stewards true receive,
  And gladly as Thou blessest us,
    To Thee our first-fruits give.

3 O hearts are bruised and dead,
    And homes are bare and cold,
  And lambs, for whom the Shepherd bled,
    Are straying from the fold!

4 To comfort and to bless,
    To find a balm for woe,

To tend the lone and fatherless,
    Is angels' work below.

5 The captive to release,
    The lost to God to bring,
  To teach the way of life and peace,—
    It is a Christ-like thing.

6 And we believe Thy Word,
    Though dim our faith may be;
  Whate'er we do for Thine, O Lord,
    We do it unto Thee.

Wm. Waltham Howe, 1860.

Various Occasions: Harvest.

254
Come, Ye Thankful People, Come.

7, 7, 7, 7. D.

A Nischke.

1. Come, ye thankful peo - ple, come, Raise the song of har - vest home!

All is safe - ly gath - er'd in, Ere the win - ter storms be - gin;

God, our Mak - er, doth pro - vide; All our wants are well sup - plied;

Come to God's own temple, come; Raise the song of harvest home! A - men.

2 What is earth but God's own field,
Fruit to His own praise to yield?
Wheat and tares together sown,
Unto joy or sorrow grown;
First the blade, and then the ear,
Then the full corn shall appear:
Lord of harvest, grant that we
Wholesome grain and pure may be!

3 E'en the Lord our God shall come,
And will take His harvest home;
From His field, in that great day,
All offences purge away;

Give His angels charge at last
In the fire the tares to cast,
And the fruitful wheat to store
In His garner evermore.

4 Even so, Lord, quickly come
To Thy final harvest home:
Gather Thou Thy people in,
Free from sorrow and from sin;
There for ever purified,
In Thy presence to abide:
Come, with all Thine angels, come,
Raise the glorious harvest home.

Alford, 1844 *and* 1865.

Sing to the Lord of Harvest.

HOLY CHURCH. 7, 6, 7, 6. D.

A. H. BROWN.

1. Sing to the Lord of har - vest, Sing songs of love and praise;
With joy - ful hearts and voi - ces Your al - le - lu - ias raise:
By Him the roll - ing sea - sons In fruit - ful or - der move,
Sing to the Lord of har - vest A song of hap - py love. A - men.

2 By Him the clouds drop fatness,
  The deserts bloom and spring,
The hills leap up in gladness,
  The valleys laugh and sing;
He filleth with His fullness
  All things with large increase,
He crowns the year with goodness,
  With plenty and with peace.

3 Bring to His sacred altar
  The gifts His goodness gave,
The golden sheaves of harvest,
  The souls He died to save:

Your hearts lay down before Him,
  When at His feet ye fall,
And with your lives adore Him,
  Who gave His life for all.

4 To God the gracious Father,
  Who made us "very good;"
To Christ, who, when we wandered,
  Restored us with His blood;
And to the Holy Spirit,
  Who doth upon us pour
His blessèd dews and sunshine,
  Be praise for evermore.

John S. B. Monsell, (1811–1875).

VARIOUS OCCASIONS: NATIONAL.

256

God Bless Our Native Land!

AMERICA. 6, 6, 4, 6, 6, 6, 4.

HANDEL.
HENRY CAREY, 1739.

1. God bless our na-tive land! Firm may she ev-er stand, Thro' storm and night; When the wild tem-pests rave, Rul-er of wind and wave, Do Thou our coun-try save By Thy great might! A-men.

2 For her our prayer shall rise
To God above the skies;
    On Him we wait:
Thou who art ever nigh,
Guarding with watchful eye,
To Thee aloud we cry,
    God save the State!

John S. Dwight, 1844.

VARIOUS OCCASIONS: MORNING.

257

My Father, for Another Night.

SAWLEY. C. M.

WALSH.

1. My Fa- ther, for an- oth - er night Of qui - et sleep and rest, For all the joy of morn - ing light, Thy ho - ly Name be blest. A - men.

2 Now with the new-born day I give
   Myself anew to Thee,
That as Thou willest I may live,
   And what Thou willest be.

3 Whate'er I do, things great or small,
   Whate'er I speak or frame,
Thy glory may I seek in all,
   Do all in Jesus' Name.

4 My Father, for His sake I pray
   Thy child accept and bless;
And lead me by Thy grace to-day
   In paths of righteousness.

W. H. Baker, 1875.

258

Awake, My Soul, and With the Sun.

MORNING HYMN. L. M.

BARTHELEMON.

1. A-wake, my soul, and with the sun Thy dai-ly stage of du-ty run; Shake off dull sloth, and joy-ful rise To pay thy morn-ing sac-ri-fice. A-men.

2 Wake and lift up thyself, my heart,
And with the angels bear thy part,
Who all night long unwearied sing
High praise to the eternal King.

3 All praise to Thee, who safe hast kept,
And hast refreshed me while I slept:
Grant, Lord, when I from death shall
I may of endless life partake! [wake,

4 Lord, I my vows to Thee renew;
Disperse my sins as morning dew;
Guard my first springs of thought and
And with Thyself my spirit fill. [will,

5 Direct, control, suggest, this day,
All I design, or do, or say;
That all my powers, with all their might
In Thy sole glory may unite.

6 Praise God, from whom all blessings flow;
Praise Him, all creatures here below,
Praise Him, above, ye heavenly host,
Praise Father, Son, and Holy Ghost.

Thomas Ken, 1697.

Now That the Sun is Beaming Bright.

BRADFIELD. C. M.

J. BAPTISTE CALKIN.

1. Now that the sun is beam - ing bright, Once more to God we pray, That He, the un - cre - a - ted Light, May guide our souls this day. A - men.

2 No sinful word, no deed of wrong,
Nor thoughts that idly rove;
But simple truth be on our tongue,
And in our hearts be love.

3 And while the hours in order flow,
O Christ, securely fence
Our gates beleaguered by the foe,
The gate of every sense.

4 And grant that to Thine honor, Lord,
Our daily toil may tend:
That we begin it at Thy word,
And in Thy favor end.

John Henry Newman. Tr. 1842. a.

260

God Who Madest Earth and Heaven.

GOTT DES HIMMELS UND DER ERDEN. 8, 7, 8, 7, 7, 7.   HEINRICH ALBERT, 1642.

1. God who mad - est earth and heav - en, Fa - ther, Son, and Ho - ly Ghost,
Who the day and night hast giv - en, Sun and moon and star - ry host,

Thou whose mighty hand sustains Earth and all that she contains: A - men.

2 Praise to Thee my soul shall render,
  Who this night hast guarded me;
My omnipotent Defender,
  Who from ill dost set me free;
Free from danger, anguish, woe,
Free from the eternal foe.

3 Let the night of my transgression
  With night's darkness pass away:
Jesus, into Thy possession
  I resign myself to-day.
In Thy wounds I find relief
From my greatest sin and grief.

4 Grant that I may rise this morning,
  From the lethargy of sin;
So my soul, through Thy adorning,
  Shall be glorious within;
And I at the judgment day
Shall not be a cast-away.

5 Let my life and conversation
  Be directed by Thy Word;
Lord, Thy constant preservation
  To Thy erring child afford.
No where but alone in Thee
From all harm can I be free.

6 Wholly to Thy blest protection
  I commit my heart and mind.
Mighty God! to Thy direction
  Wholly may I be resigned.
Lord, my Shield, my Light divine,
O accept, and own me Thine!

7 Lord, to me Thine angel sending,
  Keep me from the subtle foe;
From his craft and might defending,
  Never let Thy wanderer go,
Till my final rest be come,
And Thine angel bear me home.

Heinrich Albert, 1644.
John Christian Jacobi, Tr 1722.
And Arthur Tozer Russell, 1848.

Christ, Whose Glory Fills the Skies.

RATISBON. 7, 7, 7, 7, 7, 7.

J. NEANDER.

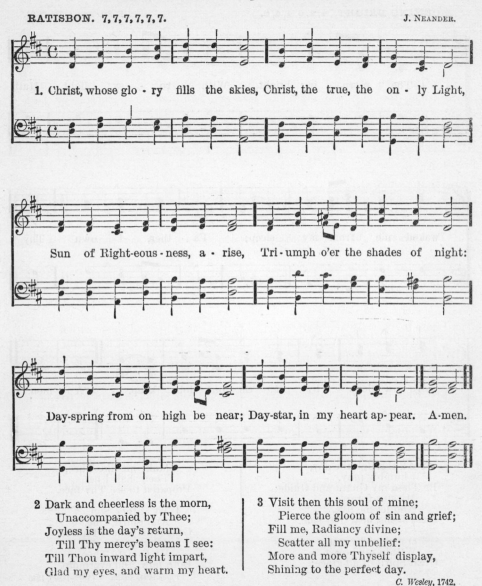

1. Christ, whose glo - ry fills the skies, Christ, the true, the on - ly Light,

Sun of Right-eous - ness, a - rise, Tri - umph o'er the shades of night:

Day-spring from on high be near; Day-star, in my heart ap- pear. A-men.

2 Dark and cheerless is the morn,
  Unaccompanied by Thee;
Joyless is the day's return,
  Till Thy mercy's beams I see:
Till Thou inward light impart,
Glad my eyes, and warm my heart.

3 Visit then this soul of mine;
  Pierce the gloom of sin and grief;
Fill me, Radiancy divine;
  Scatter all my unbelief:
More and more Thyself display,
Shining to the perfect day.

C. Wesley, 1742.

262

The Morning Bright.

MORNING BRIGHT. 4, 4, 6, 4, 4, 6.

F. SILCHER, (1789–1860).

1. The morn - ing bright, With ro - sy light, Hath waked me from my sleep; Fa - ther, I own Thy love a - lone Thy lit - tle one doth keep. A - men.

2 All through the day,
   I humbly pray,
Be Thou my Guard and Guide;
   My sins forgive,
   And let me live,
Blest Jesus, near Thy side.

3 O make Thy rest
   Within my breast,
Great Spirit of all grace;

Make me like Thee,
Then shall I be
Prepared to see Thy face.

4 To Father, Son,
   And Spirit, One,
Great God whom I adore,
   All glory be,
   My God, to Thee,
Both now, and evermore.

Thomas O. Summers, (1812–1882), 1846
Dox., Godfrey Thring, (1823 ——).

380

Every Morning Mercies New.

BARNBY'S HYMNARY, Tune 57. 7, 7, 7, 7, 7, 7.   EDWARD J. HOPKINS, (1818 ——), 1872.

1. Ev - 'ry morn - ing mer - cies new Fall as fresh as ear - ly dew;

Ev - 'ry morn - ing let us pay Trib - ute with the ear - ly day;

For Thy mer - cies, Lord, are sure; Thy com-pas-sion doth en - dure. A-men.

2 Still the greatness of Thy love
Daily doth our sins remove;
Daily, far as east from west,
Lifts the burden from the breast;
Gives unbought to those who pray
Strength to stand in evil day.

3 Let our prayers each morn prevail,
That these gifts may never fail;
And, as we confess the sin

And the tempter's power within,
Feed us with the Bread of Life;
Fit us for our daily strife.

4 As the morning light returns,
As the sun with splendor burns,
Teach us still to turn to Thee,
Ever-blessed Trinity,
With our hands our hearts to raise,
In unfailing prayer and praise.

Horatius Bonar, (1808-1889).

Various Occasions: Evening.

264

All Praise to Thee, My God, This Night.

TALLIS' CANON. L. M.

Thomas Tallis (1520—1585), 1560.

1. All praise to Thee, my God, this night, For all the bless-ings of the light; Keep me, O keep me, King of kings, Be-neath Thine own Al-might-y wings. A-men.

2 Forgive me, Lord, for Thy dear Son,
The ill that I this day have done:
That with the world, myself, and Thee,
I, ere I sleep, at peace may be.

3 Teach me to live, that I may dread
The grave as little as my bed;
To die, that this vile body may
Rise glorious at the awful day.

4 O when shall I, in endless day,
For ever chase dark sleep away,
And hymns divine with angels sing
In endless praise to Thee, my King?

5 Praise God, from whom all blessings flow;
Praise Him, all creatures here below;
Praise Him above, ye heavenly host;
Praise Father, Son, and Holy Ghost.

Thomas Ken, 1697. a.

Abide With Me! Fast Falls the Eventide.

EVENTIDE. 10, 10, 10, 10.

W. H. Monk, 1861.

1. A-bide with me! fast falls the ev-en-tide; The darkness deep-ens;

Lord, with me a-bide! When oth-er help-ers fail, and com-forts

flee, Help of the help-less, O a-bide with me! A-men.

2 Swift to its close ebbs out life's little day;
Earth's joys grow dim, its glories pass away;
Change and decay in all around I see;
O Thou who changest not, abide with me.

3 I need Thy presence every passing hour:
What but Thy grace can foil the tempter's power?
Who like Thyself my guide and stay can be?
Through cloud and sunshine, O abide with me!

4 I fear no foe, with Thee at hand to bless:
Ills have no weight, and tears no bitterness.
Where is death's sting? where, grave, thy victory?
I triumph still, if Thou abide with me!

5 Hold Thou Thy Cross before my closing eyes,
Shine through the gloom, and point me to the skies:
Heaven's morning breaks, and earth's vain shadows flee;
In life, in death, O Lord, abide with me!

Henry Francis Lyte, 1847.

266

Jesus, Tender Shepherd, Hear Me.

BATTY. 8, 7, 8, 7.

MORAVIAN, 1745.

1. Jesus, tender Shepherd, hear me;
Bless Thy little lamb to-night; Through the darkness
be Thou near me; Keep me safe till morning light. A - men.

2 All this day Thy hand has led me,
    And I thank Thee for Thy care;
Thou hast warmed me, clothed and fed me:
    Listen to my evening prayer.

3 May my sins be all forgiven;
    Bless the friends I love so well;
Take us, Lord, at last, to heaven,
    Happy there with Thee to dwell.

Mary L. Duncan, 1841.

384

Sun of My Soul, Thou Saviour Dear.

HURSLEY. L. M.

GERMAN. HAR. BY W. H. MONK.

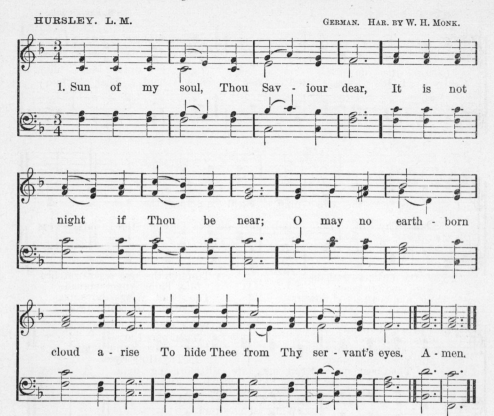

1. Sun of my soul, Thou Sav - iour dear, It is not night if Thou be near; O may no earth - born cloud a - rise To hide Thee from Thy ser - vant's eyes. A - men.

2 When the soft dews of kindly sleep
My weary eyelids gently steep,
Be my last thought, how sweet to rest
For ever on my Saviour's breast.

3 Abide with me from morn till eve,
For without Thee I cannot live;
Abide with me when night is nigh,
For without Thee I dare not die.

4 If some poor wandering child of Thine
Have spurned to-day the voice divine,
Now, Lord, the gracious work begin;
Let him no more lie down in sin.

5 Watch by the sick; enrich the poor
With blessings from Thy boundless store;
Be every mourner's sleep to-night,
Like infant slumbers, pure and light.

6 Come near and bless us when we wake,
Ere through the world our way we take,
Till in the ocean of Thy love
We lose ourselves in heaven above.

J. Keble, 1827.

268

Now the Day is Over.

6, 5, 6, 5.

S. BARING-GOULD.

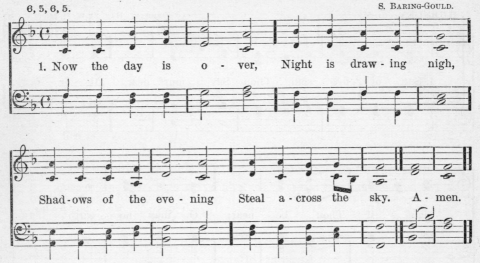

1. Now the day is o - ver, Night is draw - ing nigh,

Shad - ows of the eve - ning Steal a - cross the sky. A - men.

2 Now the darkness gathers,
  Stars begin to peep,
Birds, and beasts, and flowers
  Soon will be asleep.

3 Jesus, give the weary
  Calm and sweet repose,
With Thy tenderest blessing
  May my eyelids close.

4 Through the long night-watches
  May Thine Angels spread
Their white wings above me,
  Watching round my bed.

5 When the morning wakens,
  Then may I arise
Pure and fresh and sinless
  In Thy Holy Eyes.

6 Glory to the Father,
  Glory to the Son,
And to Thee, blest Spirit,
  While all ages run.

S Baring-Gould, 1865.

269

Our Day of Praise is Done.

FAREWELL. S. M.

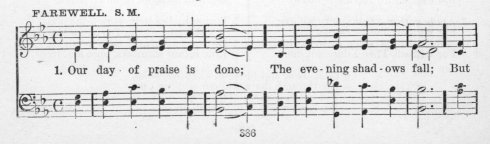

1. Our day of praise is done; The eve - ning shad - ows fall; But

Our Day of Praise is Done.—Concluded.

pass not from us with the sun, True Light that lightenest all. A-men.

2 Around the throne on high,
Where night can never be,
The white-robed harpers of the sky
Bring ceaseless hymns to Thee.

3 Too faint our anthems here;
Too soon of praise we tire:
But oh, the strains how full and clear
Of that eternal choir!

4 Yet, Lord, to Thy dear will
If Thou attune the heart,
We in Thine angels' music still
May bear our lower part.

5 'Tis Thine each soul to calm,
Each wayward thought reclaim,
And make our life a daily psalm
Of glory to Thy Name.

6 A little while, and then
Shall come the glorious end;
And songs of angels and of men
In perfect praise shall blend.

J. Ellerton, 1868.

270

The Day is Done.

FRESHWATER. 4, 4, 8. T. B.

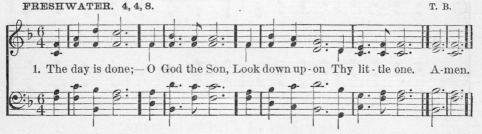

1. The day is done;— O God the Son, Look down up-on Thy lit-tle one. A-men.

2 O Light of Light
Keep me this night,
And shed round me Thy presence bright.

3 I need not fear
If Thou art near;
Thou art my Saviour, kind and dear.

4 Thy gentle eye
Is ever nigh,
It watches me when none is by.

5 Thy loving ear
Is ever near
Thy little children's prayers to **hear.**

6 So happily
And peacefully
I lay me down to rest in **Thee.**

7 To Father, Son,
And Spirit, One
In heaven and earth, all praise be done.

P. Caroline Dunsterville, 1882.

271

God, That Madest Earth and Heaven.

TEMPLE. 8, 4, 8, 4, 8, 8, 8, 4.

E. J. HOPKINS.

1. God, that mad-est earth and heav-en, Dark-ness and light;

Who the day for toil hast giv-en For rest the night;

May Thine an-gel-guards de-fend us, Slum-ber sweet Thy mer-cy send us,

Ho-ly dreams and hopes at-tend us, This live-long night. A-men.

God, That Madest Earth and Heaven.—Concluded.

2 And when morn again shall call us
   To run life's way,
May we still, whate'er befall us,
   Thy will obey.
From the power of evil hide us,
In the narrow pathway guide us,
Nor Thy smile be e'er denied us,
   The live-long day.

3 Guard us waking, guard us sleeping;
   And when we die,
May we in Thy mighty keeping
   All peaceful lie.
When the last dread call shall wake us,
Do not Thou, our God, forsake us,
But to reign in glory take us,
   With Thee on high,

1st stanza, R. Heber, 1827.
2nd stanza, W. Mercer, 1864.
3rd stanza, Whately, 1855.

Now the Light Has Gone Away.   272

MUEDE BIN ICH, GEH ZUR RUH. 7, 7, 7, 7.   LIEDERBÜCHLEIN, 1842.

1. Now the light has gone a-way, Sav-iour, list-en while I pray,

Ask-ing Thee to watch and keep, And to send me qui-et sleep. A-men.

2 Jesus, Saviour, wash away
All that has been wrong to-day;
Help me every day to be
Good and gentle, more like Thee.

3 Let my near and dear ones be
Always near and dear to Thee;
O bring me and all I love
To Thy happy Home above.

4 Now my evening praise I give;
Thou didst die that I might live,
All my blessings come from Thee,
O how good Thou art to me!

5 Thou my best and kindest Friend,
Thou wilt love me to the end!
Let me love Thee more and more,
Always better than before.

From the German. Frances Ridley Havergal, 1869.

273

Star of Morn and Even.

PALGRAVE. 6, 6, 5, 5, 5, 5.   JAMES TILLEARD (1827—1876).

1. Star of morn and e - ven, Sun of heav - en's heav -
en, Sav - iour high and dear, Toward us turn Thine ear;
Thro' what -e'er may come, Thou canst lead us home. A - men.

2 Though the gloom be grievous,
Those we leaned on leave us,
Though the coward heart
Quit its proper part,
Though the tempter come,
Thou wilt lead us home.

3 Saviour pure and holy,
Lover of the lowly,
Sign us with Thy sign,
Take our hands in Thine,
Take our hands and come,
Lead Thy children home!

4 Star of morn and even,
Shine on us from heaven,
From Thy glory-throne
Hear Thy very own!
Lord and Saviour, come,
Lead us to our home.

Francis Turner Palgrave, (1824 —), 1862.

Saviour, Breathe an Evening Blessing.

SARDIS. 8, 7, 8, 7.

BEETHOVEN.

1. Sav - iour, breathe an eve - ning bless - ing, Ere re - pose our
spir - its seal; Sin and want we come con - fess - ing;
Thou canst save, and Thou canst heal. A - men.

2 Though destruction walk around us,
  Though the arrow past us fly,
  Angel-guards from Thee surround us;
  We are safe if Thou art nigh.

3 Though the night be dark and dreary,
  Darkness cannot hide from Thee;
  Thou art He Who, never weary,
  Watchest where Thy people be.

4 Should swift death this night o'ertake us,
  And our couch become our tomb,
  May the heavenly night o'ertake us,
  Clad in bright and deathless bloom.

James Edmeston, 1820.

GENERAL.

275

God Make My Life a Little Light.

C. M.

FR. PIRA.

1. God make my life a little light, With in the world to glow,— A little flame that burneth bright Wherever I may go. A-men.

2 God make my life a little flower
   That giveth joy to all,
   Content to bloom in native bower,
   Although the place be small.

3 God make my life a little song
   That comforteth the sad,
   That helpeth others to be strong,
   And makes the singer glad.

4 God make my life a little staff,
   Whereon the weak may rest,
   That so what little strength I have
   May serve my neighbors best.

5 God make my life a little hymn
   Of tenderness and praise,
   Of faith that never waxeth dim,
   In all His wondrous ways.

Matilda Betham Edwards, 1873.

In the Vineyard of Our Father.

8, 7, 8, 7, 8, 7.

1. In the vine-yard of our Fa-ther, Dai-ly work we find to do;

Scatter'd gleanings we may gath-er, Though we are but young and few;

Lit-tle clus-ters, lit-tle clus-ters, Help to fill the gar-ners, too. A-men.

2 Toiling early in the morning,
   Catching moments through the day,
Nothing small or lowly scorning,
   So along our path we stray;
   ‖: Gathering gladly :‖
Free-will offerings by the way.

3 Not for selfish praise or glory,
   Not for objects nothing worth,
But to send the blessed story
   Of the gospel o'er the earth,
   ‖: Telling mortals :‖
Of our Lord and Saviour's birth.

4 Up and ever at our calling,
   Till in death our lips are dumb,
Or till—sin's dominion falling—
   Christ shall in His kingdom come;
   ‖: And His children :‖
Reach their everlasting home.

5 Steadfast, then, in our endeavor,
   Heavenly Father, may we be;
And, for ever and for ever,
   We will give the praise to Thee;
   ‖: Hallelujah! :‖
Singing all eternally.

Thomas MacKellar, 1845.

277

When Morning Gilds the Skies.

BEIM FRUEHEN MORGENLICHT. 6, 6, 6, 6, 6, 6.   FRANCONIAN MELODY.

1. When morning gilds the skies, My heart a-wak-ing cries: To Je-sus Christ be praise! A-like at work and pray'r, To Je-sus I re-pair; To Je-sus Christ be praise! To Je-sus Christ be praise! A-men.

2 When evil thoughts molest,
With this I shield my breast:
  To Jesus Christ be praise!
Does sadness fill my mind
A solace here I find:
  To Jesus Christ be praise!

3 The night becomes as day,
When from the heart we say:
  To Jesus Christ be praise!
The powers of darkness fear,
When this sweet chant we hear:
  To Jesus Christ be praise!

4 In heaven's eternal bliss
The loveliest strain is this:
  To Jesus Christ be praise!
Let earth, and sea, and sky
From depth to height reply:
  To Jesus Christ be praise!

5 Be this, while life is mine,
My canticle divine:
  To Jesus Christ be praise!
Be this the eternal song,
Through all the ages on:
  To Jesus Christ be praise!

From the German. Author unknown.
Tr. Edward Caswall, (1814–1878). Abridged.

Work for the Night is Coming.

ALPHA. 7, 6, 7, 5. D.

J. H. WALKER.

1. Work, for the night is com - ing; Work, thro' the morn - ing hours;

Work while the dew is spark - ling; Work 'mid spring- ing flow'rs;

Work, when the day grows bright - er, Work in the glow - ing sun;

Work, for the night is com - ing When man's work is done. A - men.

2 Work, for the night is coming,
  Work through the sunny noon;
Fill brightest hours with labor,
  Rest comes sure and soon:
Give every flying minute
  Something to keep in store:
Work, for the night is coming
  When man works no more.

3 Work, for the night is coming,
  Under the sunset skies;
While their bright tints are glowing
  Work, for daylight flies:
Work till the last beam fadeth,
  Fadeth to shine no more;
Work, while the night is darkening
  When man's work is o'er.

A. L. Walker, 1868.

279

Jesus, and Shall it Ever Be.

FEDERAL STREET. L. M.

H. K. OLIVER.

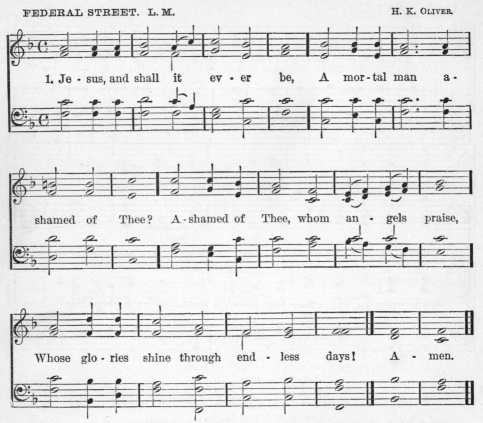

1. Je - sus, and shall it ev - er be, A mor - tal man a-
shamed of Thee? A - shamed of Thee, whom an - gels praise,
Whose glo - ries shine through end - less days! A - men.

2 Ashamed of Jesus! sooner far
  Let evening blush to own a star;
  He sheds the beams of light divine
  O'er this benighted soul of mine.

3 Ashamed of Jesus! just as soon
  Let midnight be ashamed of noon;
  'Tis midnight with my soul, till He,
  Bright Morning Star, bid darkness flee.

4 Ashamed of Jesus! that dear Friend
  On whom my hopes of heaven depend!
  No; when I blush, be this my shame,
  That I no more revere His Name.

5 Ashamed of Jesus! yes, I may,
  When I've no guilt to wash away,
  No tear to wipe, no good to crave,
  No fears to quell, no soul to save.

6 Till then—nor is my boasting vain—
  Till then I boast a Saviour slain!
  And O, may this my glory be,
  That Christ is not ashamed of me!

Joseph Grigg, 1738.
And Benjamin Francis, 1787.

Christian, Seek Not Yet Repose.

VIGILATE. 7, 7, 7, 3.

W. H. MONK.

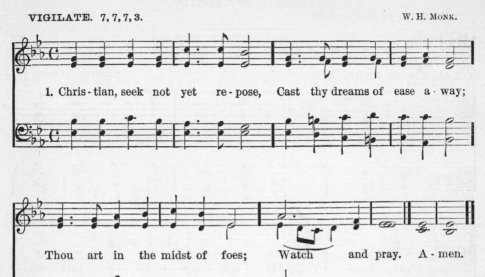

1. Chris-tian, seek not yet re-pose, Cast thy dreams of ease a-way;

Thou art in the midst of foes; Watch and pray. A-men.

2 Gird thy heavenly armor on,
   Wear it ever, night and day;
   Near thee lurks the evil One;
   Watch and pray.

3 Listen to thy sorrowing Lord,
   Him thou lovest to obey;
   It is He, Who speaks the word,
   Watch and pray.

4 'Twas by watching, and by prayer,
   Holy men of olden day
   Won the palms and crowns they wear;
   Watch and pray.

5 Watch, for thou thy guard must keep;
   Pray, for God must speed thy way:
   Narrow is the road and steep:
   Watch and pray.

Charlotte Elliott, 1839.

Last Things.

281

Let Me Go, Let Me Go.

LASST MICH GEHN. P. M. (*First tune.*)　　　　　LITHUANIAN FOLKSONG.

1. Let me go, let me go, Lord, to me Thy pres - ence show, Thith - er still my heart is turn - ing, For Thy heav'n - ly courts is yearn - ing, There Thy per - fect rest to know, There Thy per - fect rest to know. A - men.

Let Me Go, Let Me Go.—Concluded.

2 Sweetest Light, sweetest Light,
  Sun that scatt'rest clouds in flight,
  O when shall I come before Thee,
  When shall I with saints adore Thee,
  Dwelling in Thy presence bright!

3 Ah, how clear, ah, how clear,
  Ring the angel voices there!
  While my soul for wings is sighing,
  Wings o'er vale and mountain flying—
  Now in Zion to appear.

4 What shall be, what shall be,
  All the joy laid up for me,
  Lord, I know not, eyes are holden
  Till Jerusalem the Golden
  In its beauty I shall see.

5 Paradise! Paradise.
  Fairest fruits delight our eyes,
  Where the Tree of Life is planted,
  Bliss beyond our dreams is granted;
  Bring us, Lord, to Paradise!

Gustav Knak, 1840.
Tr. H. R. Krauth, 1877.

Let Me Go, Let Me Go.

6, 7, 8, 8, 7, 7. (*Second tune.*)　　　　　　　A. VOIGTLÄNDER, 1858.

1. Let me go, let me go, Lord, to me Thy pres-ence show Thith-er still my heart is turn-ing, For Thy heav'n-ly courts is yearn-ing, There Thy per-fect rest to know. A-men.

282

I'm but a Stranger Here.

ST. EDMUND. 6, 4, 6, 4, 6, 6, 6, 4.

A. S. SULLIVAN.

1. I'm but a stran-ger here, Heaven is my home; Earth is a des-ert drear, Heaven is my home. Dan - ger and sorrow stand Round me on ev-'ry hand, Heaven is my fa-ther-land, Heaven is my home. A-men.

2 What though the tempests rage?
  Heaven is my home;
Short is my pilgrimage,
  Heaven is my home.
And Time's wild wintry blast
Soon shall be overpast,
I shall reach home at last;
  Heaven is my home.

3 There at my Saviour's side,
  Heaven is my home;
May I be glorified;
  Heaven is my home:

There are the good and blest,
Those I love most and best,
Grant me with them to rest;
  Heaven is my home.

4 Grant me to murmur not,
  Heaven is my home;
Whate'er my earthly lot,
  Heaven is my home.
Grant me at last to stand
There at Thine own Right Hand
Jesus, in Fatherland:
  Heaven is my home!

Thomas R. Taylor, 1836.

Heaven.

O Paradise, O Paradise.

PARADISE. P. M.

JOSEPH BARNBY.

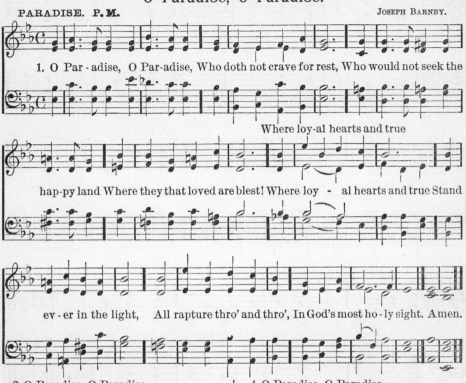

1. O Par - adise, O Par-adise, Who doth not crave for rest, Who would not seek the
Where loy-al hearts and true
hap-py land Where they that loved are blest! Where loy - al hearts and true Stand
ev - er in the light, All rapture thro' and thro', In God's most ho - ly sight. Amen.

2 O Paradise, O Paradise,
  The world is growing old;
Who would not be at rest and free
  Where love is never cold?
Where loyal hearts and true, etc.

3 O Paradise, O Paradise,
  'Tis weary waiting here;
I long to be where Jesus is,
  To feel, to see Him near;
Where loyal hearts and true, etc.

4 O Paradise, O Paradise,
  I want to sin no more,
I want to be as pure on earth
  As on thy spotless shore;
Where loyal hearts and true, etc.

5 O Paradise, O Paradise,
  I greatly long to see
The special place my dearest Lord
  In love prepares for me;
Where loyal hearts and true, etc.

6 Lord Jesus, King of Paradise,
  O keep me in Thy love,
And guide me to that happy land
  Of perfect rest above;
Where loyal hearts and true, etc.

F. W. Faber, 1862.

284

Hark! Hark, My Soul!

ANGELS OF JESUS. 11, 10, 11, 10, 9, 11.

BARNBY.

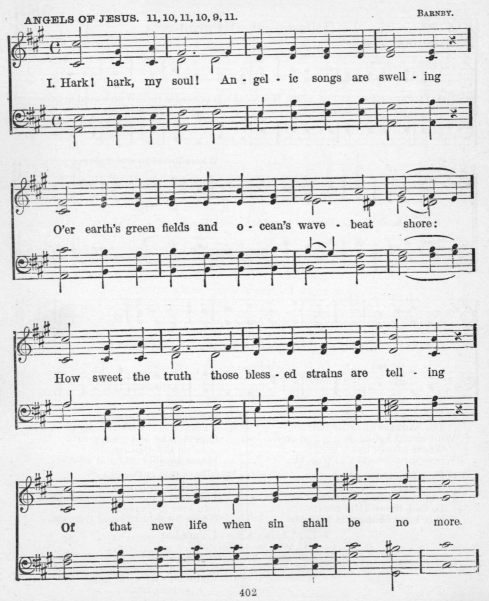

1. Hark! hark, my soul! An - gel - ic songs are swell - ing

O'er earth's green fields and o - cean's wave - beat shore:

How sweet the truth those bless - ed strains are tell - ing

Of that new life when sin shall be no more.

Hark! Hark, My Soul!—Concluded.

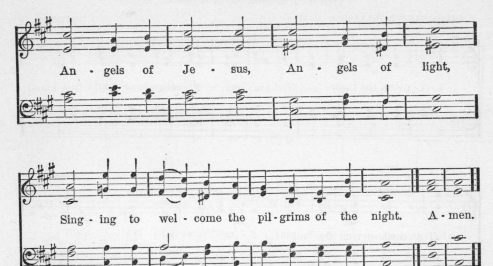

An - gels of Je - sus, An - gels of light,

Sing - ing to wel - come the pil - grims of the night. A - men.

2 Onward we go, for still we hear them singing,
　"Come, weary souls, for Jesus bids you come:"
And, through the dark, its echoes sweetly ringing,
　The music of the Gospel leads us home.
　　Angels of Jesus, Angels of light,
　　Singing to welcome the pilgrims of the night.

3 Far, far away, like bells at evening pealing,
　The voice of Jesus sounds o'er land and sea,
And laden souls, by thousands meekly stealing,
　Kind Shepherd, turn their weary steps to Thee.
　　Angels of Jesus, Angels of light,
　　Singing to welcome the pilgrims of the night.

4 Rest comes at length; though life be long and dreary,
　The day must dawn, and darksome night be past;
All journeys end in welcome to the weary,
　And heaven, the heart's true home, will come at last.
　　Angels of Jesus, Angels of light,
　　Singing to welcome the pilgrims of the night.

5 Angels, sing on! your faithful watches keeping;
　Sing us sweet fragments of the songs above;
Till morning's joy shall end the night of weeping,
　And life's long shadows break in cloudless love.
　　Angels of Jesus, Angels of light,
　　Singing to welcome the pilgrims of the night.

F. W. Faber.

285

Around the Throne of God in Heaven.

CHILDREN'S PRAISES. C. M (*With refrain.*)

ARR. BY H. E. MATTHEWS.

1. A - round the throne of God in heav'n, Thous-ands of chil - dren stand;

Chil - dren whose sins are all for - giv'n, A ho - ly, hap - py band,

Sing-ing Glo - ry, Glo - ry, Glo - ry be to God on high. A - men.

2 In flowing robes of spotless white,
　See every one arrayed;
Dwelling in everlasting light,
　And joys that never fade,
　　Singing Glory, Glory, etc.

3 What brought them to that world above—
　That heaven so bright and fair,
Where all is peace and joy and love?
　How came those children there,
　　Singing Glory, Glory, etc

4 Because the Saviour shed His Blood
　To wash away their sin:
Bathed in that pure and precious flood,
　Behold them white and clean,
　　Singing Glory, Glory, etc.

5 On earth they sought the Saviour's grace,
　On earth they loved His Name;
So now they see His blessed Face,
　And stand before the Lamb,
　　Singing Glory, Glory, etc.

Anna Houlditch.

For Ever With the Lord.

NEARER HOME. S. M. D.

J. Woodbury. Arr. by A. Sullivan.

1. For ev-er with the Lord! A-men! so let it be;
Life from the dead is in that word, 'Tis im-mor-tal-i-ty.

2. Here in the bod-y pent, Ab-sent from Him I roam,
Yet night-ly pitch my mov-ing tent A day's march nearer Home. A-men.

3 My Father's House on high,
  Home of my soul! how near
At times to faith's far-seeing eye
  The golden gates appear!

4 Ah, then my spirit faints,
  To reach the land I love,
The bright inheritance of saints,
  Jerusalem above!

5 For ever with the Lord!
  Father, if 'tis Thy will,
The promise of that faithful word
  E'en here to me fulfil.

6 Be Thou at my right hand,
  Then can I never fail;
Uphold Thou me, and I shall stand,
  Fight, and I must prevail.

7 So when my latest breath
  Shall rend the veil in twain,
By death I shall escape from death
  And Life eternal gain.

8 Knowing as I am known,
  How shall I love that word,
And oft repeat before the throne,
  "For ever with the Lord!"

James Montgomery, 1853.

287

Hark! the Sound of Holy Voices.

SANCTUARY. 8, 7, 8, 7. D.

J. B. DYKES.

1. Hark! the sound of ho - ly voi - ces Chant-ing o'er the crys - tal sea,

Al - le - lu - ia, Al - le - lu - ia, Al - le - lu - ia, Lord, to Thee;

Mul - ti - tudes, which none can num - ber, Like the stars in glo - ry stand,

Clothed in white ap-par - el, holding Palms of vic - t'ry in their hand. A-men.

2 Patriarch, and Holy Prophet,
  Who prepared the way of Christ,
King, Apostle, Saint, Confessor,
  Martyr and Evangelist,
Saintly Maiden, Godly Matron,
  Widows who have watched to prayer,
Joined in holy concert, singing
  To the Lord of all, are there.

3 They have come from tribulation,
  And have washed their robes in blood,
Washed them in the blood of Jesus;
  Tried they were, and firm they stood;
Mocked, imprisoned, stoned, tormented,
  Sawn asunder, slain with sword,
They have conquered death and Satan
  By the might of Christ the Lord.

4 Marching with Thy cross their banner,
  They have triumphed, following
Thee, the Captain of salvation,
  Thee, their Saviour and their King.
Gladly, Lord, with Thee they suffered,
  Gladly, Lord, with Thee they died;
And by death to life immortal
  They were born and glorified.

5 Now they reign in heavenly glory
  Now they walk in golden light,
Now they drink, as from a river,
  Holy bliss and infinite:
Love and peace they taste for ever,
  And all truth and knowledge see
In the beatific vision
  Of the Blessèd Trinity.

Christopher Wordsworth, 1862.

Jerusalem, Thou City Fair and High.

JERUSALEM, DU HOCHGEBAUTE STADT.

MELCHIOR FRANK, 1580—1639.

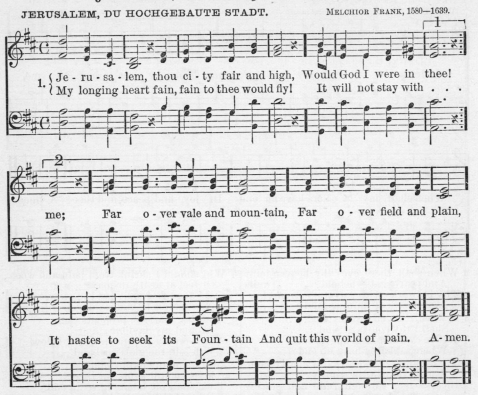

1. { Je - ru - sa - lem, thou ci - ty fair and high, Would God I were in thee!
   { My longing heart fain, fain to thee would fly! It will not stay with . . .

me; Far o - ver vale and moun-tain, Far o - ver field and plain,

It hastes to seek its Foun - tain And quit this world of pain. A - men.

2 O happy day, and yet far happier hour,
    When wilt thou come at last?
  When fearless to my Father's love and
    Whose promise standeth fast, [power,
    My soul I gladly render,
    For surely will His hand
    Lead her with guidance tender
    To heaven, her fatherland.

3 O Zion, hail! Bright city, now unfold
    The gates of grace to me!
  How many a time I longed for thee of old,
    Ere yet I was set free
    From yon dark life of sadness,
    Yon world of shadowy nought,
    And God had given the gladness,
    The heritage I sought.

4 O what the tribe, or what the glorious
    Comes sweeping swiftly down? [host,
  The chosen ones on earth who wrought the
    The Church's brightest crown, [most,
    Our Lord hath sent to meet me,
    As in the far off years,
    Their words oft came to greet me
    In yonder land of tears.

5 Innumerous choirs before the shining
    Their joyful anthems raise, [throne
  Till heaven's glad halls are echoing with
    Of that great hymn of praise, [the tone
    And all its host rejoices,
    And all its blessed throng
    Unite their myriad voices
    In one eternal song.

John Matthew Meyfart, 1630.
Miss Winkworth. Tr. 1858.

Jerusalem, My Happy Home.

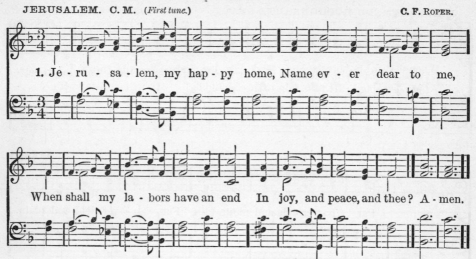

JERUSALEM. C. M. (*First tune.*) C. F. ROPER.

1. Je - ru - sa - lem, my hap - py home, Name ev - er dear to me,

When shall my la - bors have an end In joy, and peace, and thee? A - men.

2 When shall these eyes thy heaven-built
    And pearly gates behold?   [walls
  Thy bulwarks with salvation strong,
    And streets of shining gold?

3 O when, thou city of my God,
    Shall I thy courts ascend,
  Where evermore the angels sing,
    Where sabbaths have no end?

4 There happier bowers than Eden's bloom,
    Nor sin nor sorrow know:
  Blest seats! through rude and stormy
    I onward press to you.   [scenes

5 Why should I shrink from pain and woe,
    Or feel at death dismay?
  I've Canaan's goodly land in view,
    And realms of endless day.

6 Apostles, martyrs, prophets there
    Around my Saviour stand;
  And soon my friends in Christ below
    Will join the glorious band.

7 Jerusalem, my happy home!
    My soul still pants for thee;
  Then shall my labors have an end,
    When I thy joy shall see.

Composite, 1801. a.
From Francis Baker, 1628.

Jerusalem, My Happy Home.

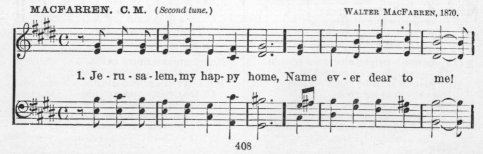

MACFARREN. C. M. (*Second tune.*) WALTER MACFARREN, 1870.

1. Je - ru - sa - lem, my hap - py home, Name ev - er dear to me!

Jerusalem, My Happy Home.—Concluded.

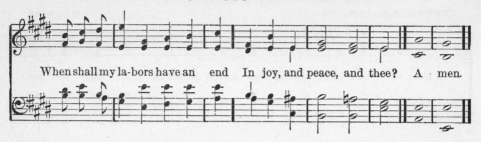

When shall my la-bors have an end In joy, and peace, and thee? A men.

There is a Happy Land.

290

HAPPY LAND. 6, 4, 6, 4, 6, 7, 6, 4.

HINDOO MELODY.

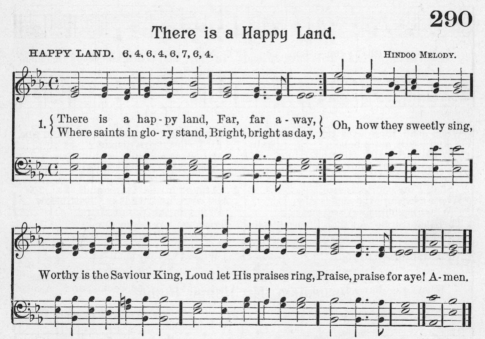

1. { There is a hap-py land, Far, far a-way, } Oh, how they sweetly sing,
   { Where saints in glo-ry stand, Bright, bright as day, }

Worthy is the Saviour King, Loud let His praises ring, Praise, praise for aye! A-men.

2 Come to that happy land,
  Come, come away;
 Why will ye doubting stand,
  Why still delay?
 Oh, we shall happy be,
 When, from sin and sorrow free,
 Lord, we shall live with Thee,
  Blest, blest for aye.

3 Bright, in that happy land,
  Beams every eye;
 Kept by a Father's hand,
  Love cannot die.
 Oh, then, to glory run,
 Be a crown and kingdom won,
 And, bright above the sun,
  We reign for aye.

Andrew Young, 1838.

291

Jerusalem the Golden.

EWING. 7, 6, 7, 6. D.

A. EWING, 1853.

1. Je - ru - sa - lem the gold - en, With milk and hon - ey blest!

Be - neath thy con - tem - pla - tion Sink heart and voice op - press'd,

I know not, O I know not What so - cial joys are there,

What ra - dian - cy of glo - ry, What light be - yond com - pare! A - men.

2 And when I fain would sing them,
  My spirit fails and faints,
And vainly would it image
  The assembly of the saints,
They stand, those halls of Zion,
  Conjubilant with song,
And bright with many an angel,
  And all the martyr throng:

3 There is the throne of David;
  And there from care released,
The song of them that triumph,
  The shout of them that feast;
And they who, with their Leader,
  Have conquered in the fight,
For ever and for ever
  Are clad in robes of white!

Bernard de Morlaix, about 1150.
John Mason Neale. Tr.

PROCESSIONALS.

The Son of God Goes Forth to War.

292

PATMOS. C. M. D.

ADAPTED FROM H. J. STORER.

1. The Son of God goes forth to war, A king-ly crown to gain.

His blood-red ban-ner streams a-far, Who fol-lows in His train?

Who best can drink His cup of woe, Tri-umph-ant o-ver pain;

Who patient bears His cross be-low, He fol-lows in His train. A-men.

2 The martyr first, whose eagle eye
  Could pierce beyond the grave,
Who saw his Master in the sky,
  And called on Him to save:
Like Him, with pardon on his tongue,
  In midst of mortal pain,
He prayed for them that did the wrong:
  Who follows in his train?

3 A glorious band, the chosen few,
  On whom the Spirit came: [knew,
Twelve valiant saints, their hope they
And mocked the cross and flame:

They met the tyrant's brandished steel,
  The lion's gory mane;
They bowed their necks the death to feel;
  Who follows in their train?

4 A noble army, men and boys,
  The matron and the maid,
Around the Saviour's throne rejoice,
  In robes of light arrayed:
They climbed the steep ascent of heaven
  Through peril, toil, and pain:
O God! to us may grace be given
  To follow in their train!

R. Heber, 1827.

293

Onward, Christian Soldiers.

ST. GERTRUDE. 6, 5, 6, 5. D.

A. S. SULLIVAN.

1. On - ward, Chris - tian sol - diers, March - ing as to war,

With the Cross of Je - sus Go - ing on be - fore.

Christ, the Roy - al Mas - ter, Leads a - gainst the foe:

For - ward in - to bat - tle, See His ban - ners go.

Onward, Christian Soldiers.—Concluded.

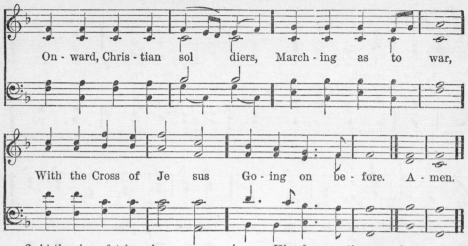

On - ward, Chris - tian sol diers, March - ing as to war,

With the Cross of Je sus Go - ing on be - fore. A - men.

2 At the sign of triumph,
    Satan's armies flee :
On, then, Christian soldiers,
    On to victory.
Hell's foundations quiver,
    At the shout of praise;
Brothers, lift your voices,
    Loud your anthems raise.
        Onward, Christian soldiers,
        Marching as to war,
        With the Cross of Jesus
        Going on before.

3 Like a mighty army,
    Moves the Church of God :
Brothers, we are treading
    Where the saints have trod.
We are not divided,
    All one body we,
One in hope, in doctrine,
    One in charity.
        Onward, Christian soldiers,
        Marching as to war,
        With the Cross of Jesus
        Going on before.

4 What our Lord established
    That we hold for true:
What the saints believed
    That believe we too.
Long as earth endureth
    Men that Faith will hold—

Kingdoms, nations, empires,
    In destruction rolled.
        Onward, Christian soldiers,
        Marching as to war,
        With the Cross of Jesus
        Going on before.

5 Crowns and thrones may perish,
    Kingdoms rise and wane,
But the Church of Jesus
    Constant will remain.
Gates of hell can never
    'Gainst that Church prevail :
We have Christ's own promise,
    And that cannot fail.
        Onward, Christian soldiers,
        Marching as to war,
        With the Cross of Jesus
        Going on before.

6 Onward, then, ye faithful,
    Join our happy throng,
Blend with ours your voices,
    In the triumph-song :
Glory, laud, and honor,
    Unto Christ the King :
This, through countless ages,
    Men and angels sing.
        Onward, Christian soldiers,
        Marching as to war,
        With the Cross of Jesus
        Going on before.

S. Baring-Gould, 1865.

294

We March, We March to Victory.

G. F. Cobb.

We March, We March to Victory.—Concluded.

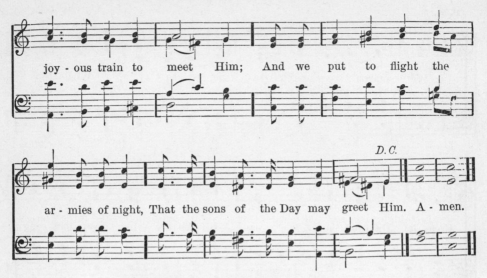

joy - ous train to meet Him; And we put to flight the ar - mies of night, That the sons of the Day may greet Him. A - men.

2 Our sword is the Spirit of God on high,
  Our helmet His salvation;
And our banner the Cross of Calvary,
  And our watchword: THE INCARNATION.
    We march, we march, etc.

3 We tread in the might of the Lord of hosts,
  And fear not man nor devil;
For our Captain Himself guards well our coasts,
  To defend all His Church from evil.
    We march, we march, etc.

4 He marches in front of His banner unfurled
  Which He raised that His own might find Him;
And the holy Church throughout all the world
  Fall in rank and march behind Him.
    We march, we march, etc.

5 And the angel choir with its song awaits
  Our march to the Golden Sion;
For our Captain has broken the brazen gates,
  And burst the bars of iron.
    We march, we march, etc.

6 Then onward we march, our arms to prove,
  With the Banner of Christ before us,
With His eye of love looking down from above,
  And His holy Arm spread o'er us.
    We march, we march, etc.

G. Moultrie.

295

Stand Up! Stand Up for Jesus!

1. Stand up! Stand up for Je - sus! Ye sol - diers of the Cross;
2. Stand up! Stand up for Je - sus! The trum - pet call o - bey;

Lift high His roy - al ban - ner, It must not suf - fer loss.
Forth in the might - y con - flict, In this His glo - rious day.

From vic - t'ry un - to vic - to - ry His ar - my He shall lead,
Ye that are men now serve Him, A - gainst un - num - bered foes;

Till ev - 'ry foe is van - quished, And Christ is Lord in - deed.
Let cour - age rise with dan - ger, And strength to strength op - pose.

Stand Up! Stand Up for Jesus!—Concluded.

CHORUS.

Stand up! Stand up for Je - sus! Ye sol - diers of the Cross;

ORGAN.

Lift up His roy - al ban - ner, It must not suf - fer loss. Amen.

3 Stand up! Stand up for Jesus!
    Stand in His strength alone;
  The arm of flesh will fail you,
    Ye dare not trust your own.
  Put on the Gospel armor,
    Each piece put on with prayer;
  Where duty calls or danger,
    Be never wanting there.—CHO.

4 Stand up! Stand up for Jesus!
    The strife will not be long;
  This day the noise of battle,
    The next the victor's song.
  To him that overcometh,
    A crown of life shall be;
  He with the King of Glory
    Shall reign eternally!—CHO.

George Duffield, Jr. (1818 —), 1858. *Abridged.*

296 Brightly Gleams Our Banner.

BRIGHTLY GLEAMS OUR BANNER. 6, 5, 6, 5. D. (*With refrain.*)   BARNBY.

1. Brightly gleams our ban - ner, Pointing to the sky, Waving wand'rers onward
2. Je - sus, Lord and Mas - ter, At Thy sa - cred feet, Here, with hearts rejoicing,
3. Pat - tern of our child-hood, Once Thyself a child, Make our childhood ho - ly,

To their home on high. Journ'ying o'er a des - ert, Glad - ly thus we pray,
See Thy chil - dren meet. Oft - en have we left Thee, Oft - en gone a - stray,
Pure, and meek, and mild. In the hour of dan - ger Whither can we flee,

And, with hearts u - ni - ted, Take our heav'nward way.
Keep us, mighty Saviour, In the nar - row way.   } Brightly gleams our banner,
Save to Thee, our Saviour, On - ly un - to Thee?

Pointing to the sky, Waving wand'rers onward To their home on high. A-men.

4 All our days direct us
  In the way we go,
  Lead us on victorious
  Over every foe;
  Bid Thine angels shield us
  When the storm-clouds lower;
  Pardon Thou and save us
  In the last dread hour.
  Brightly gleams, etc.

5 Then with saints and angels
  May we join above,
  Offering prayers and praises
  At Thy throne of love.
  When the march is over
  Then come rest and peace,
  Jesus in His beauty!
  Songs that never cease!
  Brightly gleams, etc.

Thomas J. Potter, (1827-1873), 1867.

Soldiers of Christ, Arise.

DIADEMATA. S. M. D.

G. J. ELVEY.

1. Sol - diers of Christ, a - rise, And put your ar - mor on,
Strong in the strength which God sup-plies, Thro' His e - ter - nal Son;

2. Strong in the Lord of Hosts, And in His might - y power:
Who in the strength of Je - sus trusts Is more than conquer - or. A - men.

3 Stand then in His great might,
   With all His strength endued;
But take to arm you for the fight,
   The panoply of God:

4 That having all things done,
   And all your conflicts past,
Ye may o'ercome through Christ alone,
   And stand entire at last.

5 From strength to strength go on,
   Wrestle, and fight, and pray:
Tread all the powers of darkness down,
   And win the well-fought day.

6 Still let the Spirit cry,
   In all His soldiers, "Come,"
Till Christ the Lord descends from high,
   And takes the conqueror home.

C. Wesley, 1749.

298

Forward! Be Our Watchword.

ST. BOTOLPH. 6, 5s, 12 lines.

H. SMART.

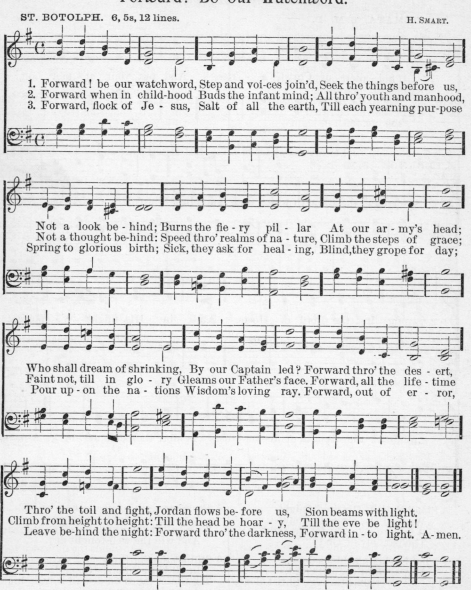

1. Forward! be our watchword, Step and voi-ces join'd, Seek the things before us,
2. Forward when in child-hood Buds the infant mind; All thro' youth and manhood,
3. Forward, flock of Je - sus, Salt of all the earth, Till each yearning pur-pose

Not a look be - hind; Burns the fie - ry pil - lar At our ar - my's head;
Not a thought be-hind: Speed thro' realms of na - ture, Climb the steps of grace;
Spring to glorious birth; Sick, they ask for heal - ing, Blind, they grope for day;

Who shall dream of shrinking, By our Captain led? Forward thro' the des - ert,
Faint not, till in glo - ry Gleams our Father's face. Forward, all the life - time
Pour up - on the na - tions Wisdom's loving ray. Forward, out of er - ror,

Thro' the toil and fight, Jordan flows be-fore us, Sion beams with light.
Climb from height to height: Till the head be hoar - y, Till the eve be light!
Leave be-hind the night: Forward thro' the darkness, Forward in - to light. A-men.

Forward! Be Our Watchword.—Concluded.

4 Glories upon glories,
  Hath our God prepared,
By the souls that love Him
  One day to be shared;
Eye hath not beheld them,
  Ear hath never heard;
Nor of these hath uttered
  Thought or speech or word.
Forward, marching eastward
  Where the heaven is bright,
Till the veil be lifted,
  Till our faith be sight!

5 Far o'er yon horizon
  Rise the city towers,
Where our God abideth,
  That fair home is ours;
Flash the streets with jasper,
  Shine the gates with gold:
Flows the gladdening river
  Shedding joys untold:
Thither, onward thither,
  In the Spirit's might:
Pilgrim to your country,
  Forward into light.

H. Alford, 1810—1871.

Rejoice, Ye Pure in Heart! 299

LEBANON. S. M. D.   J. ZUNDEL.

1. Rejoice, ye pure in heart! Rejoice! give thanks and sing; Your festal ban-ner wave on high,
2. With all the Angel choirs, With all the saints on earth, Pour out the strains of joy and bliss,

The Cross of Christ, your King. Bright youth and snow-crown'd age, Strong men and maidens meek,
True rap-ture, noblest mirth. Your clear Ho-san-nas raise, And Al-le-lu-ias loud;

Raise high your free ex-ult-ing song, God's wondrous praises speak.
While answ'ring answers up-ward float, Like wreaths of in-cense cloud.   A-men.

3 With voices full and strong
    As ocean's surging praise,
  Send forth the hymns our fathers loved,
    The psalms of ancient days.
  Yes, on through life's long path,
    Still chanting as ye go,
  From youth to age, by night and day,
    In gladness and in woe.

4 Still lift your standard high,
    Still march in firm array,
  As warriors through the darkness toil
    Till dawns the golden day.
  At last the march shall end,
    The wearied ones shall rest,
  The pilgrims find their Father's house,
    Jerusalem the blest.

E. H. Plumptre, 1865.

300

Praise the Lord of Heaven.

DAVID. 6, 5, 6, 5. D.

T. MORLEY.

1. Praise the Lord of heav - en, Praise Him in the height, Praise Him, all ye angels, Praise Him, stars and light: Praise Him, clouds and waters, Which above the skies, When His word com-mand - ed, Did es - tab - lished rise. A-men.

2 Praise the Lord, ye fountains
    Of the deeps and seas,
Rocks, and hills, and mountains,
    Cedars, and all trees;
Praise Him, clouds and vapors,
    Snow and hail, and fire,
Stormy wind, fulfilling
    Only His desire.

3 Praise Him, fowls and cattle,
    Princes and all kings :
Praise Him, men and maidens,
    All created things :
For the Name of God is
    Excellent alone,
Over earth His footstool,
    Over heaven His throne.

T. B. Brown.

APPENDIX.

304

GOUDIMEL. S. M. D.   ADAPTED FROM GOUDIMEL. MRS. H. R. SPAETH.

305

OLIVET. 6, 6, 4, 6, 6, 6, 4.   LOWELL MASON, (1792–1872). 1832.

Amen.

306

LITANY. 7, 7, 7, 7. F. MORLEY. ARR. BY W. H. WALTER.

A - men.

307

BORTNIANSKY. 7, 7, 7, 7, 7, 7. BORTNIANSKY.

Amen.

Wm. H. Keyser & Co., Phila.

Alphabetical Index of Tunes.

CANTICLES, CREED, AND LORD'S PRAYER.

INDEX OF PSALMS.

Index of Gregorian Tones.

Index of Anglican Chants.

Double.

Index of Anglican Chants.

Single.

Composer.	Key.	Page.	Composer.	Key.	Page.
Anon	A ♯	43	Hopkins, E. J	E ♭	37
Anon	B	49	Hopkins, E. J	D	76
Anon	B	64	Hoyte, H. W	A ♯	68
Anon	G	72	Hoyte, H. W	D	76
Aldrich	E Minor	82	Hoyte, W. S	A ♯	57
Aldrich	A ♯	74	Humphreys, P	C	92
Baker, H. W	C	92	Jeckyll, C. J	D	78
Banister, H. C	C	40	Jeckyll, C. J	F	90
Barnby, J	B	64	Keeton, H	A ♭	89
Barnby, J	E ♭	72	Langdon	B	66
Barrow, I	E ♯	40	Lee	D	80
Barrow, I	E ♯	58	Macfarren, G. A	A Minor	89
Barry, C. A	A Minor	76	Macfarren, G. A	B	60
Barry, C. B	E ♭	87	Macfarren, G. A	F	69
Battishill	A ♯	64	Macfarren, G. A	G	56
Battishill	B	90	Macfarren, W	F	84
Baltishill	E ♯	58	Monk, E. G	E ♭	82
Bradley, C	A ♭	65	Monk, W. H	B Minor	80
Brown, A. H	F	86	Monk, W. H	D	78
Bullinger, E. W	F	85	Monk, W. H	E ♭	78
Chard	E Minor	76	Monk, W. H	F	86
Cooke, B	E ♯	88	Monk, W. H	G	38
Croft	A Minor	36	Monk, W. H	G	38
Crotch	D Minor	50	Novello, V	A ♯	90
Crotch	G	80	Ousely, F. A. G	E ♭	46
Dupuis	E ♭	70	Ousely, F. A. G	E ♭	66
Dyce	E ♭	80	Ousely, F. A. G	E ♯	57
Edwards	B	82	Ousely, F. A. G	G	47
Elvey, G. F	B	44	Oxford Chant	D	82
Elvey, G. F	B	78	Pearce, J	D	65
Elvey, G. F	F	47	Pring	E ♭	37
Elvey, G. F	B	64	Purcell, H	A ♯	72
Farrant, R	F	84	Purcell, J	G	75
Felton	E ♭	50	Rimbault	G	54
Felton	F	62	Round, H	E ♭	76
Fisher	C	66	Russell	F	71
Frye, C	F	36	Savage, W	C	42
Gadsby, H	B	62	Smith, B	G	72
Gadsby, H	B	87	Stainer	E ♭	49
Garrett	A ♯	71	Stewart, R. H	G	44
Garrett	B	61	Tallis, T	C	63
Goss	A ♯	70	Tallis, T	F	69
Goss	E ♭	61	Thorne, E. H	A ♯	88
Goss	F	46	Turle, J	G	60
Hackett	A ♯	68	Turle, J	G	75
Hager	F	42	Tours, B	D	90
Havergal, W. H	E ♭	63	Turpin, E. H	D	58
Havergal, W. H	F	68	Turton	A ♯	74
Heywood	G	54	Webbe, S	G	38
Heywood	F	68	Woodward	B	66
Hine	G	43	Woodward	C	56

Metrical Index.

METRICAL INDEX.

Index of First Lines.

———※———

INDEX OF FIRST LINES.